International Etiquette

*An etiquette guidance to cultivate
a professional image and an elegant life*

Lydia, Jui-Chih Peng (Author / Translator)

Kathlene, Hsin-Chi Chang (Translator)

International Etiquette

An etiquette guidance to cultivate a professional image and an elegant life

Author	Lydia, Jui-Chih Peng
Translator	Kathlene, Hsin-Chi Chang & Lydia, Jui-Chih Peng
Publisher	Yang-CHih Book Co., Ltd.
Lssuer	Jhong-Sian Ye
Editor-in-Chief	Fu Ping Yen
Address	8F, No. 258, Sec. 3, Pei-Shen Rd. Shenken, New Taipei City, Taiwan
TEL	886-2-8662-6826
FAX	(02)2664-7633
URL	http://www.ycrc.com.tw
E-mail	service@ycrc.com.tw

ISBN 978-986-298-422-2
September 2023
NT $ 500

FORWARD

In "GUANZI" within the chapter "Shepherding the people" by Guan Zhong, it uses etiquette, righteousness, integrity, and disgrace as the four dimensions of a country. If the four dimensions are not upheld, the nation is susceptible to downfall. In the four dimensions, "righteousness", "integrity", and "disgrace" are all cultivation of morality and mind. While they eventually manifest in actions, they belong to the realm of abstract personality. " Etiquette " is a form of temperance and ritual from the beginning, with clear and precise forms and norms, which may be observed through interaction. From my own experience, "Etiquette" is the best measure of personal cultivation and social civilization. Regardless of individual or society, if one practices and performs etiquette, thus, shall one create harmony and reduce conflicts.

In "The Genealogy of Confucius" within the "Records of the Grand Historian" by Sima Qian, it is mentioned, "When I arrived in the state of Lu, I saw chariots, clothes, and ceremonial vessels in Confucius' ancestral hall. Many Confucian students kept practicing etiquette accordingly, I lingered and couldn't bear to leave." We can clearly see that beauty of a society that values, and practices etiquette had deeply touched Sima Qian and kept him lingering. From this, we could understand that the longstanding emphasis on etiquette in our country is indeed an inevitable aspect.

However, with the rise of individual autonomy, emphasizing the freedom of individual behavior has become a common phenomenon, consequently, education on etiquette has been gradually neglected and proper mannerisms have become less and less important. By doing it repeatedly, the saying that goes 'the most beautiful scenery in Taiwan is the people' may become a thing of the past that cannot be regained.

As a member of Feng-Chia's general education, I always believe that the essence of general education is liberal arts, and the core is humanities. The so-called humanities refer to the respect for people, events, objects, and the universe and nature. The so-called liberal art, on one hand, is the absorption and integration of knowledge, and on the other hand is the completeness and practice of aesthetics. Etiquette embodies both the connotation and manifestation of elegance.

Professor Jui-Chih Peng has been teaching international etiquette courses at various universities, and is deeply loved by students. She is like a skilled gardener, making sure that every grass and flower thrive and blossom. In other words, every student who follows her guidance will be able to gain an understanding of international etiquette and display proper mannerism accordingly. In recent times, education authorities have emphasized the cultivation of students' international perspectives and mobility, and Professor Peng's class serves as an excellent example in this regard.

Last but not least, I would like to emphasize again that the most valuable aspect of this book is its practicality and approachability. Etiquette isn't about excessive formalities, nor should it be intimidating. Instead, it should be seamlessly integrated into every facet of our daily lives, evident in our clothing, dining, housing, and transportation. Professor Peng applied her decades of rich international work experience, and her knowledge obtained through abundant traveling and reading to crafting this educational resource that is both applicable and instructive. True merit is immeasurable, this is the forward.

何壽澎

Chi-Peng, Ho, 2023.8.10

Dean, College of Humanities and Social Sciences,

and

Director, General Education Center,

Feng Chia University

Author's Preface (from Chinese edition)

Transitioning from the aviation sector to academia, she pursued and obtained master's and doctoral degrees. She has taught for several years at two prominent universities in central Taiwan. One is the esteemed private university Feng Chia University, admired even by university presidents for its exceptional education quality, acknowledged by both businesses and parents. The other is the foremost higher education institution in Taichung, National Chung Hsing University, which has nurtured numerous top-tier talents in Taiwan.

Having instructed in the international etiquette domain for over a decade, she considers herself fortunate as both of these institutions place significant emphasis on international etiquette courses. They view these courses as crucial for nurturing students' soft skills over the next decade. Additionally, she has been granted ample authorization and support to continually refine and innovate in the realm of international etiquette education. Beyond the classroom, she has also perceived a growing demand and acceptance for learning international etiquette during her teaching engagements with government, corporate, and private organizations. Taiwan's stride towards internationalization has integrated international etiquette into everyday life, becoming an essential component for enhancing interpersonal relationships.

What is International Etiquette? What is taught in International Etiquette courses? The author perceives International Etiquette courses as a comprehensive learning endeavor that encapsulates various aspects of international norms related to dining, clothing, housing, transportation, education, recreation, as well as business and diplomatic interactions. Previously, understanding International Etiquette required exposure to various international contexts and learning, often involving trial and error or even learning from embarrassing situations. The phrase "When in Rome, do as the Romans do" captures this idea – adapting to local customs. Continuously evaluating others' cultures based on our own experiences or expressing our preferences could lead to feeling out of place in a foreign setting, inhibiting the enjoyment of different customs and cultures. Etiquette in different countries can often be quite contrary; for instance, while most Western countries uphold the concept of "Lady First" and emphasize gentlemanly conduct, Japan, which CNN deemed one of the world's most polite nations, has different norms, where women often serve men in social contexts. Understanding, respecting, and embracing diverse perspectives are integral aspects of International Etiquette.

Does understanding International Etiquette equate to having an "international perspective"? The term "international perspective" implies sensitivity to global affairs, an interest in places beyond one's own country, and the ability to comprehend them. According to the author, possessing an international perspective primarily involves accepting the manners and "improprieties" of various nations, which encompasses adaptability to diverse cultures and respecting differences. It even extends to appreciating these distinctions, ultimately enabling seamless integration. Dr. Liu Birong, an expert in international negotiations, once remarked, "Your international perspective determines how vast your world is." Learning International Etiquette to understand the customs of different countries is just a step; genuine international perspective involves accepting and comprehending these customs from the cultural standpoint of the other side. "Respect" and "understanding" precisely encapsulate the core values of International Etiquette.

Over the past decade, schools at all levels in Taiwan have actively pursued internationalization, gradually recognizing the significance of International Etiquette courses. Reflecting on the author's experience, upon graduating from university, she had the opportunity to attend a formal banquet in Washington, D.C., alongside diplomats from various countries. Faced with an array of cutlery, she felt apprehensive about making mistakes and becoming a subject of amusement. During that period, there were no hospitality-related majors, and International Etiquette was not a subject of study. Without proper exposure to etiquette, she entered society and had to learn and accumulate experiences through trial and error.

In recent years, hospitality majors have gained popularity, and many higher education institutions have introduced International Etiquette courses in their general education curriculum. The introduction of the Ministry of Education's International

Etiquette certification in 2007 has further contributed to the growing recognition of this art of living. Teachers from various schools, as well as secretaries of clubs or event organizers, attend her International Etiquette training courses based on business demands. Among them, a junior high school director from a remote area in Hualien, despite the long and challenging journey, attended the course, leaving a deep impression on the author.

This experience planted the idea of publishing an International Etiquette textbook in her mind. The author hopes this could serve as a practical tool for teachers involved in promoting International Etiquette education in schools, offering convenience to those seeking to elevate their lifestyle and learn about International Etiquette.

Reflecting on the initiation of teaching the subject of "International Etiquette," the author began by reading various International Etiquette books available in the market. These books were authored by diplomats, hospitality industry professionals, tour guides, models, beauty experts, and more. Drawing from her personal experience of two to three decades in the international aviation field, coupled with a background in hospitality studies, and enriched by speaking engagements at universities, corporations, and associations, she developed her own teaching methodology. Through a process of reform and refinement, the author condensed and organized these insights into this book.

However, the scope of International Etiquette is extensive, with each unit representing a distinct expertise that merits further in-depth exploration. Due to space limitations, the content can only touch the surface. The content has been drawn from a wide range of resources, including academic journals, relevant books, and online articles. The author aimed to align it as closely as possible with current events. Yet, International Etiquette is a subject that evolves constantly and rapidly. She humbly seeks the guidance and corrections from esteemed scholars and experts in this field, as it is a subject that is both "progressive" and subject to constant change.This book is dedicated to the mentors, educators, and friends who have supported the author throughout her journey. Your encouragement has been instrumental in her continuous growth. The author would love to extend her gratitude to her family, who have always been her pillars of strength. Writing this book has been possible thanks to the guidance from experts in the fields of diplomacy and the service industry. A special acknowledgment goes to the leadership and faculty of Feng Chia University and National Chung Hsing University for their continuous care and support, which allowed the course "International Etiquette and Professional Image" to evolve from its inception in Chinese to including English classes and even online English courses. As this book is published, the author holds deep appreciation for all those who have contributed along the way.

彭瑞芝 Lydia Peng

2022/03/01

AUTHOR'S PREFACE

Since the publication of my Chinese work, "國際禮儀：空姐教你如何塑造觀光餐旅的專業形象", I have consistently felt the demand for an English version of the textbook. Consequently, I translated this book in the following year.

I teach "International Etiquette" courses in both Chinese and English at several universities and that brings me great joy and satisfaction. Additionally, my English classes are conducted in an English-Medium Instruction (EMI) format, with classes entirely delivered in English. Each semester, my class comprises a diverse mix of foreign students and proficient local students, contributing to the course's multicultural atmosphere. Nonetheless, the various English accents of students from different countries also pose a challenging aspect to the classroom. As a result of that, it prompted me to believe that having an English textbook as a companion could provide students with a reference to better understand the lesson. For students with weaker English-speaking skills, with a book as their reference could encourage them to participate more actively in class discussions.

The Ministry of Education is currently actively promoting English Medium of Instruction (EMI) teaching. International Etiquette is a subject that is relatively relatable yet interesting, making it highly suitable for incorporation into various departments as EMI courses. For local students, this International Etiquette book also serves as an excellent tool for learning English. When using it, I recommend using it alongside the Chinese version. This approach allows students to learn international etiquette while simultaneously enhancing their English proficiency.

I have published this English textbook with the hope that it can contribute to the promotion of English teaching at all levels of schools. For teachers conducting classes in English, this book serves as a convenient English teaching resource. It also includes carefully designed course activities, group discussions, and practical exercises, ensuring the ease of implementation within the curriculum.

My student, Kathlene Chang, was a participant in my International Etiquette

English class at National Chung Hsing University, and subsequently served as my teaching assistant for the International Etiquette course for four consecutive semesters. She made significant contributions to the translation work of this book.

Jui-chih, Peng 2023.8.23

Contents

Part 1

Etiquette Introduction

Etiquette is a universal aspect of our daily lives, and what we consider to be habitual behavior may also be part of international etiquette. Take, for example, the direction in which one starts when having a buffet in a restaurant - the answer is clockwise. This queuing manner is not just unique to Taiwan, but can be easily integrated as a worldwide etiquette. China is often cited as a country where etiquette is deeply ingrained in its culture, with the earliest known book related to etiquette being the "Book of Rites", compiled by Dai Sheng in the Western Han Dynasty. The six arts in ancient China included "rites, music, archery, charioteering, reading and writing, and arithmetic", with "rites" being given the highest priority. This underscores the importance placed on learning and acquiring proper etiquette in Chinese Confucianism. With the advancement of technology and transportation, physical barriers between countries are being broken down, exposing us to foreign cultures and people. Therefore, it is increasingly important for us to understand international etiquette and expand our global perspectives, in order to foster greater mutual understanding when interacting with others.

Chinese Book of Rite.

Source: Taiwan Digitalarchives

Six arts of Confucius

Source: Internet

Chapter

1

Etiquette Introduction

- Definition and Categories of Etiquette
- The origin and history of international etiquette

The term "international" refers to the differences among various countries, cultures, or tribes around the world. On the other hand, "etiquette" pertains to the social interactions and courtesies between people. With political and commercial exchanges, the world has gradually established a common etiquette. However, certain countries still have distinctive etiquettes that are preserved through traditional customs, habits, and experiences. While it is often said that we should "respect the guest", international etiquette dictates that the opposite is true - we should "respect the host". This is because according to standardized international etiquette, the guest should prioritize the host's needs and perspectives, regardless of where they are.

Definition and Categories of Etiquette

How do you define "Etiquette" and "International etiquette"? What do these terms consist of respectively? What are the relevant terms to these words?

I. Definition of International Etiquette

Definition of Etiquette

In China, the character "禮" originally referred to the act of worshiping the gods. The ancient form of the character, written as "豊", depicted two strings of precious jade placed on a sacrificial vessel, while the character "示" next to it represented the sacrificial table. Thus, the character "禮" carries connotations of reverence towards the gods and the rituals and rules associated with such worship. In the Book of Rites, it is mentioned in the "Rules of Propriety" chapter that going and not coming is indecent, coming and not going is indecent. Manners themselves are timeless and develop over time, while the desire to seek good luck and avoid evil is a fundamental human instinct. Learning manners can help one avoid problems and show respect for oneself and others. The character "儀", written with "人" on the left and symbolizing a solitary individual,

Ancient form of the character 『禮』

Ancient form of the character 『儀』

and power, authority, and ceremony on the right, represents how one presents oneself in terms of appearance and behavior.

In the West, Weber's dictionary defines "Etiquette" as the accepted or necessary forms, ceremonies, or rituals in social relations, workplaces, or formal occasions. Etiquette is a social aesthetic that involves the art of displaying or interacting with people. It encompasses a set of rules and conventions that govern behavior and reflect social norms and values.

Etiquette is essential for building and maintaining positive relationships and fostering mutual respect and understanding in various social contexts. It encompasses everything from basic manners, such as saying "please" and "thank you," to more

Etiquette is an art of social connection

https://www.independent.co.uk/voices/comment/a-short-history-of-modern-manners-84587 30.html

complex customs and rituals, such as table manners or proper business etiquette.

Definition of International Etiquette

International etiquette is a general term that encompasses all forms of etiquette related to interactions between different countries, including their unique customs and traditions. The common saying "When in Rome, do as the Romans do" applies to international etiquette, emphasizing the importance of respecting and adapting to the customs and traditions of the host country when traveling abroad. The Ministry of Foreign Affairs of the Republic of China defines "international etiquette" as the norms that govern interactions between people from different cultures and nations. These norms have evolved over time, largely influenced by Western civilization, but regional traditional rituals continue to play a significant role. The practice of international etiquette is essential in promoting mutual understanding, respect, and cooperation among individuals and nations.

II. Types of etiquettes

The relevant words to etiquette include "Etiquette", "Protocol", "Codes of Conduct" etc.

1. Etiquette: Etiquette is a widely used term that encompasses the social customs and practices of respect between individuals across the world. It involves the display of courtesy, consideration, and politeness in various social situations. Simple actions such as opening doors for the elderly or women, as well as welcoming guests, are considered essential components of proper etiquette. By adhering to these gestures, individuals can demonstrate their respect for others and foster a more harmonious and respectful social environment.

2. Protocol: Protocol is a widely used term in the context of international etiquette, with a focus on the proper etiquette to be followed by individuals, countries, organizations, or businesses, without giving undue importance to social status. Examples of such protocols can be seen by visiting the protocol department of

the Ministry of Foreign Affairs.

3. Ceremony: Ceremony refers to a formal or public event held to commemorate a significant achievement, occasion or anniversary. Examples of ceremonies include weddings, graduations, commencements, and inaugurations. These events typically involve ritualized activities, such as speeches, presentations, and performances, and are often accompanied by special attire or decorations. Ceremonies play an important role in many cultures and are often steeped in tradition and symbolism.

4. Formality: It refers to conforming to a set of formal and traditional requirements or procedures, such as dress code, language use, and behavior, for a particular event, situation, or environment. Failure to meet these requirements is considered informal.

5. Procedure: Procedures are a set of standardized steps or actions that are followed in a particular way or sequence to achieve a specific goal or objective. They are often referred to as Standard Operating Procedures (SOPs) and are an integral part of many formal processes and organizations.

6. Manner: Manner is a set of behaviors that are considered good and refined and are typically learned at home or in one's social surroundings. Examples of manners include not talking with a mouth full of food and following specific etiquette rules, such as table manners, executive manners, and court manners.

7. Courtesy: Courtesy refers to the display of good manners and behavior without needing reminders or prompting. An example of courtesy is giving up a seat for someone in need. Compared to manners, which are more specific, courtesy is more abstract and reflects a willingness to go above and beyond basic etiquette.

8. Code of Conduct: A code of conduct is a set of basic principles that guide behavior according to specific rules or regulations in particular settings, such as companies, schools, or societies.

9. Custom: Custom refers to traditional practices that are passed down and often observed on special occasions, such as eating 「Zongzi」 or rice dumpling, and crazy for the Mazu Pilgrimage in March.

10. Politeness: Politeness refers to the accepted norms of behavior in society and is

demonstrated through respectful and considerate interactions with others. For example, gift exchange can be an example of mutual respect and politeness.

Types of Etiquette

Etiquette	Protocol：The Protocol Department of Foreign Affairs
	Ceremony：Wedding Ceremony、Inaguration Ceremony
	Formality：Formal，Informal
	Procedure：Standard Operating Procedure（SOP）
	Manner：Table Manner、Executive Manner
	Courtesy：Courtesy Seating
	Codes of Conduct：The School Codes of Conduct
	Custom：A Traditional Behavior of Certain Group of People
	Politeness：Treat each other with courtesy.

Source: Thesaurus.plus

The origin and history of international etiquette

I. Origin of Etiquette

Etiquette originated in Western countries during the 12th century and evolved into a more structured form during the 16th century. Its roots can be traced back to the social hierarchies that existed in ancient civilizations, such as the Egyptian Empire where classes ranged from slaves to pharaohs. Similarly, in Europe, different classes existed, including royals, middle class, workers, and peasants. The royals established standards of behavior for the lower classes to follow in order to avoid offense.

Source:https://alancientrivervalleycivilizations.weebly.com/

In eastern countries, etiquette has a long history dating back to at least two thousand years ago. The Chinese Philosopher Confucius once remarked, Don't talk when you eat, don't talk when you go to bed. emphasizing the importance of showing consideration and avoiding offensive behaviors. In ancient China, social classes were organized into servants, civilians, scholars, baronage, and emperors, with specific regulations on various aspects of life, including eating habits. Prior to the Qin and Han dynasties, civilians in China typically ate only two meals a day, while eating three meals a day was reserved for baronage, and emperors could have up to four meals a day. The concept of "lunch" as a distinct mealtime gradually emerged during the Tang dynasty, further highlighting social distinctions.

Source:https://slideplayer.com/amp/1388577/

II. Evolution of international etiquette

Etiquette evolution and development in Europe:

1. The "Prisse Papyrus" is a historical document from ancient Egypt that dates back to the 12th century. French scholars discovered it in Thebes, and it is now housed in the Bibliothèque Nationale de France in Paris. The papyrus contains a series of maxims and admonitions that focus on the morality of conduct.

2. The "Maxims of Ptah-Hotep," written by the former Egyptian Prime Minister Ptah-Hotep, was a guide to proper behavior and etiquette for young people during the 3rd century BC in Egypt.

3. During the period of 1419-1467 in the common era, Philip III, Duke of Burgundy, lived a lavish lifestyle. He wrote rules for the domestic life of the royal household on cards, which served as a clear guide for his personal attendants.

4. Desiderius Erasmus Roterodamus, a Dutch philosopher and Catholic theologian, is widely regarded as one of the most important scholars of the northern Renaissance between 1469 and 1536. He authored a book called "On Civility in Children," which is considered the

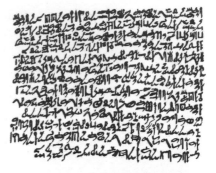

Ancient Egyptian writing

Ptah-Hotep

Philip III, Duke of Burgundy

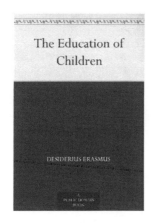

The book of The Education of Children   Desiderius Erasmus Roterodamus

first treatise in Western Europe on the moral and practical education of children. Although it was translated into various languages, its contents became outdated over time.

5. In the 16th century, the term "Etiquette" originated in France. During the reign of King Louis XVI (1638-1715), norms for courtesy and behavior were established. The French court even created elaborate etiquette guidelines for royalty, which included the use of linen.

6. 17th century: "The Accomplished Ladies' Rich Closet of Rarities," a book on ladies and table manners was published in London in 1663

With the evolution of Western etiquette, it is evident that the concept of "etiquette" has transformed over time to suit different historical backgrounds. Etiquette can be regarded as a civilizing process that adapts to changes in politics, economics, society, culture, and human evolution.

First etiquette book for ladies

Class activities I

The objective of this chapter is to trigger the interests in international etiquette while learning. Think of any daily occasion where international etiquette is applied. Try classifying such etiquette.

1. Ask students what are their expectation and intentions to learn about international etiquette
2. Allow students to clear their doubts about international etiquette
3. Encourage students to name out some of their daily encounters with etiquette and try classifying the etiquette respectively.

延伸閱讀

Etiquipedia，禮儀百科，https://etiquipedia.blogspot.com
中華民國外交部禮賓處，https://www.mofa.gov.tw/Organization.aspx?n=60&sms=85#hash28
外交部，有禮走天下，https://www.mofa.gov.tw/Upload/WebArchive/314/國際禮儀手冊
國家教育研究院雙語詞彙，禮記，https://terms.naer.edu.tw/detail/1315098/
華廈訓評國際禮儀接待員乙級證照參考資料

Chapter

2

Why the need to learn international etiquette?

- Why do we learn about international etiquette?
- Etiquette differences among countries
- Etiquette trend

Why is learning etiquette important? Consider a scenario where etiquette doesn't exist in our daily lives. This would lead to confusion and even embarrassment, potentially causing a negative impact on our interactions with others. However, with the knowledge of various types of etiquette, we can apply appropriate behavior in different settings. For example, when dining with a group, proper etiquette ensures that everyone knows where to sit and avoids confusion. Etiquette is not only relevant, but it is also a form of life knowledge that can be as basic as common sense.

In today's globalized world, we no longer need to travel abroad to interact with people from different cultures. By learning international etiquette, we can be more civilized and respectful when communicating with foreigners. Additionally, it helps us to become more elegant and charming, leaving a good impression and raising the national standard.

Why do we learn about international etiquette?

Learning international etiquette is essential because it provides a framework for how we should interact with others and the world around us. Chinese society places great importance on manners and etiquette as it is believed that having good manners can help prevent conflicts and tensions. However, etiquette is not an innate quality and must be learned through education and practice. The Protocol Department of the Ministry of Foreign Affairs is responsible for managing international affairs. Before visiting a foreign country, heads of state and ministers are expected to study and understand the culture of the country to avoid unintentionally breaching any cultural taboos. This is especially crucial in the realm of political diplomacy.

I. Knowing yourself and knowing others to be favorable everywhere

Acquiring knowledge of international etiquette is akin to obtaining a travel passport. If one intends to broaden their network, having a command of etiquette is indispensable. Assimilating into the local society and comprehending their customs can offer numerous

Culture diversity

benefits, including building social status, facilitating business negotiations, or cultivating diplomatic relationships.

II. Etiquette is not an innate humanity, it is cultivated through learning

Our understanding of our own country's culture often comes from our upbringing and education. However, when we travel to other countries, it's important to make an effort to learn about their customs and etiquette. For example, in Chinese culture, it is common to pick up bowls and chopsticks to eat, but in South Korea, this is seen as improper as bowls and chopsticks are often made of metal or steel which conduct heat. Koreans prefer to use utensils and not hold the bowl in their hands. It's crucial to keep an open mind and learn about these cultural differences to avoid misunderstandings and show respect towards the host country's culture.

III. Diversity in etiquette and being updated

Experiencing cultural shock is a common occurrence when encountering cultural differences. Sometimes, the differences can be so significant that it leaves one in awe.

For instance, the hand gestures that are deemed acceptable in one culture might be considered impolite or even offensive in another. For example, the "OK" sign that we commonly use in Western cultures is viewed as vulgar in Brazil. Similarly, the "V" sign we make when taking pictures is considered a rude gesture in the UK. As society evolves, traditional beliefs and practices that were once deemed acceptable might no longer hold true. Therefore, it is important to remain open-minded and continue to learn about international etiquette to navigate through cultural differences.

IV. Creating a good first impression

The way you behave and conduct yourself reflects your character and moral values. In our society, people often form opinions based on first impressions. As the saying goes, "You never get a second chance to make a first impression." Therefore, it is essential to present oneself in a neat and presentable manner when interacting with others. Equally important is having a good understanding of etiquette. This knowledge allows one to feel comfortable in social situations and avoid coming across as impolite or awkward.

V. Learning international etiquette is a virtue

Having a good attitude towards learning international etiquette is crucial in order to acquire the relevant knowledge for different social settings. The purpose of learning etiquette is not to become arrogant or feel superior, but to transform oneself into a more cultured and refined person. For instance, understanding various dining etiquette and knowing how to eat French cuisine does not make one extraordinary, but rather it is important to remain humble and not become complacent when interacting with people from different backgrounds.

The adage "It is better to travel 10,000 miles than to read 10,000 volumes of books" emphasizes the importance of practical experience. However, reading international etiquette books and applying what you have learned can also help you develop a deep understanding and respect for diverse people and cultures around the world, making you

Who needs to learn international etiquette

International etiquette is not typically taught as an official subject in traditional education. However, its usefulness becomes apparent when we enter the real world and apply it in our daily lives. This realization has led to a growing recognition of the importance of international etiquette in recent years, with educational institutions beginning to incorporate it into their curricula. By doing so, they aim to instill higher standards and manners in their students.

This book is suitable for people who want to learn international etiquette, this includes...

1. Teachers and students of all levels : Education institutions are often tasked with teaching students about international etiquette, but many educators are not experts in this area. Therefore, it is crucial for educators to master international etiquette themselves before imparting knowledge to their students. In addition, providing guidance books can further assist learners in acquiring this knowledge quickly and effectively.

2. Business needs : The demands of the business world require individuals to possess a thorough understanding of international etiquette, particularly in professions that involve organizing events or visits by executives. Private organizations, including secretaries, public relations consultants, and corporate personnel, must also possess such knowledge in order to excel in their roles.

3. Global business needs : Organizations that engage in international affairs, such as schools with international programs or companies conducting business transactions across borders, require knowledge of international etiquette in order to effectively communicate and establish relationships with people from different cultures.

Learning international etiquette can provide a competitive edge in future employment opportunities. It can improve personal presentation and add value to specific roles or departments, making it a valuable asset in the workforce. In fact, everyone should strive to learn etiquette. Take Japan as an example, where good manners are instilled from a young age. In times of crisis, such as natural disasters, people remain calm and wait patiently for government assistance or head to emergency shelters, instead of taking advantage of the situation. This is a result of good mannerism becoming a national norm in Japan. Therefore, international etiquette not only reflects an individual's worth but also a country's potential.

a well-informed and cultured individual. The true purpose of international etiquette is to help you develop an inner sense of tolerance and acceptance that radiates outward, leading to personal growth and a more harmonious world.

Difference in etiquette among various countries

International etiquette is a complex and diverse subject that requires a certain level of adaptability. Each country has its own set of customs and practices, and understanding them can help us interact with locals in a more appropriate manner. Developing these soft skills allows us to be more flexible and adaptable, which can be particularly valuable when traveling or working abroad.

There are plenty of differences in etiquette between countries and here are the few interesting cultural differences :

I. Wine toasting etiquette in China

The practice of toasting has its roots in ancient times and was initially considered a form of worship or reverence. In China, toasting originated from the emperor's practice of offering alcohol to courtiers, who were expected to accept it without hesitation. Over time, the practice of toasting has evolved and is now commonly used to signify loyalty, friendship, and even courage. Toasting is also a prominent feature in business negotiations and serves as a way to build and maintain connections, demonstrating politeness and sincerity. Refusing a toast in Chinese culture is considered a sign of disrespect, so it is best to accept it. However, recent efforts to promote safe drinking practices have led to initiatives like "don't drive after drinking" campaigns in Taiwan, and some officials in China are also attempting to change the norm around toasting to reduce negative consequences, such as car accidents. It is always better to call a taxi or use public transportation after a gathering and avoid causing unnecessary problems. Ultimately, the purpose of such gatherings is to enjoy oneself and strengthen relationships, not to endanger oneself or others.

II. Bowing manners in Japan

Japanese etiquette emphasizes paying attention to details and aesthetics in daily activities, and has been around for ages. Etiquette is seen as a form of art, emphasizing body postures, which is a self-cultivation (Ikegami, 2005). Japanese etiquette classes put strong emphasis on postures, tones, and attitudes, as a verbal greeting alone is not enough. Bowing is a common form of greeting in Japan and is seen everywhere. Japanese children are taught to bow as early as preschool age (Hayashi, Mayumi, &Tobin, 2009). There are three types of bows: the 15-degree bow, 30-degree bow, and

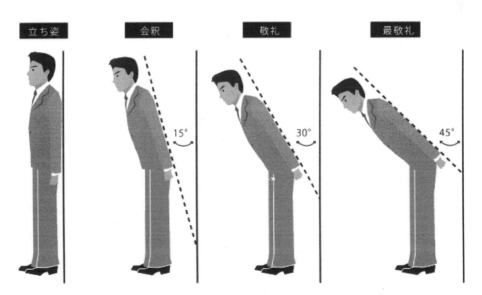

Multiple ways of Japanese bowing

Source: berlinippon.com

45-degree bow. One should bow according to the degree of politeness, and each bow has a respective duration to maintain. To practice the most formal 45-degree bow, one should stand with feet together, hands clasped below the waist, bow with straight back hold for three seconds, in the mean time express proper greeting before rising. This is the bowing procedure in Japanese culture, and it is how respect is expressed. Japanese etiquette training focuses on both verbal and non-verbal behaviors, and such conduct reflects certain levels of respect and hierarchy. To the Japanese, knowing how to bow correctly is very important.

III. Mannerism in Taiwan

We often hear that "the most beautiful scenery in Taiwan is the people". This is because the Taiwanese have certain standards and courtesy. A research study on Taiwan society has concluded that whether a person is polite or impolite is mainly based on if the person is respectful, thoughtful and has self-discipline (Su, 2019). Additionally, appropriateness, harmony, upbringing, knowing how to say "please, thanks and sorry", politeness, gratitude, kindness and understanding the boundaries are also crucial. The good mannerisms among the Taiwanese nourishes their land and on top of that, it also greatly attracts many foreigners as the Taiwanese are welcoming and passionate. This in turn increases its global competitiveness and also attracts huge tourism, thus highlighting the country's immense potential.

IV. Business Etiquette in Russia

When conducting business in Russia, it is crucial to conduct thorough research on potential business partners to understand their background and source of funds. It is also important to remain neutral and polite when dealing with partners until you become familiar with them. Building a strong working and social network is necessary to do business in Russia, as Russians often invite their business associates to private social gatherings. Rejecting such invitations is considered rude, and it is a missed opportunity to experience Russian culture firsthand. Punctuality is viewed as a sign of trust and reliability in Russia, but being overly strict about it can be seen as assertive and rude. Late arrivals due to circumstances such as traffic or getting lost on the way are generally acceptable, but being late for more than 15 minutes is not. Russians take pride in their railway system, but it is considered taboo to discuss WWII or monarchy-related topics when interacting with them. Russians often showcase their wealth through expensive accessories such as watches, jewelry, and handbags.

V. Time concept in India

As a former British colony with a history dating back 200 years, India has inherited the British hierarchical system and maintains the use of titles such as "Madam" and "Sir". Social order and status are of great importance to Indians, influenced by the caste system and religious beliefs. Following a well-defined hierarchy is essential for maintaining social structures. While punctuality is considered a fundamental etiquette across many cultures, it is viewed differently in India. Time management is more flexible and things do not always run like clockwork. Being late to a meeting or experiencing interruptions during meetings is considered normal and not unprofessional. The business culture in India is slow-paced and informal, with many Indians believing in the need for flexible schedules to accommodate others. Leaving some allowance in your daily schedule can serve as a buffer for unexpected events such as meeting delays or traffic jams. Visitors to government officials or Muslim businessmen should be prepared to wait as needed, including for prayer breaks (Dezan et al., 2012).

VI. American's casual wear

When traveling, it is common to see Americans dress very casually or underdressed. This is because Americans value individual freedom and believe that dressing as they please is a way to express that freedom. Of course, everyone has the right to present themselves to the world in their own way, and such freedom can break down stereotypes related to gender, age, and wealth. A few centuries ago in the United States, one's social rank could be easily determined by their clothing, making it impossible to hide their status. However, today, both the rich and the poor can choose to wear whatever they like, as long as it is comfortable and suits their style. For example, Apple founder Steve Jobs was known for always wearing a black t-shirt, making it his signature style. However, Americans still tend to dress appropriately for formal occasions such as dinner parties or dining at expensive restaurants. Wearing appropriate attire for a given setting or event is considered good etiquette

VII. Proper dining posture in Japan and Korea

In Japan and Korea, it is customary to remove shoes when sitting at a low dining table with legs crossed. This dining style may pose a challenge for some Westerners who are not accustomed to it. The Japanese have traditionally valued the "sit upright" posture as a way of showing respect and courtesy.

Seiza, the Japanese proper way of sitting

Source: Daily news

VIII. American loves chewing gum while Singapore does not allowed gums

Americans have a reputation for their love of chewing gum. However, this behavior has sometimes been viewed as inappropriate, such as when former US President Barack Obama was criticized for chewing gum during formal occasions, including the funeral of South African President Mandela and the 70th anniversary of the Normandy landing, as well as when he welcomed Queen Elizabeth II. While some argue that chewing gum has benefits, such as freshening breath and calming nerves, many countries frown upon chewing gum at formal events. For example, Singapore has even banned the sale and import of gum in order to maintain cleanliness, as it is difficult to remove gum from the ground. Bringing gum into the country can result in a fine.

President Obama chewed gum at India's Republic Day parade

Chewing gum banned in Singapore

IX. Shower in the night or day

In Taiwan, it is common for the majority of the population to shower at night before going to bed, while in America, most people prefer to shower in the morning. According to a research study conducted in the United States on shower preferences, the results showed that people generally prefer taking showers in the morning. This is because they believe that showering in the morning helps to invigorate the body and mind, and presenting

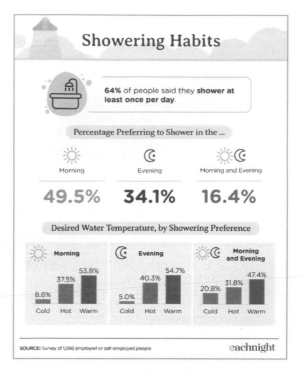

Showering Habits

Source: eachnight.com

oneself as clean and neat is considered a form of civility. Since Americans often spend their daytime in indoor air-conditioned environments, they may only need to wash their face and brush their teeth before going to bed at night, unless they have engaged in vigorous exercise or activities during the day.

Etiquette trend

Pandemics have had a significant impact on social interaction. As society and the human population evolve, international etiquette must adapt accordingly. For instance, the recent COVID-19 pandemic has led to a global norm of wearing masks, which has greatly reduced close human interactions. Nonetheless, people have come up with innovative ways to greet each other. During summit meetings, leaders have replaced hugs or handshakes with elbow bumps as a new form of greeting. Additionally, maintaining

During covid pandemic, European politicians greeted one
another by bumping elbows instead of shaking hands or hugs

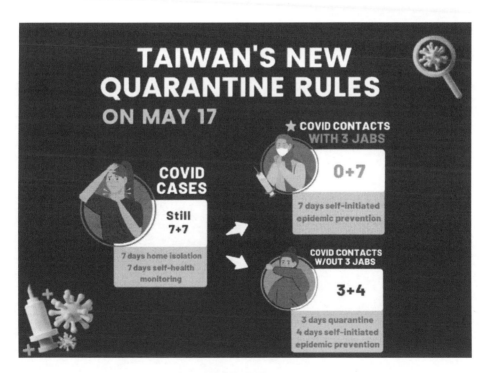

Source:taiwannews.com.tw

social distance, regular hand-washing, wearing masks, and self-quarantine after traveling have become new norms for social interaction.

I. WFH: Work from Home

Due to the pandemic, remote work have become increasingly popular. Many have realized that work can be done just as efficiently online, saving lots of travel time, and thus showing a clear shift towards virtual meetings rather than physical ones. Even though one does not have to be present physically, there are still many things that need to be prepared beforehand to ensure that the virtual meeting goes smoothly. Here are some useful tips for online meetings:

1. Ensure a clean and tidy background that is suitable for work.
2. Ensure proper attire, tidiness and make sure one can be seen within the camera frame.
3. Pretest audio and camera to avoid unnecessary interruption. When the speaker is speaking, remain attentive and silent
4. The meeting host should take the time difference into consideration to decide an

awkward moments during video conference

Source: YouTube

ideal conference time to fit all.

5. Ensure that the meeting has no interruption. When one has to be away from the camera, make sure that camera is turned off to avoid potential awkwardness

II. Metaverse virtual world

The metaverse is a rapidly growing virtual world that offers many new forms of human interaction, including virtual worlds and currency. It extends real life into the virtual world, where everyone has another identity or even multiple identities that are interchangeable. In the virtual world, people can easily form their own circles of friends regardless of distance, age, or their real-life identity. For example, a typical college student in real life could be a wealthy businessman in another universe, where they would have to learn new ways of networking and proper social etiquette. As the metaverse continues to evolve, new etiquette standards are emerging, making it important for individuals to adapt to these new social norms and keep themselves up to date.

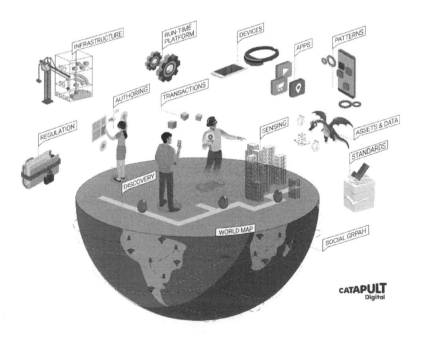

metaverse, virtual world

Source: https://medium.com/digital-catapult

 ## Class activities 2

1. In your past experiences, which countries have you been to? Share some of the cultural differences you encountered
2. Please share some of your personal encounters and opinions towards the differences in etiquette in different countries.
3. Discuss the advantages and disadvantages of online classes or meetings. What are some of the etiquette one should be aware of?
4. What types of etiquette should there be in the metaverse ?

延伸閱讀

Denton, J., & Tang, H., (2017). *The Practical Use of International Etiquette* (Second Edition). 書林 出版社

Dezan Shira & Associates and C. Devonshire-Ellis (2012). *Doing Business in India.* India Briefing, DOI: 10.1007/978-3-642-27618-7_3,

Dunn C. D. (2018). Bowing Incorrectly: Aesthetic Labor and Expert Knowledge in Japanese Business Etiquette Training. In: Cook H., Shibamoto-Smith J. (eds.) *Japanese at Work. Communicating in Professions and Organizations*. Palgrave Macmillan, Cham. https://doi.org/10.1007/978-3-319-63549-1_2

Froide, G. M., & Verheul, M. (2016). *An Experts' Guide to International Protocol*. Amsterdam University Press.

Hayashi, A., Mayumi, K., & Tobin, J. (2009). The Japanese Preschool's Pedagogy of Feeling: Cultural Strategies for Supporting Young Children's Emotional Development. *Ethos, 37*(1), 32-49.

Ikegami, E. (2005). *Bonds of Civility: Aesthetic Networks and the Political Origins of Japanese Culture*. New York: Cambridge University Press.

Mao, Y., Tian, X., & Wang, X., (2021). I will empty it, be my guest: A pragmatic study of toasting in Chinese culture. *Journal of Pragmatic, 180*, 77-88.

Medinskaya, O., & Randau, H. R., (2021). Etiquette: Do's and Don'ts. *Russia Business*, 255-263: Springer.

Su, H.Y. (2019). The metapragmatics of Taiwanese (im) politeness: Conceptualization and evaluation of limao. *Journal of Pragmatics, 148*, 26-43.

Etiquipedia，禮儀百科，https://etiquipedia.blogspot.com (2021/11/2)

Part 2

Dining Etiquette

It is said: "Food and drink are the paramount desires of people." Food and drink, as the most basic human needs, have numerous rules and etiquette, especially in ancient China, making it difficult to grasp their full extent. Among the highest standards of cuisine throughout history, the Qing Dynasty's "Imperial Banquets" are renowned, with Empress Dowager Cixi's Western Kitchen surpassing even the Emperor's dining arrangements. Not only could it prepare over 4,000 dishes, but it also offered more than 400 types of desserts, with a wide variety of choices. Historical records mention that Empress Dowager Cixi (1835-1908) had two main meals, two additional meals, and six small snacks each day. Each main meal consisted of over 100 dishes, requiring six dining tables to accommodate them. Of course, the Empress Dowager didn't consume all the dishes herself. Whenever she fancied a particular dish, the eunuchs would serve her a portion. According to the ancestral rules of the royal family, even for the most delicious dish, she was not allowed to eat more than three bites, to ensure that no one knew the Emperor's preferences. Empress Dowager Cixi's dining occasions were grand, with the Emperor, Empress, and concubines all present to attend to her. American artist Katharine

Augusta Carl (1865-1938), who painted a portrait of Empress Dowager Cixi, recorded in her book "With the Empress Dowager of China" that during meals, the Dowager sat facing south at one end of the table, which was adorned with countless silver bowls and plates filled with extraordinarily rare delicacies.

Food and dining are important social activities, with diverse culinary traditions and unique food contents and utensils in different countries. How we appropriately navigate and engage at the dining table depends on our international dining experiences and understanding of foreign foods and cultures. Before delving into dining etiquette, it is essential to understand what factors contribute to a delightful dining experience. Additionally, gaining knowledge of the factors influencing dining etiquette in various countries is crucial.

Empress Dowager Cixi's dining scene.

Image source: Internet

Chapter

3

The Connotation of Dining Etiquette

- Factors Contributing to the Formation of International Cuisine
- Types of Dining

Dining is an essential part of life and a significant activity for interpersonal communication. Whether it's socializing with friends and family or engaging in business meetings, dining plays a crucial role. Having delightful dining experiences brings harmony and success to our lives. Creating a wonderful dining experience encompasses the following conditions:

1. Good Food: Delicious and appetizing food that excels in visual appeal, aroma, and taste, providing a delightful sensory feast for the eyes, nose, and palate.

2. Good Environment: A well-designed seating arrangement, excellent views, and appropriate privacy contribute to a pleasant dining experience.

3. Good Service: Proficient and attentive service that combines the staff's expertise and professional appearance with well-trained service etiquette.

4. Dining with the Right People: Dining can elevate relationships between individuals, especially when shared with the right company, enhancing the overall experience.

5. Good Atmosphere: Pleasant lighting, a favorable ambiance, meticulous table settings, and suitable background music create a favorable dining atmosphere.

6. Human Touch: The genuine efforts and attentiveness of hosts, guests, chefs, or service staff can enhance the dining experience and leave a positive impression.

Factors Contributing to the Formation of International Cuisine

Have you ever wondered why Japanese cuisine often features raw fish, Koreans love kimchi, and Southeast Asian dishes are known for their spicy and tangy flavors? The formation of cuisine in different countries is influenced by various factors. Understanding these factors is essential for gaining basic knowledge and respect for the dining etiquette of a particular culture. Especially with the spirit of "being flexible to the host's preferences," it allows the host to conveniently prepare meals using local ingredients, while guests can fully appreciate and enjoy the local delicacies.

I. Geography

The geographical location of a region or country plays a significant role in the formation and dietary habits of its cuisine. It is often said that "people eat what is available in their surroundings." For example:

1. Japan

Being an island nation with mountainous terrain and limited plains, Japan's geographical environment is not suitable for large-scale animal husbandry. However, surrounded by abundant seafood resources, Japanese cuisine, known as "washoku," focuses on showcasing the natural flavors of ingredients. Raw food preparation allows for the full expression of the ingredients' freshness and natural essence, resulting in the development of Japanese raw food culture.

2. Korea

When dining in Korea, you will always find a variety of kimchi dishes on the table. This is because Korea experiences cold winters, making it challenging to obtain fresh vegetables. To overcome this, they harvest and preserve vegetables as kimchi during the summer season. The consumption of spicy chili peppers during cold weather helps to keep warm, and the high vitamin C content in chili peppers aids in preventing colds and boosting immunity. Therefore, a wide range of kimchi varieties are served in Korean cuisine. Kimchi is not just a common food item; it is considered a national treasure in Korea. The process of making kimchi is fermentation, not pickling. It is regarded as a healthy food and a source of pride for Koreans. Respecting Korean kimchi means respecting Korean culture, and it has become an important cultural gift in international exchanges.

3. Thailand

Thai cuisine is known for its bold and spicy flavors. The hot climate in Thailand often reduces appetite, so adding spicy and tangy condiments helps stimulate the taste buds and increase appetite. Additionally, the use of acidic ingredients in Thai cuisine helps preserve food and prevents spoilage in high temperatures during the summer season.

4. China

China's vast territory and diverse geographical features result in different climate conditions across regions. It is often said, "Southern Chinese prefer rice, while Northern Chinese enjoy wheat-based foods." In the southern part of China, where the climate is humid and hot, rice is the primary staple crop. In contrast, the colder and drier climate in the north is more suitable for growing wheat and other cereal crops, making flour-based dishes more prevalent.

II. Culture

Culture refers to the values, beliefs, attitudes, or customs accepted by a group or individual. Eastern and Western cultures differ significantly in terms of food and dining habits. Easterners use chopsticks to eat rice, while Westerners use knives and forks to eat steak. Regardless of the eating utensils used, they should be understood and respected. Foreigners who want to understand the culture of a country should also learn to use such tools in dining, following the local customs. It is important not to offend or undermine the essence of another country's food culture unknowingly. For example, Dolce &

Eating with chopsticks series advertisement

Gabbana's controversial video of eating pizza with chopsticks caused offense among the Chinese community and resulted in sanctions imposed on the brand by China, greatly damaging the company's image. This demonstrates a lack of respect for the food culture of another country.

1. Food

Different countries may find foreign foods unpalatable or unfamiliar. However, one should express gratitude for the host's special preparations. Hosts should also understand that foreign visitors may have difficulty accepting unfamiliar and unconventional foods. Therefore, when selecting food, extra consideration should be given. For example, "pig's blood" is a type of blood product that may be taboo for foreign guests or certain religious groups and should be avoided. Strong-flavored foods like "stinky tofu" with its distinct odor often make foreigners hesitant to try it. Some foreigners may find the unique smell of "tea eggs" commonly found in Taiwanese convenience stores off-putting. On the other hand, Asians may have difficulty accepting foods like "Blue Cheese" from Italy, which is made with blue mold. It can be said that different foods have their own preferences and enthusiasts, and we should respect and understand that. As guests in a foreign land, even if we personally cannot accept certain foods, we should respect the culinary preferences of others and avoid showing disdain or discomfort, which can make the person enjoying the food feel embarrassed. Since we are in a foreign land, we should try various international cuisines to broaden our experiences. However, when trying new foods, we should also pay attention to our own digestive system to avoid getting sick from the change in diet. For example, Huaxi Street, also known as "Snake Alley" in the past, attracted many foreigners to visit. There was a case where three pilots from an airline tried drinking snake blood from Huaxi Street and ended up in the hospital. As a result, the airline had to cancel flights the next day, affecting the travel plans of over three hundred passengers.

2. Tableware

There are three widely popular ways in which humans eat: with their fingers, with a fork, or with chopsticks. Finger food is mainly found in countries such as Africa, the Middle East, and India. The use of forks for eating is prevalent in Europe, North America, and South America. The use of chopsticks for rice is primarily seen in East Asian countries. Chopsticks, as one of the symbols of Chinese cuisine, have an ancient origin, and it is difficult to determine who exactly invented them. The earliest discovered chopsticks in China were made of bronze. Historical records mention King Zhou using delicate ivory chopsticks. The history of chopsticks dates back approximately four thousand years. Using hands for eating, as seen in countries like India, is actually a sign of respect towards deities because food is considered a gift from the gods and nature. Eating with hands establishes a connection with the gods. We also have instances of using hands for eating in our daily lives, such as when enjoying crab or eating chicken with our hands. Hands are versatile, convenient, and allow for a more enjoyable eating experience. Moreover, eating with hands limits the amount of food taken at a time, preventing mouth burns. Additionally, it eliminates the need for utensils, which is environmentally friendly!

3. Dining etiquette

Dining etiquette: In some countries like the Philippines, Cambodia, Korea, and Egypt, finishing all the food on the plate signifies telling the host, "I'm not full yet." In Vietnam, elders advise not to finish all the food to show consideration for others, as leaving some food symbolizes having someone in mind. In Japan, China, and Taiwan, finishing all the food on the table indicates satisfaction with the host's culinary skills. Other dining etiquettes include not placing chopsticks upright in a rice bowl in China and holding the rice bowl properly while eating. In contrast, Koreans do not lift the rice bowl when eating because homeless people on the streets eat directly from the rice bowl due to the absence of tables. In practical terms, Korean steel bowls tend to conduct heat, making it uncomfortable to lift the bowl.

◆China

Chopsticks should not be placed upright in a rice bowl. When eating fish, it should not be flipped over, as it symbolizes a capsized boat. During a company banquet, if the boss positions the chicken head towards someone, it signifies that person may be laid off. Noodles should not be cut because longer noodles symbolize longevity (similar to the long mochi eaten during the Japanese New Year). When dining together, there is a concept of using public chopsticks and serving spoons. It is advised to avoid mixing or stirring the food on the communal plate, and it is considered impolite to make noise while eating soup or rice.

◆Japan

It is customary to loudly say "Itadakimasu" before starting a meal, which means "I humbly receive." After finishing a meal, it is common to say "Gochisousama deshita," which means "Thank you for the meal." Additionally, in Japan, making sounds while eating noodles is considered a way to express enjoyment, and the act of creating airflow by making noise helps to cool down the hot broth and prevent burning one's mouth. In Japanese funerals, chopsticks are used to pass on the bones of the deceased, so it is not common for Japanese people to use chopsticks to transfer food to others at the dining table.

◆Japan and Korea

It is common to see kneeling while eating in Japan and Korea. In ancient China, before the Western Jin Dynasty, people also used to eat while kneeling. Before the Qin and Han Dynasties, there were no tables or chairs, and people would sit on reed mats placed on the floor. Food utensils, such as rectangular stands or trays, were placed in front of them. They would kneel on the mats and eat, a practice known as "jizuo" or "kneeling eating." It was not until the invention of the stool that people started eating while sitting. Kneeling or sitting cross-legged while eating is still prevalent in Korea and Japan. Those who enjoy kneeling eating believe that this posture increases blood flow to the stomach, aids in digestion, and prevents bloating.

◆Thailand and the Philippines

The main utensils in Thailand and the Philippines are spoons and forks. The spoon

Thai people hold a spoon in their right hand and a fork in their left hand

Italians eat pasta with only forks and plates

is held in the right hand, and the fork is held in the left hand. The fork is used to push the food onto the spoon before eating. It is important not to put the fork directly into the mouth. In contrast, Western countries typically use a knife and fork, holding the knife in the right hand and the fork in the left hand. However, when enjoying Italian pasta, the fork is held in the right hand and the spoon in the left hand. Using the fork, the pasta is twirled around the spoon and then eaten. Interestingly, Italians eat pasta with only a fork and no spoon, so using a knife to eat pasta would make Italians shake their heads in disapproval.

III. Custom

Certain countries or regions have unique customs, which in turn shape their special dietary habits. Taking Taiwan's festival customs as an example:

1. Chinese New Year

On New Year's Eve, families gather around a hot pot to enjoy a grand feast known as the "Reunion Dinner." The dining table is adorned with symbolic dishes such as fish (representing abundance), longevity noodles (symbolizing long life), and dried tofu for Hakka people (signifying prosperity). It is also customary to have chicken during the New Year because the word for chicken sounds like "auspicious" in Chinese and is homophonous with the word for "home" in Taiwanese. Therefore, eating chicken carries the meaning of starting a prosperous life.

2. Lantern Festival

During the Lantern Festival, people eat tangyuan as they resemble the shape of a full moon, symbolizing family reunion ("tuan yuan" in Chinese).

3. Qingming Festival

Qingming Festival combines ancestor worship and reverence for nature. It is an important traditional festival when people visit and clean ancestral graves. Traditional offerings include rice cakes, kuei (sticky rice cakes), and pastries. The red tortoise-shaped pastries represent longevity, and it is customary to distribute these "tomb-sweeping cakes" to local children, symbolizing the continuation of ancestral virtues.

4. Dragon Boat Festival

The Dragon Boat Festival originated from an ancient Chinese festival called "Jie Long Ri" or "Duanwu Festival." People would take preventive measures against diseases during this time as it was believed that the air was heavily contaminated. Consuming realgar wine and mung bean cakes were believed to have cooling and detoxifying effects. Although most people associate Dragon Boat Festival with dragon boat races and eating zongzi (sticky rice dumplings), which are related to the patriotic poet Qu Yuan, these activities are actually part of the ritual ceremonies dedicated to deities.

5. Mid-Autumn Festival

The Mid-Autumn Festival is a time of harvest and gratitude towards ancestors and the Earth God for the bountiful crops. Mooncakes and pomelos are commonly enjoyed during this festival. Mooncakes, with their round shape, symbolize "reunion" and "togetherness." In recent times, it has become a tradition for families to gather and enjoy mooncakes while appreciating the moon and having a barbecue, signifying the importance of cherishing family reunions.

6. Customs in other countries

In Italy, during Christmas, people enjoy a special fruit bread called "Panettone," which is a traditional Christmas treat and gift. It is often paired with sparkling wine. In India, during the festival of Diwali (also known as the Festival of Lights), which falls in the Indian lunar month of Kartika, people eat almond sweets as a way to invite good fortune and ward off evil spirits. These customs and traditions greatly influence the culinary lifestyle. Whether foreign friends visit our country, or we travel to other countries, we can embrace and enjoy the local customs, special culinary cultures, and festive celebrations according to local traditions and time. By doing so, we embody the spirit of international etiquette and celebrate with understanding and joy.

IV. Weather

Weather also deeply influences culinary habits. For example, as mentioned earlier, Korean kimchi is served on Korean tables even during winter. The tangy and spicy sauces found in Southeast Asia are also a result of climatic factors. Due to the tropical

Panettone bread eaten at Christmas in Italy

climate in the region, people have relied on strongly flavored spices to preserve their ingredients. The use of aromatic spices in their cuisine awakens the taste buds and enhances appetite. Countries such as Indonesia, the Philippines, Thailand, and India incorporate a wide range of aromatic spices in their dishes.

On the other hand, the Inuit people residing in the far northern regions of North America experience average temperatures below minus eight degrees Celsius throughout the year. The cold weather conditions lead to their food sources primarily relying on high-fat fish and meat, with little consumption of vegetables and fruits. The polar climate makes it difficult for plants to grow, resulting in a limited availability of plant-based food. The Inuit people have a unique culinary tradition called "Kiviak," which is considered one of the darkest dishes in the world. It involves fermenting seabirds and is a test of courage for outsiders to challenge the local practice of consuming raw food.

The weather conditions greatly shape the availability of ingredients and the preservation methods employed in different regions, leading to diverse culinary cultures around the world.

V. Religion（Please refer to Chapter 6 for Religion etiquette ）

Religion has a significant impact on the dietary practices and rituals of individuals. When hosting guests, it is important to understand their religious beliefs, as for many people, religious faith is sacred and deeply ingrained. The world's three major religions include:

1. Buddhism

Vegetarianism is emphasized and encouraged among Buddhists. Based on a compassionate standpoint, they believe that consuming meat is detrimental to one's health. Buddhist vegetarianism also includes avoiding pungent spices such as garlic, onions, and chives. Regarding alcohol consumption, Buddhism places emphasis on wisdom and believes that excessive drinking leads to moral misconduct. To advance spiritual cultivation and achieve mental clarity, Buddhists practice abstinence from alcohol.

2. *Hinduism*

Hinduism strictly prohibits the consumption of beef. Additionally, most Hindus abstain from eating pork due to the widespread belief that it is impure. Uncooked fish and smoked fish are also considered unsuitable. However, they can consume lamb, poultry, other types of fish, and dairy products. In fact, India encourages vegetarianism, and half of its population practices vegetarianism, particularly among Hindus. The Jain branch of Hinduism follows even stricter dietary rules, abstaining from all food that may cause harm to living beings. Abstaining from alcohol is a common practice among Indians, including Hindus.

3. *Islam*

Islam, also known as Muslim, has dietary guidelines known as Halal food. Muslims do not consume pork and abstain from alcohol. The certification of Halal food is stringent, requiring the slaughter to be performed by a Muslim. The process involves recitation of religious verses and ensuring the animal's death occurs with the least amount of pain through bleeding. Muslims also avoid consuming animals that have died naturally because their cleanliness cannot be guaranteed. Additionally, Muslims have fixed prayer times throughout the day and observe a month-long period called "Ramadan." Ramadan occurs in the ninth month of the Islamic calendar, during which Muslims fast from dawn to sunset. However, breastfeeding women, those who are ill, and tourists are exempt from fasting. Muslims use the month of Ramadan to practice self-restraint, experience the struggles of the less fortunate, and reflect on their personal spirituality.

VI. **Modern Development**

The level of a country's development is most evident in its dining customs. African tribes, living a primitive lifestyle, introduce their children to hunting from a young age.

They use leaves as plates and their hands as utensils, sitting on the ground. In some regions, tribes lead extremely basic lives, pushing the limits of human endurance by relying on bare-handed consumption due to limited resources. In contrast, in ancient historical countries like France, England, and China, dining practices are often steeped in elaborate traditions. Both Chinese and Western cuisines place great importance on sophisticated tableware and lavish presentations. The level of a country's development also influences the cooking methods employed in its cuisine, ranging from rudimentary techniques to the intricate flavors and artistic plating associated with Michelin-starred restaurants.

Types of Dining

Dining can vary in terms of time and type, and the complexity can also differ.

I. Categorization by Time

1. Breakfast

The word "breakfast" is formed by combining "break" and "fast," indicating the first meal after breaking the overnight fasting period. Breakfast is generally divided into American Breakfast (AB), Buffet Breakfast (BB), Continental Breakfast (CB), English Breakfast/Full Breakfast, as well as other variations such as German-Austrian breakfast, French breakfast, and Italian breakfast. Asian breakfast options are also diverse, including Chinese breakfast, Japanese breakfast, Southeast Asian breakfast, and more. In hotels, the type of breakfast offered may vary based on the size of the hotel, regional characteristics, and the number of guests staying on a particular day. Especially during the pandemic when the number of guests has decreased, adaptability in breakfast offerings has become an important operational concern for hotels.

◆Continental Breakfast is relatively light and generally provides:

1. Bread: toast, rolls, croissants, pastries, butter and jam

2. American ham, Italian sausage, Italian ham

3. Lettuce salad, fresh fruit

4. Dairy products such as milk, cheese, yogurt

5. Breakfast cornflakes, cereal, oatmeal

6. Juice, coffee, tea, milk, mineral water

◆English Breakfast / also known as Full Breakfast, generally provides the following meals on a large plate

1. Omelet, sausage, bacon or ham, blood sausage

2. Green beans, roasted tomatoes, and roasted mushrooms

3. Toast with strong English tea, coffee and juice

In Europe, hotels typically offer guests a choice between an English breakfast or a continental breakfast. Continental breakfast is typically more carbohydrate-heavy, while English breakfast tends to be protein-focused. Additionally, some European hotels may provide a "cold buffet" option, featuring cold dishes and room-temperature bread rather than hot food.

◆American Breakfast is typically more abundant and generally includes:

American Breakfast: Typically, American breakfast is more abundant and includes

1. Various egg dishes such as sunny-side up, scrambled eggs, omelets, and breakfast burritos.

2. It also features items like bacon, ham, sausages, and hash browns.

3. Additionally, it offers pancakes, waffles, bagels, toast, pastries, cornflakes, and oats.

4. The beverage options usually include fruit juice, milk, coffee, and tea.

◆Wiener Breakfast (German-Austrian Breakfast):

This breakfast typically includes coffee, bread, boiled eggs, cheese, ham, and bacon.

◆French Breakfast

A French breakfast often consists of café latte, hot chocolate, sliced French bread, croissants, and raisin bread rolls.

◆Italian Breakfast

Italian breakfast options include latte, cappuccino, bread, bread rolls, and croissants. Italians enjoy coffee in the morning, and latte is typically consumed during breakfast, paired with various types of bread.

◆Buffet Breakfast

Buffet breakfast offers a wide variety of choices. In many international hotels that accommodate guests from different countries and cultures, buffet breakfast tends to provide a selection of international breakfast options. The aim is to cater to guests' preferences and create a "home away from home" experience.

◆Chinese Breakfast

Chinese Breakfast: Chinese breakfast includes items like sesame pancakes, fried dough sticks, soy milk, egg wraps, rice balls, pan-fried buns, porridge, and various pickled vegetables.

◆Japanese Breakfast

A Japanese breakfast often consists of steamed rice steeped in green tea, miso soup, udon noodles, natto, and pickled vegetables, among other Japanese foods.

◆South Asia Style Breakfast

Vietnamese breakfast may include beef noodle soup (pho), fresh shrimp rice noodle rolls, while Indian breakfast can feature spiced rice, flatbreads, and vegetable pancakes. In Malaysia, a popular breakfast is bak kut teh (pork rib soup), while Indonesian breakfast may

Nasi uduk

include nasi uduk (coconut rice) and beef noodle soup or meatball soup.

2. Brunch

Brunch is a combination of breakfast and lunch, typically enjoyed around midday, usually between 11 am and 2-3 pm.

3. Lunch

Lunch is a midday meal typically served between 12 pm and 2 pm. It is an important mealtime for business interactions and meetings.

4. Tea Party

A tea party is held between breakfast and lunch or between lunch and dinner.

5. Cocktail Party

A cocktail party is a social gathering where guests are served alcoholic beverages and hors d'oeuvres. There is usually no formal seating arrangement, and guests are free to move around. Cocktail parties can be held before or after a formal dinner, allowing more opportunities for interaction among guests. The invitation should indicate the start and end time of the cocktail party.

6. Dinner

Dinner is typically served after 6 pm and is considered the most formal meal of the day. It is often a family or personal mealtime, and it is customary to invite couples together when hosting a dinner.

7. Soiree

A soiree is an evening event that includes dinner and entertainment, such as music performances, games, and dancing. The term comes from the French word "Soir," meaning evening or night.

Difference between supper and dinner

Dinner is the largest meal of the evening, typically served between 5 pm and 8 pm. On the other hand, Supper is an older term that also refers to the evening meal. In comparison to Dinner, Supper generally implies a lighter portion.

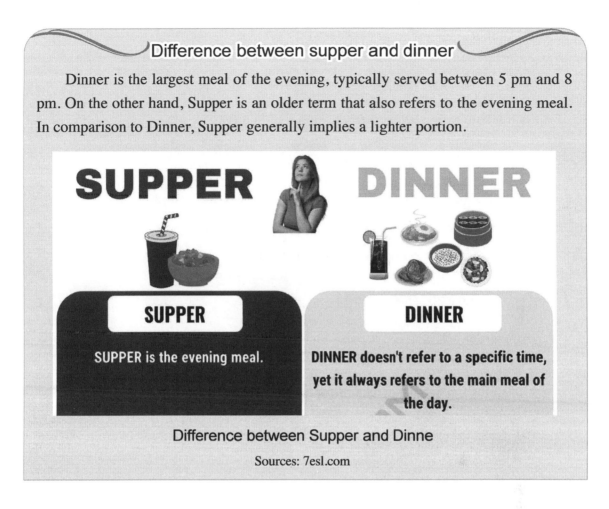

Difference between Supper and Dinne

Sources: 7esl.com

8. Gala Dinner

A gala dinner is a large-scale party or banquet that often includes a fixed-seating formal dinner or a buffet-style meal. It is usually accompanied by entertainment, such as awards ceremonies or themed activities. Guests are expected to dress formally, often in black-tie attire.

II. Categorized by types

1. State Banquet

A state banquet refers to a formal banquet held for visiting heads of state or dignitaries attending important international conferences. It is the highest-level diplomatic banquet.

2. Garden Party

A themed outdoor event, such as a charity garden party.

3. Buffet

A buffet is a meal where food is displayed on a table or buffet line, and guests serve themselves. There are no assigned seats, and guests can eat at their own pace, enjoying more freedom in terms of portion sizes and food choices.

4. Hi-Tea, Afternoon Tea

Afternoon tea originated from the Victorian era in England and is typically served between lunch and dinner. It usually takes place from around 3:30 pm to 5 pm. Afternoon tea is not a full meal and is often accompanied by cakes and sandwiches.

Difference between High Tea and Afternoon Tea

Sources: theteacupoflife.com

Three-Tier Petit Four Stand for Afternoon Tea:

Petit four refers to small cakes or biscuits that are typically enjoyed with coffee after a meal. In afternoon tea, the three-tier stand is used to display different items on each tier. Generally, savory snacks such as sandwiches or scones are placed on the bottom tier, followed by sweet cakes on the second tier, and the top tier typically holds chocolates or macarons. The order of consumption is to start with the savory items before moving on to the sweet ones. This is because consuming sweet treats can affect our appetite. Therefore, when enjoying afternoon tea, it is customary to start from the bottom tier and work our way up, progressing from savory to sweet.

Afternoon Tea Decoration

 ## Class activities 3

1. Ask students to discuss their dining experiences at restaurants. Which factors determine a pleasant dining experience and what makes them feel disappointed? Why?
2. Divide students into groups and have them research the breakfast foods of different countries. They can share their findings in class.
3. Divide students into groups and have them research traditional festival foods from various countries and their symbolic meanings. They can present their findings in class.
4. Divide students into groups and have them research different countries of their eating method and content of their meal.

延伸閱讀

Black, R. (2019). *Essential Guide for Table Manners, Business Meals, Sushi, Wine, and Tea Etiquette*. Celestial Arc Publishing.

Mason, L. (2018). *Book of Afternoon Tea*. National Trust.

Meier, M. (2020). *Modern Etiquette Made Easy*. Skyhorse Publishing.

中村義裕（2017）。《日本傳統文化事典》。遠足文化。

行政院國情簡介──宗教信仰在台灣，https://www.ey.gov.tw/state/D00B53C98CD4F08F/0fe638e7-c0bf-401e-b9f2-3db11eecd508

張玉欣、郭忠豪、蔡倩紋（2020）。《世界飲食文化》。華立圖書。

Chapter

4

Fine Dining

- Chinese Dining Etiquette and Table Setting
- Japanese Dining Etiquette and Table Setting
- Western Dining Etiquette and Table Setting
- Seating Arrangements in Dining Etiquette

A joyful and beautiful dining feast always brings happiness. From the artistic environment of the restaurant to the smiles radiated by the waiters to the tantalizing aroma of the food. All of these enhances the dining experiences. And what is a delightful meal without fine wine? The clinking of glasses and the sound of laughter make life even more enjoyable.

🤝 Chinese Dining Etiquette and Table Setting

A delightful dining feast includes a clean and elegant environment with well-arranged dining tables. It also involves the cultivation of both hosts and guests in their dining etiquette. A well-designed table setting can enhance the guests' mood, create a pleasant dining atmosphere, and whet the appetite. The table setting could be chosen based on the host's temperament, preferences, and tastes. Excessive elaborateness and overly complex formalities might sometimes detract from the joy of savoring delicious food. We will introduce some of the most common dining styles in the following :

I. Chinese dining etiquette

1. the correct chopstick etiquette: "The Dragon Holds the Pearl, the Phoenix Nods."

龍含珠 鳳點頭

Correct Way of Holding Chopsticks and Bowls - "The Dragon Holds the Pearl, the Phoenix Nods."

Chopsticks are a quintessential part of Chinese culture. If you were to ask every Chinese person whether they know how to use chopsticks, you would likely receive the answer, "Of course! I've been using them for many years!" However, is that really the case? In fact, not all Chinese people necessarily know how to use chopsticks. Based on many years of teaching experience, over 80% of students in class do not know how to use chopsticks correctly. Some even hold chopsticks in awkward and incorrect ways. There are two main reasons why Chinese people may struggle with chopsticks:

- Every individual comes from a different family background, and the "enlightener" who teaches the use of chopsticks varies. Typically, this enlightener is a mother or another family member. It's worth understanding and discussing whether the enlightener themselves know how to use chopsticks correctly and can pass on this knowledge accurately.

- Chinese people typically start learning to use chopsticks around their kindergarten years. Some parents may become impatient and put unnecessary pressure on their children, causing them to grasp chopsticks with excessive force. The muscles in their hands and fingers become tense and numb, leading them to continue using this incorrect way of holding chopsticks until adulthood without realizing whether they are doing it correctly. Interestingly, foreign students in the classroom often use chopsticks better and more accurately than local students. This is because foreign students learn to use chopsticks as adults when their hand muscles are fully developed, and they are motivated by interest rather than feeling pressured.

The correct method of holding chopsticks is "The Dragon Holds the Pearl, the Phoenix Nods." When sitting, maintain an upright posture with the left hand holding the bowl and the right hand holding the chopsticks. When holding the bowl with the left hand, place the thumb on top and the four fingers parallel below, resembling a dragon opening its mouth and holding a precious pearl. On the other hand, holding the chopsticks with the right hand is like a phoenix. When the tips of the chopsticks open and close, it resembles the nodding of a phoenix. This posture of holding the bowl and chopsticks is both correct and elegant

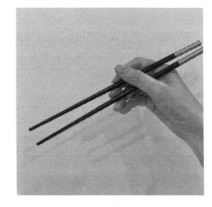

Correct Way of Holding Chopsticks

Here are the 6 steps of the correct way to use

chopsticks:

- Align the chopsticks, and hold them at the upper third section of the chopsticks.
- Slightly separate the two chopsticks and place them between the thumb and index finger.
- Use the thumb, index finger, and middle finger to gently hold the upper chopstick.
- Place the index finger lightly on top of the upper chopstick, allowing the chopstick to rest on the fingernail of the middle finger.
- Gently secure it with the thumb, while the index and middle fingers are responsible for moving the upper chopstick.
- The pinky finger rests lightly against the ring finger, and the second chopstick gently rests on the fingernail of the ring finger.

The key to properly holding chopsticks is to remain relaxed. It is important to keep the muscles in your hand as relaxed as possible, similar to playing a musical instrument or singing, where relaxed muscles are essential for smooth control. By staying relaxed, you can handle chopsticks correctly and with ease.

2. The Incorrect Ways of Holding Chopsticks

- Crossed Index Finger: This grip is very similar to the correct way of holding chopsticks, with the difference being that the index finger crosses over the top chopstick in an attempt to increase control. The reason behind this is excessive

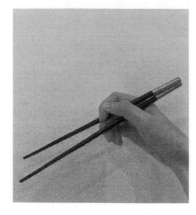 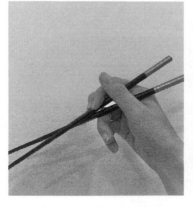 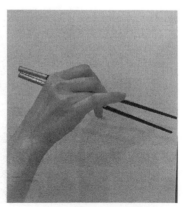

Incorrect way I:
Cross index finger

Incorrect way II
Chaotic five-finger grip

Incorrect way III
Lotus finger grip

tension in the hand muscles. This is the most common incorrect way of holding chopsticks.

- Chaotic Five-Finger Grip: The five fingers are spread out haphazardly, with the chopsticks placed in the center of the ring finger. The emphasis is on the intersection of the crossed chopsticks. This grip results in a disorganized finger position and incorrect use of force.

- Lotus Finger Grip: In this style, the chopsticks are held by the thumb, exerting more force on the ring finger. As a result, the pinky finger is raised, and when picking up food, the back of the hand tends to face upward.

- Fist Grip: This grip involves holding the chopsticks in a closed fist with all fingers together, and the chopsticks are used by holding them within the palm. This grip

Incorrect way IV
Fist grip

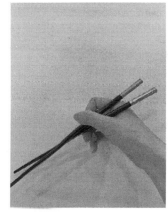

Incorrect way V
Pen grip

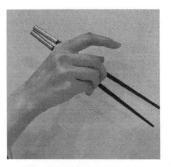

Incorrect way VI
Raised finger grip

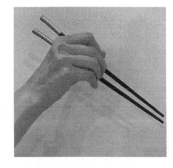

Incorrect way VII
Back chip grip

is often seen in children and resembles stabbing or scooping food rather than grasping it.

- Pen Grip (Crossed Grip): This style involves crossing the chopsticks, similar to holding a pen. The index finger and middle finger are responsible for placing them on the upper and lower chopsticks, respectively. This type of chopstick grip is also quite common.

- Raised Finger Grip: The index finger is raised, and the chopsticks are controlled using the middle finger and ring finger. This grip can make the person sitting across feel pointed at or uncomfortable.

- Back Clip Grip: Generally, when picking up food, the back of the hand should not face upward. In this grip, all fingers are together, with the emphasis on the middle finger, and the back of the hand faces upward.

3. Table Etiquette

- In Chinese dining, the table is typically round, and in the center of a large round table, there is a small rotating table known as "Lazy Susan." The purpose of this small round table is to rotate the dishes for easy access by everyone. The order of starting the meal is to allow the main guests to begin first. If there are no main guests, then the person closest to where the dishes are placed should start first, but the juniors should always let seniors start first as a sign of courtesy.

  When rotating the Lazy Susan, it should be done in a clockwise direction. If you miss the dish you want to pick up, patiently wait for the table to rotate again and bring it back in front of you. Avoid forcefully pulling back the Lazy Susan in a "rewinding" manner. However, if the table has already completed a full rotation, and everyone has taken what they wanted, adjustments can be made as needed.

- In fact, in Western buffet-style dining as well, the practice is to take food in a clockwise direction. When taking food, it is important to use a clean plate and follow the clockwise direction. It is advisable to avoid engaging in conversations while taking food. It is recommended to take small portions that can be finished in each round rather than taking excessive amounts. Some establishments

Lazy Susan, the Chinese rotating table

may charge extra for food wastage, but regardless of such policies, wasting food is generally viewed unfavorably. It is important to cultivate the virtue of appreciating and cherishing food.

- Avoid making loud chewing noises while eating, as it can be bothersome to nearby diners and create a negative impression. Refrain from sneezing, coughing, yawning, or blowing your nose during the meal; if necessary, use a handkerchief or napkin to cover your mouth.

- Talking with food in your mouth may result in spitting food, causing embarrassment for yourself and inconvenience to others. The proper approach is to pause the conversation momentarily, quickly swallow the food, and wipe your mouth with a napkin before continuing to talk.

- Engaging with your mobile phone or answering calls at the dining table is considered impolite. Respect your dining companions and place your phone on silent in your pocket or bag. Enjoy the meal and engage in pleasant conversations with those around you.

- Always use serving chopsticks and spoons when sharing dishes. There are two common practices for serving chopsticks: some restaurants place a

Serving set of utensil

set of serving chopsticks on each dish for communal use, while others provide two sets of chopsticks per person—one for personal use and one for public use.

- When picking up food, avoid digging or searching in the serving dish for your preferred portion. Do not put the chopsticks in your mouth to suck or taste, and refrain from using chopsticks as a conductor's baton to point at others or objects. Additionally, do not use your chopsticks to take food from someone else's bowl. These actions go against proper table manners and can leave a negative impression on others.

- If utensils fall to the ground during the meal, signal a waiter for assistance and wait for them to provide new utensils. Do not pick up fallen utensils by yourself, and avoid using utensils from neighboring tables, as it may cause inconvenience to the restaurant and its staff.

- Avoid using toothpicks at the dining table. If necessary, you can discreetly use a napkin to cover your mouth while quickly using a toothpick. Additionally, ladies should not touch up their lipstick at the table. Many restaurants provide a dedicated space called the Powder Room, equipped with mirrors, chairs, and a vanity for such purposes. It's a more comfortable and appropriate area for personal grooming.

II. Chinese table setting

- The more formal table setting includes placing the chopsticks on the right side of the plate with the tips facing upwards. The inner pair of chopsticks is for personal use, while the outer pair is for sharing (public chopsticks). For dishes that require the use of knives and forks, the server will provide them before

Chinese-style dining lounge

Chinese table setting

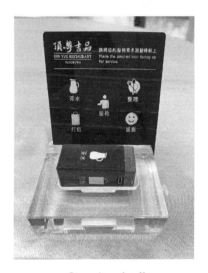

Service bell

Standard items on Chinese table setting

serving the respective dish.

- The teacup is placed on the right side of the plate, and the soup bowl is placed on the left side of the plate. The soup spoon should be placed inside the soup bowl (avoid placing it upside down on the plate to prevent soup from dripping and soiling the tablecloth).

- On the left side of the plate, a towel and a towel holder are placed.

- Apart from decorative flowers and vases, the basic table setting includes toothpicks, vinegar, and soy sauce. Some restaurants provide a service bell, where guests can indicate their needs by turning the corresponding item face up. The server will then attend to the requested service, which may include tea refills, packing leftovers, tidying up, or indicating satisfaction.

Japanese Dining Etiquette and Table Setting

Japan is a country known for its emphasis on etiquette. Japanese people value the principle of "おめいわく かげないよに" , which means "do not cause trouble or inconvenience to others." This mindset of self-imposed requirements is instilled in individuals from their early education and within the family. When traveling to Japan, interacting with Japanese people, or dining at Japanese restaurants, it is important to pay special attention to etiquette to avoid offending others or causing embarrassment. Here are several Japanese dining etiquette guidelines:

I. Japanese Dining Etiquette

- Before starting the meal, wait until everyone received their meal. It is customary to say "Itadakimasu" (いただきます), which means "I humbly receive." After finishing the meal, it is polite to say "Gochisousama deshita" (ごちそうさまでした), which means "Thank you for the meal."

Japanese sushi bar

- Japanese cuisine usually provides a moist hand towel called "oshibori." In winter, it is warm, and in summer, it is cold. The oshibori is meant for wiping hands only and should not be used to wipe sweat, face, or glasses.

- When eating, it is considered impolite to make noise while chewing, except when eating ramen. However, in international settings, it is important to adapt to international etiquette and avoid making noise while eating.

- Japanese table settings differ from Chinese cuisine. In Japanese cuisine, chopsticks are placed horizontally with the tips pointing to the left. At no time should the chopsticks be placed "resting" on the bowl. After finishing the meal, it is best to place the chopsticks back on the dish or in the chopstick holder.

- The proper way to handle a soup bowl is to lightly hold it with the left hand and lift the lid with the right hand. If the lid is difficult to open due to steam, you can press down on the sides of the bowl with your left hand to release the air, making it easier to open the lid. Place the lid on the table to avoid wetting the surface. Since soup spoons are not commonly used in Japanese cuisine, the usual method for drinking soup is to use chopsticks to eat the larger ingredients and then bring the bowl to your mouth to sip the soup. After drinking, place the lid back on the bowl neatly.

Japanese miso soup

- In Japanese cuisine, the order of eating is from light to rich flavors. Therefore, when eating sashimi, it is recommended to start with white fish such as shrimp and scallops, and end with fattier fish like tuna.

- When eating sushi, it is best to eat one piece at a time and avoid biting it in half, as it may appear clumsy. When bringing the food to your mouth, do not use your free hand underneath to assist or prevent sauce from dripping. Instead, use a plate or a napkin.

- Wasabi should not be mixed directly with soy sauce. Many Taiwanese people's way of eating sushi is not correct in this case

- It is considered impolite to leave the table to go to the restroom during the meal. This disrupts the dining pace, and make others wait for your return before continuing. It can inconvenience the sushi chefs and other diners at the counter or in the same group.

- Some Japanese restaurants require you to take off your shoes, so it is important to keep your feet clean and hygienic. If your feet have an odor, especially after a long day at work, consider bringing an extra pair of socks to put on or replace the ones you are wearing. When removing your shoes, place them with the toes facing outward to facilitate putting them back on when leaving.

Japanese tatami dining room

Source: lovepic.com

- The complete order of serving in a traditional Japanese meal is as follows:
  (1) Sakizuke (appetizer)→(2) Owan (soup)→(3) Mukōzuke (sashimi)→(4) Hassun (assorted small dishes)→(5) Yakimono (grilled dish, often fish or beef)→(6) Agemono (deep-fried dish, like tempura)→(7) Nimono (simmered dish)→(8) Sunomono (vinegared dish, like salad)→(9) Mushimono (steamed dish, like chawanmushi or steamed egg)→(10) Gohan + Shiojiru (rice and miso soup) + Kōmono (pickles)→(11) Mizumono (dessert).

- When eating soba noodles, it is considered more elegant to take one bite of the noodle and then dip it in the soba sauce. It is not customary to pour soy sauce over the entire bowl of soba noodles to avoid making them overly salty.

II. **Japanese Table Setting**

Japanese dining often includes a counter seating arrangement where the chef prepares the dishes in front of the guests and serves them one by one onto their plates for immediate enjoyment. This type of table setting is relatively simple and typically includes chopsticks, plates, soy sauce dishes, tea cups, etc. Another common Japanese dining style is the kaiseki cuisine (かいせきりょうり), where all the dishes are presented on a single plate for the guests to enjoy. The chopsticks are placed below the plate, closer to the person, with the tips pointing to the left. The white rice is placed on the left side, and the soup bowl is on the right side, allowing guests to start with the soup and side dishes before picking up the rice bowl to eat alongside the main dish in front of them.

Seating arrangement in front of the counter

Kaiseki cuisine table setting

Japanese New Year's Cuisine

Japanese New Year's cuisine, known as "osechi ryori", is prepared for the celebration of the new year, which falls on January 1st according to the Gregorian calendar.

Japanese New Year's Cuisine - Osechi Ryori

Osechi ryori consists of various dishes arranged in a stacking box called "juubako" (重箱). The layered juubako symbolizes the accumulation of good fortune and joy. Typically, formal osechi ryori consists of four layers, but nowadays, the number of layers and the variety of dishes may vary depending on the region and individual family preferences. Unlike the hot dishes traditionally eaten for the New Year's Eve dinner in Taiwan, osechi ryori is served cold. Any leftovers can be stored in the refrigerator and enjoyed the next day. On the day right before the new year, it is customary to eat "toshikoshi soba" (年越しそば), which is buckwheat noodles. As buckwheat noodles are easily bitten and broken, they symbolize "breaking away from the misfortunes of the past year." By eating them on the last day of the year, people hope for a long and slender life, or to overcome any hardships like the buckwheat plant, which thrives in adverse conditions without falling ill.

Western Dining Etiquette and Table Setting

I. Western Dining Etiquette

1. Proper use of linen napkin: How should a linen napkin be placed?

Western-style restaurant

- When you take your seat, do not immediately use the linen napkin. Wait for the hostess to unfold her napkin before using yours.
- The linen napkin is used to

wipe your mouth or cover a portion of your face when needed. Do not use it to wipe sweat or glasses.

- If your napkin or utensils fall, signal the server for assistance. They will provide you with fresh utensils and a new napkin. Never take utensils or napkins from a neighboring empty table

- Fold the napkin in half and place it on your lap. Do not tie it around your neck or tuck it into your collar. Use the inner side of the napkin to wipe your mouth and discreetly place it back on your lap, ensuring any food stains or lipstick marks are not visible.

- For female guests who are concerned about leaving a lipstick mark on the glass, it is recommended to lightly dab the napkin on your lips. Ladies should avoid touching up their lipstick at the table. If necessary, excuse yourself temporarily to the powder room to freshen up.

- If you need to leave the table temporarily during the meal, signal your nearby dining companion and place your napkin on the armrest or backrest of your chair. When you have finished your meal and wish to leave the table, place your napkin on the left side of the table, specifically to the left of the main plate (or above the bread plate). Do not place it on top of the main plate, especially if there are still dishes or sauces on it. Also, avoid placing it on the right side of the table, as the cutleries are placed there.

Proper use of a napkin

2. Use of Cutlery:

- Cutlery should be used from the outside in, according to the order of the courses.

- Regardless of whether you are left-handed or right-handed, the general rule is to hold the knife in the right hand and the fork in the left hand.

- However, it is a complete different setting when it comes to eating pasta. Fork is on the right and the spoon is on the left. This allows you to twirl the pasta onto the spoon for consumption.

- The fork and soup spoon should both be facing upwards, meaning the part that touches the mouth should not be in close contact with the tabletop.

- Do not place unnecessary utensils on the table.

- Typically, beverages are served from the right side, while dishes are served from the left side. Dishes for guests sharing the same table should be brought out simultaneously, ensuring synchronized service timing.

- After using cutleries, do not place them back on the table (they should be placed on the plate) to allow the server to remove them.

- When enjoying a steak, the recommended cutting method is to start from the lower left corner and cut from left to right.

Preferred cutting method for
steak, from left to right

Placement of cutlery during
the meal

Placement of cutlery at the
end of the meal

- During the meal, if you need to leave the table, notify others and then leave your knife and fork on the plate in a crossed position, forming an inverted "V" shape, or place the knife at 4 o'clock and the fork at 8 o'clock on the plate. This makes it convenient to pick up the cutleries when you return to the table. If you have finished your entire meal, place the knife and fork together on one side of the plate at 4 o'clock, indicating that you are finished with the meal.

3. Table Etiquette:

- Assisting women to their seats: When a man serves a female friend, it not only expresses friendliness towards her but also demonstrates his gentlemanly demeanor and shows that he is a well-mannered person.
- Left-handed individuals: Although left-handed individuals should not alter the table setting, western dining etiquette maintains the use of the knife in the right hand and the fork in the left. Many foreigners are left-handed. In the case of Chinese-style meals where chopsticks are held in the left hand, it is polite to acknowledge the person on the left and inform them that you are left-handed

and ask for their understanding. This way, both parties will be mindful and leave some extra space for each other while dining.

- Serving sequence for Western meals:

The dining sequence is as following: Appetizer→Soup→Salad→Main course →Cheese and fruit→Dessert.

Sequence of Serving Western Dishes

- Beverage Order:

  1. When seated, start by ordering an apéritif (Otherwise, champagne is also a good option), or if someone prefers, they can choose beer or whiskey.

  2. After ordering the main course, one can opt for a suitable wine pairing or seek recommendations from the sommelier.

  3. Before the main course is served, there is usually a palate cleanser known as sorbet. This helps awaken the taste buds for the main dish and clears the flavors of the appetizers consumed earlier.

  4. The cheese and fruit served after the main course are not considered post-meal fruits. Cheese aids digestion, and the accompanying fruits (such as a small amount of grapes or cantaloupe) enhance the flavor of the cheese.

  5. After the meal, it is common to enjoy sweeter, high-alcohol beverages such as

port wine or liqueurs like Baileys Irish Cream.

- When should salad be served, before or after the main course?

  In the United States, salads are typically served before the main course, often followed by soup and bread. However, in European countries like Italy and France, salads are served after the main course and before dessert. This is because salads are rich in fiber, aiding digestion and cleansing the palate to prepare for dessert.

- Go Dutch? Splitting the bill: Considerations for whether each person should pay their own bill:

  1.People: Among peers, classmates, or unfamiliar opposite-sex friends, it is common for each person to pay their own bill.

  2.Timing: Should the bill be split beforehand or afterward? It depends on the situation and can be coordinated by one person. If there are important guests or elders present, whether to split the bill immediately should be carefully considered.

  3.Location/Occasion: Some restaurants do not allow splitting of the bill.

  4.Purpose: Splitting the bill avoids any sense of indebtedness and eliminates pressure in social settings among friends. However, in a business context, splitting the bill may carry different implications. Therefore, whether to "Go Dutch" should be considered before the meal.

- Toasting

  There are many celebratory occasions where toasting is done during a meal, and the Chinese and Western traditions differ:

  1.Chinese Banquet: The host initiates the toast by inviting the guests, and the guests respond. After the host finishes toasting around the table, guests can individually offer toasts. Chinese toasting customs often involve clinking glasses, and it is customary to drink the entire contents of the glass to show respect.

  2.In Western toasting, it usually takes place at the end of the meal. The host explains the purpose and invites everyone to raise their glasses. It is not

Toasting in Celebration with Friends

necessary to clink glasses; a simple gesture of raising the glass is sufficient. It is considered impolite to damage the host's precious crystal glasses by clinking them. It is also incorrect to imitate the improper movie gesture of tapping a spoon on a glass to get everyone's attention at the end of a dinner. However, when dining with close friends at home, one can be more casual and enjoy the joy of clinking glasses.

II. Western Table Setting

The table setting in dining reflects the host's style and taste in home banquet, while in a restaurant, it showcases the establishment's style and attention to detail. A pleasant dining experience includes a comfortable dining environment and ambiance, and the table setting is one aspect that leaves a lasting impression. The texture of the table setting encompasses visual appeal and tactile sensations, from the cutlery and plates to the small vases and salt and pepper shakers on the table, as well as the decorative elements of napkins/tablecloths.

Western Table Setting

1. Table Setting Elements

- Tableware: High-quality tableware depends on the material. If you opt for silverware, it's essential to regularly polish it to prevent tarnishing. When arranging tableware, consider wearing gloves to avoid leaving fingerprints on the polished cutleries.

- Glasses: Essential glassware for table setting includes water glasses and appropriate wine glasses. The choice of wine glasses should align with the wine selection. Check that the glasses are clean, free from dirt or odors, and undamaged.

- Tablecloth/Napkins: The tablecloth should have a certain thickness to prevent slipping. It should be aligned and centered on the table, ensuring that the overhang is not too long to avoid accidents.

- Tablecloths can be decorative or functional. Decorative tablecloths can feature intricate and beautiful designs, such as roses or birds of paradise, primarily serving as table decor. Functional napkins, on the other hand, are meant for guests to place on their laps and use for wiping their mouths. Overly complex folding or intricate designs are not suitable for functional napkins.

Napkin - Rose

Students in classroom practicing
the folding of the napkins

2. Key points for Western table setting:

- Knives are placed on the right side, forks on the left side, with the knife blade facing towards oneself.

- Fork tines and spoons are placed facing upward, away from the tablecloth, as this side tends to contact with mouth.

- An oval soup spoon is used for clear soups, while a round soup spoon is used for thick soups.

- The plate is placed in the center, with a napkin placed on top. The bread plate is on the left, and the beverage glass is on the right.

- Dessert forks are set above the plate, with the dessert spoon placed above and facing left, and the dessert fork placed below and facing right.To learn how to properly arrange the knives and forks, students can watch the online video "Anna Post - How to set the table" at https://www.youtube.com/watch?v=KoU1XiQJ1vo.

International Etiquette Commonly Used English Vocabulary:

Chopstick	Chopstick stands	Silverware	Utensil
Linen	Tablecloth	Serviette	Set a table
cutlery	Placemat/ table cloth	Cloth napkin/paper napkin	Eat outside in
Dinning sequence	Hors d'oeuvre	Soup Salad	Cheese & fruit Dessert

Table Setting Demonstration

Seating Arrangements in Dining Etiquette

Seating arrangements in dining are a skillful practice that requires thoughtful consideration of social etiquette and venue decoration. It's important to arrange seats based on the guests' seniority, status, and importance within the occasion. A well-organized seating plan can greatly honor the guests, while mistakes can potentially disrupt the atmosphere of the gathering. Therefore, it should be handled with great care.

The seating arrangements in dining etiquette should first establish a distinction between seniority and juniority, and then arrange the table and seats accordingly. The following list provides a guide:

Dinning seating order

	Honor	Humble
Differentiated by Gender	Female	Male
Differentiated by Age	Senior	Junior
Differentiated by Rank	Higher Rank	Lower Rank
Differentiated as Host or Guest (Visiting)	Host	Visitors
Differentiated as Host or Guest (Invited)	Invited Guest	Host
Differentiated by Purpose	Guest	Salesperson
Differentiated by Number of Participants	Group	Individual

Once the seniority is clarified, it's important to consider the left and right directions, with the perspective of facing away from the stage or towards the exit. In the context of a wedding, where the bride and groom are seated with their backs to the stage and facing the guests, the seating arrangement at the main table typically has the bride seated on the right side of the groom. To her right, you would find her parents and elders or matchmakers, while to the left of the groom, you'd find his parents and elders or matchmakers. For other guest tables, the arrangement is such that when facing away from the stage towards the exit, the tables to the right are for the bride's relatives, and the tables to the left are for the groom's relatives.

I. **Chinese-style seating arrangement** (This information is based on the "International Etiquette Handbook" by the Ministry of Foreign Affairs)

1. *Chinese-style round table seating arrangement - Variation One*

Explanation: The male and female hosts sit side by side, with the man on the left and the woman on the right. The couples are seated in pairs from top to bottom and from right to left.

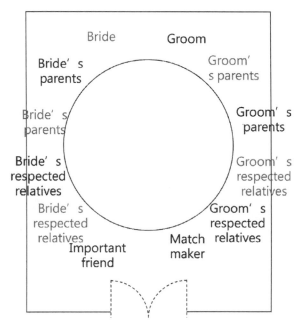

Seating arrangement for main table in a wedding banquet

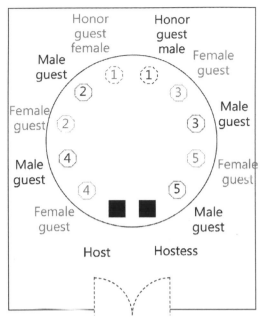

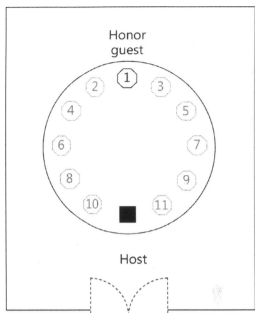

Chinese-style round table seating
arrangement - Variation One

Chinese-style round table seating
arrangement - Variation Two

2. Chinese-style round table seating arrangement - Variation Two

Explanation: The guest of honor sits opposite the host, with higher-ranking individuals seated from top to bottom and from right to left.

3. Chinese-style round table seating arrangement - Variation Three

Explanation: When there is no prominent guest and the host holds a higher status than the banquet guests, the host can be seated in the center of the table. The higher-ranking guests are seated from top to bottom, and the seating arrangement follows accordingly.

II.Western dining table arrangement

1. Seating arrangement for two round table-Variation One

Explanation: The seating arrangement follows the Western style round table seating arrangement. The host and hostess sit facing each other at the first round table. Co-host

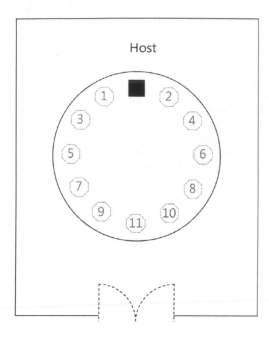

Chinese-style round table seating
arrangement - Variation Three

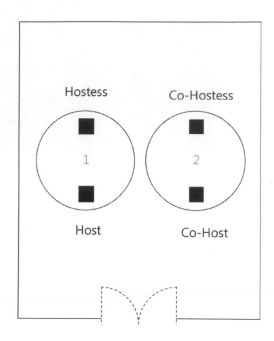

Seating arrangement for two round
table-Variation One

and co-hostess is designated to preside over
the second round table.

2. *Seating arrangement for two round table-Variation Two*

Explanation: The guests of honor sit
facing the host and hostess, host and hostess
sit separately.

3. *Various table arrangement*

Explanation: The seating arrangements
for groups of two to five tables are illustrated
in the diagram below.

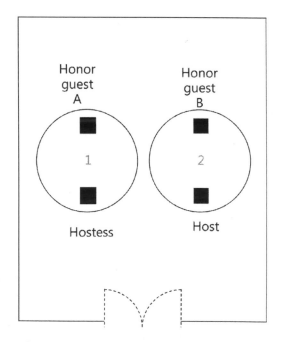

Seating arrangement for two round
table-Variation Two

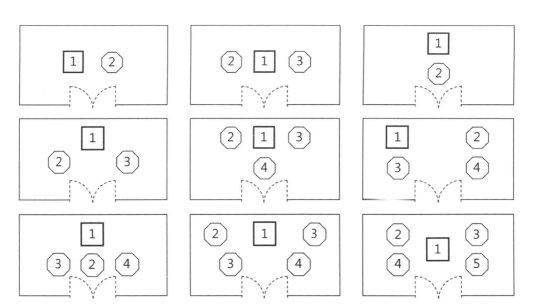

Various table arrangement

III. Western dining seating arrangement

1. Seating arrangement for long tables - Variation One

Explanation: There are 6 guests including the host and hostess. The host and hostess sit facing each other, with guests divided between the two ends of the table

2. Seating arrangement for long tables - Variation Two

Explanation: There are 8 guests, including the host and hostess. Male and female guests are seated alternately, with men facing men and women facing women. The seats closer to the host and hostess are considered more honorable

3. Seating arrangement for long tables - Variation Three.

Explanation: With total 12 diners, the host and hostess sit opposite each othe in the center, and the two ends of the long talbe are the last seats.

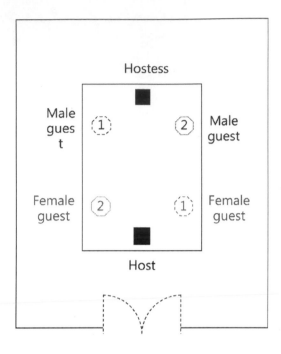

Seating arrangement for long tables
- Variation One

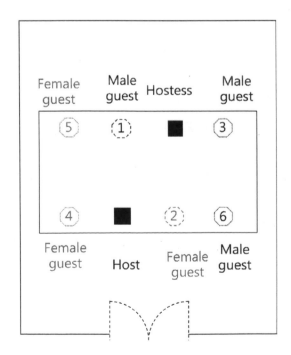

Seating arrangement for long tables
- Variation Two

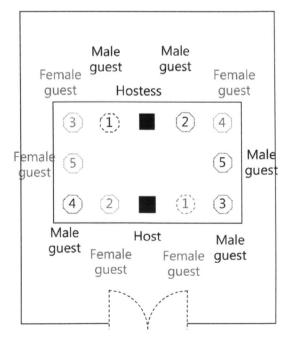

Seating arrangement for long tables
- Variation Three

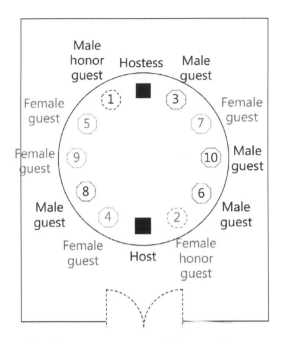

Seating arrangement for western
round table-Variation One

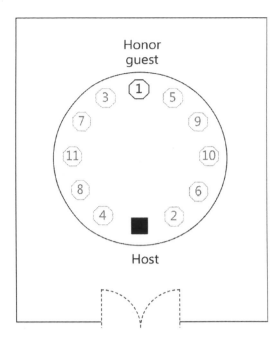

Seating arrangement for western
round table-Variation Two

4. Seating arrangement for western round table-Variation One

Explanation: The male and female hosts sit opposite each other, with the male guest of honor seated to the right of the hostess, the female guest of honor seated to the right of the host.

5. Seating arrangement for western round table-Variation Two

Explanation: The host and the guest of honor sit opposite each other, and the seating order starts from the host's right side.

IV. Teppanyaki Seating Arrangement

Teppanyaki is a top choice for business banquets, offering high-quality ingredients, skilled chef performances, friendly tableside conversations, luxurious decor, and impeccable service. It has captivated the hearts of many local and foreign diners. The deliciousness of Teppanyaki lies in the fact that most ingredients are not heavily

The magnificent and luxurious style of a teppanyaki restaurant.

Opposite of chef is considered the most honorable, while the sides are considered less prestigious.

seasoned, and the high temperature of the iron griddle allows the food to retain its natural flavors. In Japan, it is considered a premium dining experience. The seating arrangement for Teppanyaki also follows a hierarchical structure. The seats directly facing the chef are considered prestigious positions, while the seats on the sides are considered less prominent.

V. General Seating Arrangement Guidelines

Seat arrangement is of great importance. The social ranking, position and friendship between the host and the guests should be carefully considered. The following are the four general principles of seating arrangement:

Honor the right
- Hostess sit at the right of the host at the same table
- When host and hostess sit at the same table, Hostess's right side is the most honorable guest
- When host and hostess sit separately, most honorable guest sit with hostess at the right table

Sit separately
- According to international etiquette, Male/Female, Husband/Wife, Western/Asian sit separately
- In Chinese gathering, husband and wife could sit together

3P policy
- Position, Political situation, personal relationship should be considered to make party more harmonious.

Honorable seat
- Honorable guest should be seated away from the entrance
- The center table is most honorable, then the right table, left is the last

General Seating Arrangement Guidelines

 **Class activities 4**

1. Please prepare Chinese-style bowls and chopsticks as well as Western-style knives and forks for the students to use. The teacher should inspect each student's posture to ensure correctness.
2. When taking a seat, gentlemen should pull out chairs for their female friends. The teacher will pair male and female students for practice.
3. Practical exam design - Napkin Folding: Please have the students fold at least four types of napkin folds, noting that napkins are categorized as decoration linen (used for decoration) and dining linen (used for dining). Complex folding techniques are more suitable for decorative purposes

The folding styles for dining linen napkins include:

- "Steps to Success" (French fold)
- Ji Gong Hat
- Kimono
- Boots
- Bamboo Shoots After the Rain
- Land God
- Starry Brilliance

The folding styles for decoration linen napkins include:

- Rose
- Bird of Paradise (placed on top of a water glass)
- Lotus Stand (placed under silverware or a teapot)
- Cutlery Wrap/Menu Wrap (used to hold cutlery or menus)

延伸閱讀

山本素子（2021）。《日本文化的圖解小百科：如何過年、過節、品茶道，專為外國人解說的文化小百科》。原點。

告訴你筷子的最正確用法，有80％的人都搞錯方式了！，https://clickme.net/32263

林雨荻（2011）。《禮儀實務》（四版）。華立圖書。

林慶弧（2013）。《國際禮儀》（二版）。新文京。

連娟瓏（2019）。《國際禮儀》（七版）。新文京。

Chapter

5

In-Flight Dining

- The history of In-Flight Dining
- Catering service in the cabin
- Dining etiquette in the cabin

According to the Ministry of Foreign Affairs, more than 16 million Taiwan citizens traveled abroad in 2018. Of this number, only 3% traveled for business purposes, while 80% traveled for sightseeing, and the remaining 20% for domestic business travel. However, due to the outbreak of the epidemic at the end of 2019, the number of Taiwanese traveling abroad dropped sharply to only 2.5 million per year. The tourism industry has been severely hit for two consecutive years, as countries closed their borders and the government promoted an epidemic prevention policy of not traveling abroad unless it is necessary for family visits or business purposes. Cumbersome quarantine procedures, rigorous testing requirements, and the added costs of anti-epidemic hotel stays further reduced the willingness of Taiwanese citizens to travel abroad. Despite this, the number of tourists visiting outlying islands Penghu, Jinmen, and Matsu reached a new record. This trend, referred to as "Pseudo-abroad", highlights the surge in domestic tourism as an alternative to international travel. More than 1.06 million travelers traveled by air, and 250,000 by sea, showing Taiwanese citizens' strong interest in air travel. Airlines are now offering "pseudo-overseas flights" and "non-landing flights" to meet this demand. This trend can be seen as an innovative response from the aviation industry, fueled by the most anticipated "meal service aboard the plane" . The history of in-flight catering has evolved over a century, adapting to changes in food trends, health trends, and advances in aircraft technology.

EVA Air's "pseudo-overseas flights"

Source: businesstoday.com.tw

The history of In-Flight Dining

Originally, airplanes were exclusively used for military purposes, but during World War II, airports were built in many cities, and the war drove significant advancements in aviation technology. Commercial air travel began in the 1920s and 1930s, with the Douglas DC-3 aircraft being the most successful at the time due to its high capacity, setting a new milestone in aviation history. Throughout different eras, there have been changes in the trend of in-flight food, the innovation of cooking methods, and the definition and pursuit of "advanced" food, which have all contributed to the development of aviation catering and created a fascinating story in the industry's history.

I. In 1919

Handley-Page Transport (later known as Scottish Airlines) made history by becoming the first airline to provide food and beverages onboard their flights. On October 11, passengers flying from London to Paris were given cold lunch boxes containing sandwiches, fried chicken, and fruit salad. Airplanes at that time were not equipped with cooking or heating facilities due to weight restrictions, only cold food could be provided. On European flights, more luxurious cold meals such as lobster salad, cheese and fruit plates, and ice cream were served, along with champagne. As air travel was not yet common during this time, most meals remained relatively unchanged.

II. In 1922

Daimler Airways (which later became part of British Airways) became the first airline to introduce flight attendants, who would greet boarding passengers with a glass of juice. This was a significant development in the history of aviation, as flight attendants would go on to play an important role in ensuring the safety and comfort of passengers during flights.

Trans World Airlines Inflight Service

Image source: travelandleisure.com

III. In 1936

United Airlines introduced the world's first sky kitchen, where flight attendants provided menus and prepared hot meals on board while considering the influence of high altitude on the flavors of the food. Pan American World Airways (Pan-Am) even had a restaurant on board, complete with white tablecloths and buffet service for passengers. At the time, many people were unfamiliar with high-altitude flying and could easily feel nervous or afraid. However, with the food and service provided by flight attendants brought comfort to passengers. The aircraft relied on human eyesight for navigation and hence the planes are limited to flying at lower altitudes, which increased the chances of encountering turbulence and food spillage. As a solution, some airlines used the apron and allowed guests to enjoy meals during refueling on the ground.

IV. In 1946

after World War II, there was a need for a new approach to provide in-flight meals. Cold food boxes were not ideal and lacked the necessary nutrition for soldiers on the front lines. As a solution, Trans World Airlines (TWA) developed a method to freeze and reheat meals on board for long-distance flights. This process involved quickly freezing freshly cooked meals and packaging them for delivery. The meals were then reheated and served on board the aircraft. This innovation paved the way for frozen and reheated meals to be offered as a standard practice in the aviation industry.

V. In 1950

Pan Am took in-flight dining to the next level with high-end dining services. Flight attendants dressed in uniforms would serve passengers between tables, while formal table settings and high-end china plates were used. The airline served a full

Northwest Airlines VIP Lounge

Image source: northwestairlineshistory.org

set of French cuisines on flights from New York and Baltimore to Bermuda. Northwest Airlines also stepped up its in-flight dining game by introducing a VIP room called the "Fujiyama Room", where passengers could enjoy a variety of luxurious meals such as fruits, cheese, shrimp with pineapple.

VI. During the 1950s and 1960s

Aviation technology continued to advance, resulting in the development of faster and larger aircraft with increased passenger capacity. In response, Pan Am partnered with Maxim's, a renowned Parisian restaurant, to provide French cuisine on board their flights. This collaboration paved the way for Pan Am to offer a top-notch dining experience, including presidential service in first class, featuring appetizers, main courses, and desserts to create a complete dining experience for passengers.

VII. In 1973

The introduction of "first class" marked a peak in the choice of in-flight meals. The

Luxury in-flight service

Image Source: Reader's Digest

Air France in-flight dining

Image Source: lovefood.com

first-class meal service process took about two hours, compared to the thirty minutes in economy class. Air France collaborated with a French chef to adjust the recipes of the meals on the plane, taking into account factors such as hormonal changes caused by stress, high air pressure that makes the taste buds insensitive, and dry air that makes the nasal passages insensitive to food. As a result, the in-flight meals were greatly upgraded, with Singapore Airlines also collaborating with star chefs to provide more exquisite cuisine. Despite this, food on planes was still criticized for being too oily and salty due to the challenges posed by high-altitude flight. However, with the appearance of the French "Concorde" aircraft, in-flight dining had reached a new level, with passengers being served fine champagne, top truffles, and lobster on board.

VIII. 1973~1980

With the rise of low-cost airlines after the Second World War, airlines began to offer more affordable in-flight meals, often consisting of simple sandwiches or snack boxes. In the United States, Southwest Airlines started offering peanuts as a free snack during the journey, and it became a popular tradition for many airlines. However, due to the increasing number of passengers with peanut allergies, some airlines decided to stop serving peanuts on board, with some completely halting their supply of peanuts as of 2018.

IX. In 2003

airlines introduced the concept of an "Onboard Chef," marking another milestone in the history of in-flight meals. These airlines recruited chefs from four or five-star restaurants, and even Michelin three-star chefs, to serve as onboard chefs. First-class and business-class passengers received table-side service from these chefs. In addition to their catering and cooking skills, these chefs had to understand the limitations of equipment on the plane and the changes in taste buds at high altitude to deliver the best quality meals to guests, as if they were dining in a restaurant. Currently, the airlines that provide such services are:

1.Etihad Airways.
2.Gulf Air.
3.Austrian Airlines.
4.Turkish Airlines.
5.Garuda Indonesia.

Emirates has the world's largest air kitchen facility in Dubai, providing 225,000 meals a day and more than 82 million in-flight meals every year. There are 69 chefs from all over the world in the air kitchen specializing in cooking dishes from all over the world.

Turkish Airlines Onboard Chef

X. In 2019

Singapore Airlines took a groundbreaking step in in-flight catering by transforming an abandoned steel factory near Newark Airport in Newark, New Jersey into the world's largest vertical farm. The farm provides pesticide-free green vegetables for in-flight meals, showcasing a commitment to sustainability and healthy eating options for passengers.

Singapore Airlines Farm in the Sky in New Jersey, USA (Aero farm)

Image Source: aerofarms.com

Non-smoking on all flights for aviation safety

It's worth noting that passengers have the option to select their preferred seat on an airplane, such as an "Aisle Seat" or "Window Seat". In the past, planes were divided into "Smoking Seat" and "Non-smoking seats". However, due to concerns regarding the health of flight attendants and the potential fire hazards posed by cigarette butts, airlines began to prohibit smoking on domestic flights in 1990. By 1998, this ban had been extended to all international flights worldwide.

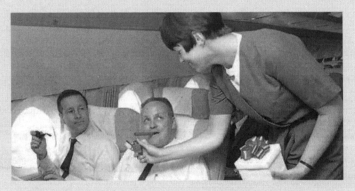

Smoking was allowed in planes in the early days.

Image Source: quitgenius.com

Catering service in the cabin

Aircraft cabins are typically categorized into three classes: First Class, Business Class, and Economy Class. Some airlines also offer a Premium/Deluxe Economy Class, which falls between Business and Economy Class. Prices vary depending on the class, with Business Class typically costing twice that of Economy Class, and First Class costing twice that of Business Class. However, pricing may also vary depending on flight location and airline strategy. The quality of the cabin experience lies in both tangible and intangible factors, such as the hardware equipment, seat comfort, and service quality. The most anticipated aspect of the flight experience is the in-flight catering service. The difference in catering service among classes lies in the quality of materials used in the meals, the popularity of celebrity chefs, and the meticulousness of service. For large aircraft or long-distance flights, the standard ratio of flight attendants to guests in first class is 1:5, with additional assistance from the chief purser to achieve high levels of refinement and customization. In Business Class, the ratio is typically 1:20, and in Economy Class, it is 1:40. Accurate calculations are required to meet the expected service standards for each class and to exceed guest expectations.

I. First Class

First-class air tickets are typically expensive, and first-class passengers usually have higher social and economic status. As a result, they have higher expectations for service, especially when it comes to in-flight services. The quality of in-flight catering and service provided by flight attendants must meet first-class standards. They must successfully make the VIP passengers feel respected through meticulous service and high-quality refreshments.

1. Greeting Champagne

Upon boarding the plane, it is customary for the flight attendant to assist the first-class guest with stowing their luggage and then offer them a glass of champagne or Mimosa (champagne and orange juice) along with nuts in ramekin. If the flight is headed to a resort island, the attendant may also serve a cocktail with a small umbrella to enhance the guest's sense of vacation and relaxation before arrival. If the guest prefers a different drink, the flight attendant can always customize it to their liking. The goal is to provide a luxurious and personalized experience that makes the first-class VIP feel respected and well-cared for.

Greeting Champagne

Image Source: mindfulmoctail.com

Tropical style greeting champagne

Image Source: pretty-palate.com

2. Meal service after takeoff

- begins with the offering of hot towels to the guests
- The chief purser personally greets each guest and inquiries about their preferred beverages.
- The folding table is then opened, covered with a tablecloth, and the guests' drinks are served.
- The first dining cart, also known as the Queen Cart, is then launched to set up tables for guests. The table is set sequentially with salt and pepper shakers, knives and forks, water glasses, wine glasses, decorative plates, bread plates, and more.
- Salad trays are served from the dining cart, with various salad dressing options available for guests to choose from. The flight attendant pours guests' preferred salad dressing and adds croutons, cheese, and pepper according to their preferences.
- Bread is offered from the breadbasket, then complement the beverages.
- Next, appetizers such as cold smoked salmon, top caviar, and foie gras, as well as hot appetizers like grilled crab cakes, are served.
- The main course is provided on a dining car, with a steak car launched for guests who prefer grilled steak. The freshly cut steak is served according to the

guest's preference of ripeness, and comes with a choice of steak sauce, usually mushroom sauce or black pepper sauce. Guests can choose their favorite side dishes and starchy mains from the dining cart, and they are placed on their dinner plate.

- Each meal is paired with a suitable wine, and guests can switch according to their preferences at any time.

- After the main meal, all leftover food, tableware, and tablecloths are collected from the guest's table to keep it tidy. The cheese and fruit trolley is then rolled out, with various cheese options freshly cut according to the guest's taste and quantity, and various cut fruits served on a fruit plate.

- Finally, the dessert and fruit dining cart is launched, with various whole cakes on the car. Slices are made on the spot according to the guest's preference, and ice cream is provided with a variety of toppings, such as chocolate sauce, almonds, and wafer rolls, according to the guest's preference and amount, and finally squeezed whipped cream.

- The last dining cart is for after-dinner drinks, including after-dinner wine such as port wine and liqueurs (including Bailey's Irish Cream etc.), as well as coffee and tea.

Cheese and fruit platter after meal in first class

Image Source : liveandletsfly.com

- After the meal, all leftover food, cutlery, and tablecloths are collected, and the table is put away for the guests.

Based on the detailed description of the first-class meal service outlined above, it typically takes around 2 hours to complete the full dinning service. However, many airlines have recently simplified their first-class service or even eliminated it altogether due to low demand. In addition, there has been a growing trend towards healthier and simpler foods, which has led to a decrease in the popularity of elaborate and intricate dining experiences. It is important to note that despite any changes in service, the first-class experience should always prioritize courteous treatment of guests. To show respect, guests should be addressed by their last name in addition to their title of Mr. or Ms.

II. Business Class

Business class passengers often travel for work and have busy schedules, which can create a lot of pressure. Therefore, the service provided in business class should be carefully tailored to meet their needs and strike a balance between efficiency and quality. While the number of guests in business class is typically 3 to 4 times higher than that of first class, the number of flight attendants serving them is usually the same. As a result, it is important to maintain a sense of decorum and speed when serving meals. Unlike the meticulous and individualized service offered in first class, business class meals are often served on larger plates and are designed to be more practical and efficient.

1. Greeting Champagne

Welcome champagne is a drink offered to passengers upon boarding the plane. This drink is typically champagne or Mimosa, which is a mix of champagne and orange juice. While first-class passengers are served with standard tall champagne glasses, business-class passengers are usually served with small ISO cup-sized cups. Flight attendants take the initiative to serve the welcome drink to passengers and offer them a choice of champagne, orange juice, or water. This gesture allows business-class passengers to quench their thirst, relax, and enjoy the flight experience.

United Airlines 787 Melbourne to San Francisco Business Class

Image source: Wayne Slezak

2. Meal service after takeoff

- The senior flight attendant/senior purser (usually in charge of business galley) greets each guest individually and asks about their drink preferences.
- Tablecloths are placed for each guest.
- Meals are served on big trays, and the necessary decorations such as salt and pepper shakers, tableware, salads, or appetizers are pre-arranged by the catering staff.
- Guests are served breads from a handheld breadbasket, and a selection of champagne, wine, and various beverages are re-filled.
- After guests have finished their salads or appetizers, only the used salad or appetizer plate is retrieved from the big tray. The main course is then served.
- Once the main course is finished, the big tray is removed, and small plates with dessert or fruit are served. Guests are also offered coffee, tea, or liqueur.
- After the meal, all leftover food, cutlery, and tablecloths are collected from the table and cleared away for the guests.

Starlux airlines in-flight meal, Michelin one star food on the list

Image Source: LaVie 行動家

III. Economy Class

1. No welcome drink

In economy class, due to the high number of passengers, no welcome drink is provided when boarding the plane. However, passengers can request for drinking water if they wish. Disposable plastic cups are used in economy class.

2. Meal service after takeoff

- Aft-Purser: The aft purser is usually in charge of the kitchen in the economy class. They would double check the special meals ordered by passengers one by one based on the Special Passenger Information List (SPIL) and ensure that there are no seat changes.

- For flights lasting more than 2 hours, a round of beverage service is typically provided before the meal is served. One flight attendant will push a half-cart, which is a beverage cart, or two people will push a full-cart down the aisle, the beverage cart is stocked with a variety of hot and cold drinks, cups, napkins, and snacks.

Flight attendants serve beverages

Image Source: istockphoto.com

- Flight attendants prioritize the delivery of special meals, and to avoid mistakes during subsequent deliveries, these meals are marked with the passenger's name and the type of special meal.

- The flight attendant pushes a meal trolley with 13-14 layers, each of which can hold three meal trays. These trays are prepared in advance by the flight kitchen, complete with basic tableware, salads, desserts, and coffee cups. The hot meals are cooked after takeoff and set to the meal tray upon the delivery to passenger. In economy class, there are usually two meal options, such as beef with potatoes or chicken with pasta. The meals provided depend on the time of departure, whether it's breakfast, lunch, or dinner.

- Once all meals have been delivered, the flight attendant will make rounds in the aisle to refill coffee and tea.

- Afterward, the empty dining cart is pushed out to collect used plates and catering items.

In general, all drinks, including alcoholic beverage such as wine, cocktails, and beer, are complimentary on international flights. On domestic flights, however, only basic beverages are likely provided, alcoholic beverage are available at an additional cost. Note that, alcohol drinks may not be served on flights to and from Islamic countries, such service could be expected when the plane has left the airspace of those countries.

It's worth mentioning that passenger should mind their tolerance of alcohol for unlimited alcohol ordering in flight. It is refrained from drinking your own bottle of alcohol during the flight. Flight attendants are responsible for monitoring passengers' alcohol consumption to ensure that they are not under the influence of alcohol.

🤝 Dining etiquette in the cabin

While the development of aircraft equipment and safety have greatly improved the level of in-flight catering, it is important to remember that the airplane is still primarily a means of transportation and not a restaurant on the ground. Proper dining etiquette in the cabin should be observed to show consideration for the hard work of flight attendants and to be respectful towards fellow passengers, especially in the crowded environment of economy class. Although convenience may be limited, familiarizing oneself with in-flight services and equipment can enhance the dining experience. Precautions for dining etiquette can be categorized into before, during, and after the flight.

I. Before boarding the plane

1. Book Special Meal

When booking special meals, please consider the difference between the departure

Infant food provided on board

place and the destination of the flight. Generally, airlines require passenger to order their special meals 2 days prior to their trip. Special meals on board include:

◆baby meal

This meal option is suitable for infants under 1 year old and typically includes three bottles of baby food such as name brand Gerber or Heinz meat puree, fruit puree, or canned milk, as well as other items that are appropriate for babies.

◆child meal

Suitable for children aged 2 to 7, the portion size will be smaller than that of adults. This special meal prioritizes foods that are easy to bite, can be eaten by hand and are more attractive to children, such as burgers, chicken nuggets, puddings, etc.

◆Religion Meal

- Non-vegetarian Indian meal (Hindu Meal): Non-vegetarian Indian meal, also known as Hindu Meal, is a type of special meal served on flights. It is suitable for non-vegetarian travelers who do not eat beef, veal, pork, smoked and raw fish. The meal contains meat such as mutton or poultry, fish, or dairy products. The meal is usually spicy and may contain curry.

- Kosher Meal: This is a pre-packaged and sealed meal that contains meat. Before

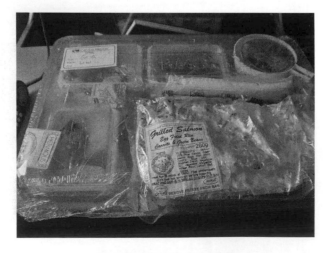

Sealed kosher meal

Image Source: wikimedia.org

serving, flight attendants should ask guests if they are willing to unpack and have the meal cooked for them. While guests will typically provide consent, this step is important in showing respect for their dietary preferences.

- Asian Vegetarian Meal: This meal is suitable for vegetarian passengers who prefer an Asian-style cuisine. It does not contain meat, fish, or seafood, and is prepared with vegetables, fruits, grains, and legumes. However, it is important to note that there is no guarantee that the meal will be prepared in the vegetarian manner as expected in all Asian countries, including Taiwan. For example, the meal may contain spices, herbs, or other ingredients that are not commonly used in vegetarian cooking, such as shallots and garlic. Therefore, if you are flying from Taiwan or other Asian countries, it is important to check the meal ingredients beforehand if you have any dietary restrictions.

- Western Vegetarian Meal: Does not contain all kinds of meat or dairy products but adopts Western cooking.

- Meal for Special Patient Care:

  ①Diabetic Meal: no sugar, less salt

  ②Gluten Free: No wheat, rye, barley, oats

  ③Low Calorie Meal: Less fat, sauces, gravy, fried food. Small amount of sugar flavored food.

  ④Low Fiber Meal: Meal with limited fiber (for example: fruits, beans, vegetables, cereal products with gluten).

  ⑤Non-Lactose Meal: A special meal for people who are lactose intolerant or allergic to dairy products. This meal does not include any foods containing milk, solid milk, dry cheese, cheese, cream, butter, lactose, and margarine.

  ⑥Low Sodium Meal: This meal option includes processed foods that do not contain natural salt or added sodium, such as baking powder, soda powder, and MSG (monosodium glutamate). The meal is prepared without adding salt in the production process.

- Non-Beef Meal: In Taiwan, where cattle have long been a valuable asset to farmers, many people prefer not to eat beef. To cater to this preference, foreign airlines entering the Taiwanese market often offer non-beef meals, which typically feature chicken or seafood as the main course instead.

The options for special meals can be selected on the airline's website. Singapore Airlines provides a relatively comprehensive list of options compared to other airlines in the industry. The following list is taken from the Singapore Airlines website:

2. *Passenger carry their own food*

Passengers have the option to bring their own meals onboard, but it is important to note that airlines may not always allow refrigeration of such meals due to health and safety concerns. Keeping food at room temperature during the journey may lead to bacteria growth potentially causing food safety issues and affecting one's travel experience. In addition, not all destinations may have comprehensive health insurance coverage, and any medical expenses incurred due to food poisoning can be costly. For those who purchase take-away meals at the airport, it is recommended to consume them on the plane as soon as possible, rather than asking flight attendants to heat them up. Heat up passenger's own food might be a potential hazard to hygiene issue.

II. When boarding a plane

- Passengers are kindly requested to tidy up their used tableware after their meal, so that flight attendants can properly organize and recycle them. However, there is no need for passengers to go out of their way to assist the flight attendants, such as collecting dishes from other passengers or taking them to the galley. In some cases, passengers may try to help by stacking the smaller items, but this may inadvertently hinder the flight attendants' ability to properly clear the larger items, such as dinner plates, from the dining area. Therefore, it is recommended that passengers simply tidy up their own space and leave the rest to the flight attendants.

- It is recommended to consume the main meal or sandwich lunch box early during the flight, rather than storing it for a long period of time. Bringing food

In-flight Meal Options by Singapore Airlines

Meals Code	Meal Content
Meals for Baby, Infant and Child Meals	
Baby Meals (BBML)	Suitable for infants less than 1 year old, this meal consists of 3 jars (approximately 80g/3oz to 110g/4oz per jar) of baby food - main course, vegetables and dessert.
Child Meal (CHML)	Suitable for children between the ages of two and below 12 years old, this meal features a Western-style main course and may contain beef, chicken, fish, pasta, vegetables, chocolate, crisps, crackers, milk and dairy products, fruit and fruit juices.
Religious Meals	
Hindu Non Vegetarian Meals (HNML)	This meal is non-vegetarian and contains meat (lamb, poultry), fish, and/ or dairy products. It is a non-vegetarian meal suitable for those who do not consume beef, veal, pork, smoked and raw fish. Typically cooked spicy or curried, its preparation and cooking style may vary.
Kosher Meals (KSML)	Prepared according to Jewish religious specifications, this pre-packed meal (which is sealed) contains meat. * Pre-packed and sealed; contains meat. Request must be made at least 48 hours before flight departure. Passengers on flight duration of 1.5 hours and below will be served a cold refreshment.
Muslim Meals (MOML)	No alcohol, pork, pig by-products, ham or bacon is used in the preparation of this meal. Its preparation and cooking style may vary.
Vegetarian meals	
Vegetarian Indian Meals AVML	This is a non-strict vegetarian meal which is prepared in an Indian style and is usually spicy. No meat, seafood or egg is allowed. This meal may include dairy products.
Vegetarian Jain Meals (VJML)	Suitable for Jains, this meal is cooked in an Indian style and is usually spicy. No meat, seafood and egg products are used in the preparation of this meal. Onions, garlic, ginger, mushrooms, and root vegetables are also not used.
Vegetarian Oriental Meals (VOML)	Typically cooked in Asian style, this meal does not contain meat, seafood, egg, and dairy products.
Vegetarian Vegan meals VGML	Typically cooked in Western style, this meal does not contain meat, seafood, egg, and dairy products.
Vegetarian Lacto-Ovo Meal(VLML)	Typically cooked in Western style, this is a non-strict vegetarian meal which can include eggs and dairy products but eliminates all meats and seafood.
Dietary Meals	
Bland Meal (BLML)	Items that cause gastric irritation will not be used in the preparation of this meal e.g., black pepper, chili powder, cocoa and alcohol.

In-flight Meal Options by Singapore Airlines

Meals Code	Meal Content
Diabetic Meal (DBML)	Sugar is not used in the preparation of this meal. Salt in restricted quantity is allowed.
Fruit Platter (FPML)	Only fresh fruits are served for this meal.
Gluten Intolerant Meal (GFML)	No wheat, rye, barley and bran in any form (including food items which may contain such ingredients) are served for this meal.
Low Fat Meal (LFML)	This meal excludes the use of animal fats or fatty foods. Food naturally high in cholesterol (e.g. prawns and poultry skin of all types) and fried foods of all types are prohibited. Only low-fat dairy products (e.g. skim milk or cottage cheese), lean meat and poly-unsaturated liquid vegetable oils are permitted.
Low Lactose Meal (NLML)	This meal excludes foods which contain milk, dry milk solids, casein, cheese, cream, butter, lactose and margarine.
Low Salt Meal (LSML)	Salt, as well as naturally salted and processed foods (e.g., baking powder, soda and MSG) are either eliminated or restricted in amount in the preparation of this meal.
Other Meals	
Seafood Meal (SFML)	This meal only serves seafood, including fish.

Source: Singapore Airlines Website.

> **As Bovine spongiform encephalopathy (BSE) has become more prevalent, passengers may be concerned about the safety of beef served on flights.**
>
> However, airline meals are prepared in advance and flash-frozen for later use, meaning that passengers may be served entrées that were prepared months ago. Despite this, passengers need not worry about epidemics such as BSE or foot-and-mouth disease as the airlines ensure the safety of their meals, and the government sets high standards for air kitchens. In the event of a medical emergency, the nearest country and airport must be landed at. Failure to do so could pose a significant threat to the health of the sick passenger.

off the plane is not advisable, especially since some countries prohibit certain agricultural products such as meat, and the United States has restrictions on certain agricultural items as well. Breaking the law or receiving a fine due to carelessness is not worth the risk. During the initial outbreak of Covid-19, passengers were heavily fined for carrying meals off the plane, and it is important to avoid making such unintentional mistakes.

- Airplane meals typically offer 2-3 main meal options. While airlines aim to provide meals that cater to passengers' preferences, there may be limitations in the number of meals available. If you have food allergies or specific dietary requirements, it is recommended that you order special meals prior to departure. If you realize this during the flight, you can politely ask the flight attendant for assistance. For longer flights, you can ask the flight attendant to reserve your preferred meal for the second meal service.

- On the plane, if you have a hearty appetite and one meal is not sufficient, you can politely request a second one from the flight attendant. However, typically, you will have to wait until all the passengers have received their meals and the flight attendants have confirmed that there is enough food before serving you a second portion. In the event that there is not enough food left, the flight attendant will provide additional bread as a substitute.

Bringing airplane meals out will result in a fine of NTD 200,000.

Image Source: Apple Daily

Celebrity is fined for bringing fruits into the country

Image source：EBC news

- Passengers who request special meals should be mindful and only order meals that cater to their actual dietary needs. For instance, it is not appropriate for adults to request children's meals. Similarly, if a passenger requests a special meal such as a fruit meal, they should ensure that it meets their requirements before ordering. If a passenger regrets their special meal request, they may find themselves in a dilemma with nothing else to eat. However, if there are any extra meals available, they may politely request the flight attendant to change their meal.

- Foods with strong odors are prohibited on airplanes. For instance, durian, which has a pungent smell, is not allowed on most airlines. While there are no written rules for other strongly scented foods, it is still important to be mindful of your fellow passengers and avoid bringing them on board. It's advisable to consider this before your flight and make a decision on whether to bring food with strong odors on board or not.

- Passengers traveling with infants should bring the formula milk that their infants are used to as whole milk or low-fat milk provided on the plane may not be suitable for young infants. When requesting assistance from the flight attendant to prepare the milk, passengers should do so politely and provide information on the ratio of hot and cold water required. Clean feeding bottles must also be provided, and passengers should not ask the flight attendants to wash the feeding bottles, as they have not received professional training in this area and cannot guarantee food safety for the children.

- Alcoholic drinks on international flights are generally served unlimitedly. Passengers should drink in moderation and avoid overindulging or drinking for the sake of entertainment. Cabin pressure at high altitudes can decrease alcohol tolerance, and passengers may not realize they are getting drunk or becoming disorderly until they reach their destination, which may result in aviation police intervention. Such behavior may result in being blacklisted by the airline, and the passenger may never be allowed to fly again.

- Alcoholic beverages served during the flight cannot be taken off the plane as there are limits on the amount of imported alcohol allowed at each airport. Exceeding these limits may result in taxes being imposed. It is important to note that alcohol is prohibited from entering Muslim countries like Saudi Arabia and Maldives. Visitors should inquire about local laws and regulations before entering such countries to avoid any violations.

- When ordering alcoholic beverages on a plane, flight attendants are required to check passengers' identification according to regulations. The legal drinking age varies by country, and it's important to note that it is calculated based on the laws of the country to which the aircraft belongs, not the passenger's country of origin. The aircraft has a "territorial" system, meaning that entering the aircraft is

Pop star Donald Cheng sorry for drunken rampage

Image Source: topick.hket.com

equivalent to entering the territory of the country to which the aircraft belongs. For instance, in Taiwan, the legal drinking age is 18 years old, while American airlines require passengers to be at least 21 to consume alcohol. All passengers on board, regardless of their citizenship, must adhere to the laws of the country to which the aircraft belongs. Violators will be punished according to those laws, and passengers should not ignore them.

III. After landing

- When the plane is preparing for landing, it is important to take the time to pack your luggage and visit the lavatory to freshen up your appearance, especially after long-haul flights lasting more than ten hours. After eating and sleeping, it is recommended to brush your teeth, freshen up and tidy up your appearance. It is also important to remember to bring an overnight kit or amenity kit, even for passengers traveling in economy class, in order to have necessary toiletries. Passengers should visit the lavatory early to groom themselves and keep their breath fresh before landing.

- Check that your personal belongings are properly stored around you. Tidy up any used blankets or newspapers and magazines you have read. Keep your surroundings neat and clean to avoid giving other passengers a negative impression. After all, this is a matter of personal upbringing. When traveling abroad, you are not only representing yourself, but also your country and race. Once you have tidied up, double-check to make sure you haven't left anything behind.

- It is recommended to leave any uneaten food on the plane. Before entering the destination country, it is important to check for contraband items such as certain agricultural products that may be prohibited. If you are carrying any such items, you should dispose of them before entering the country. You can choose to eat or discard them on the plane, but it is important to make sure that you are not carrying any prohibited items when going through customs.

- You should not rush to get off the plane when airplane is still taxing and has not come to a complete stop. Doing so may cause you to fall and get injured due to the sudden braking of the plane. Instead, wait until the seatbelt sign is turned off and then gather your belongings before disembarking. Double-check your carry-on luggage to ensure that you have not left anything behind when exit the airplane. It is also important to show respect and gratitude to the crew members by bowing, returning smiles, and saying thank you to expressing your appreciation.

Class activities 5

1. What are the differences in the services of different cabins? What do Tangible and Intangible refer to ?
2. Allow students to share their in-flight experience and the reasons for their likes and dislikes.
3. Research up the legal drinking age of other countries
4. Discuss the items that can and cannot be brought on the plane.

延伸閱讀

17 Milestones in the History of Airlines' In-Flight Meals, https://skift.com/2013/10/11/17 -milestones-in-the-history-of-airlines-in-flight-meals/

Foss, R. (2015). *Food in the Air and Space*. Rowman & Littlefield.

The history of In-Flight Dinning -Reader's Digest, https://www.rd.com/list/history-of-inflight-dining/

The most decadent airline menus throughout history, https://www.lovefood.com/gallerylist/70748/the-most-decadent-airline-menus-throughout-history

The Secret to Singapore Airlines' Delicious Meals is an Indoor, Vertical Farm in New Jersey, https://www.aerofarms.com/2020/02/27/the-secret-to-singapore-airlines-delicious-meals-is-an-indoor-vertical-farm-in-new-jersey/

What Airplane food look like through the decades-Travel and Leisure, https://www.travelandleisure.com/airlines-airports/old-airline-meals

飛機餐豬肉卷沒吃帶下飛機，她打官司像洗三溫暖！最後慘噴這麼多錢， https://tw.appledaily.com/local/20210720/VXEGQ7WSX5GF7CNPVMKM5KP5OU/

新加坡航空特殊餐點，https://www.singaporeair.com/zh_TW/hk/flying-withus/dining/specialmeals/

鄭中基重提18年前飛機鬧事，飛機急降要賠好幾百萬，https://topick.hket.com/article/2043712/

Chapter

6

Types of Religion and Dining Etiquette

- Christianity
- Islam
- Hinduism
- Buddhism

According to the 2023 World Population Review, the world's four major religions have the following populations: Christianity (2.38 billion), Islam (1.91 billion), Hinduism (1.16 billion), and Buddhism (507 million). Each religion has its unique dietary customs, which can significantly impact the people who follow them. By learning about these differences, we can understand and respect each other's eating habits, which may evolve into rituals or religious practices. When hosting guests of different religious beliefs, it is crucial to be respectful and considerate of their dietary requirements. In this chapter, we will discuss the dietary practices of the four major religions with the most significant populations. Having a fundamental understanding of these religions can help us interact with and accommodate the needs of friends or business partners from diverse backgrounds.

Religion distribution in the world

Religion	Distribution Area
Christianity	Mainly found in Europe, America, Oceania, South Korea, sub-Saharan Africa, and the Philippines.
Islam	Commonly found in the Middle East, North Africa, Central Asia, South Asia, West Africa, Pakistan, Bangladesh, Malaysia, Indonesia, as well as East Africa, the Balkan Peninsula, Russia, Europe, and mainland China.
Hinduism	Predominantly found in the Indian subcontinent, Fiji, Guyana, Trinidad and Tobago, Europe, Mauritius, Suriname, Bali, Australia, North America, and Southeast Asia.
Buddhism	Mostly found in the Indian Subcontinent, Sri Lanka, East Asia, Southeast Asia, Hong Kong, Macau, Taiwan, Eastern Mainland, Central Asia, parts of Russia, as well as Western Europe, North America, and Oceania.
Taoism	Mainly distributed in mainland China, Hong Kong, Macao, Taiwan, Singapore, Malaysia, and the entire Chinese character cultural circle (Japan, Korea, Vietnam).
Sikhism	Mostly found in the Indian subcontinent, Australia, North America, Southeast Asia, UK, and Western Europe.
Judaism	Mainly found in Israel and the Jewish Ghetto, with significant populations in North America and Europe.
Gaha'i	Widely distributed globally, with 60% of believers mainly found in India, the United States, Vietnam, Kenya, Congo, Philippines, Zambia, South Africa, Iran, and Bolivia.
Jainism	Mostly found in India and East Africa.

Religion distribution in the world

Religion	Distribution Area
Confucianism	Heavily influenced mainland China, Taiwan, and the entire East Asian region.
Shinto	Japan
Cao Dai	Found mainly in Vietnam, where it is a synthesis of various religions such as Buddhism, Catholicism, Christianity, Taoism, and Confucianism, advocating the coexistence of all gods, also known as "Great Harmony."
Cheondogyo	Korean Peninsula
I-Kuan Tao	Taiwan
Africa Traditional Religion	Africa
American Traditional Religion	America
Others	India and Asia

Christianity

Christianity is currently the world's largest religion, with approximately two billion believers spread across all continents. Christianity originated as a branch of Judaism, but gradually separated after Jesus Christ's resurrection, ascension, and the establishment of the Christian Church by his disciples. The title "Christ" in English is derived from the Greek word Χριστ (transliteration Christos), which is synonymous with the Hebrew "Messiah" used by Jews, referring to an "anointed one" who saves the world, which is attributed to Jesus. Christianity spread from the Middle East to the West in the first century. In the Middle Ages, due to different interpretations of the Bible, theology, and liturgy, three major Christian denominations were established: Catholicism, Orthodox Church, and Protestantism, which is further divided into many different sects. The common belief of all Christian denominations is the belief in one God. In terms of dietary restrictions, unlike Judaism's strict regulations, Christianity has almost no dietary restrictions due to its reformation of faith that emphasizes freedom and pluralism. This is because Christianity has replaced all the rituals and festivals of the Old Testament with

Jesus Christ himself, and fulfilled the law that God enacted through Moses, which is translated into Hebrew as Torah and regarded as the foundation of Jewish law.

I. Basic understanding of Christianity

1.Trinity

Some Chinese translate it as "Trinity", which means that one God has three persons: Holy Father , Holy Son (Jesus Christ) , and Holy Spirit Personality . In other words, this God has three different persons, all of whom have the same honor but are still the same God. This is a "mystery" that needs to be experienced to be understood. For Christians, no matter when or where, the only way to call upon the name of the only true God is to pray to Him.

2. Holy Bible

Christianity is a religion that values "classics". This classic is the "Bible", which is also the highest model of Christian faith, and it is God's revelation and teaching to mankind. The "Bible" is composed of sixty-six volumes of different lengths. It serves as both "historical documents" and "faith classics" and is also a subjective testimony of faith. Among them, the "Old Testament" has thirty-nine volumes, written in Hebrew, and is also a classic of Judaism. After the birth of Jesus, we entered the era of the New Testament. The 27 volumes of the "New Testament" were written in Greek. The contents include the Gospels, historical books, letters to the church and individuals, and apocalyptic literature that records Jesus' life and speeches.

3. Evangelism

The "Gospel" of Jesus Christ originally meant "good news" in Greek εὐαγγέλιον, translated as euaggélion, the good news announced by the messenger, and the corresponding English word is Gospel (from Old English, which may be a combination of "God spell," meaning "oracle"). It mainly refers to the salvation that God sent his only son Jesus to come to the world, died on the cross for the sins of the world, and was resurrected three days later. He rose from the dead, and whoever professes Him as Lord will be saved from sin and death. In short, the gospel is the power of God to save everyone who believes (Romans 1:16). Christians often use various opportunities to spread the gospel of Jesus Christ, because they obey the words of the Lord Jesus: "Go into all the world and preach the gospel to all peoples." (Mark 16:15). Knowing that this is their mission and responsibility, even preaching the gospel is "paying the debt of the gospel" ("Romans" 1:14), and woe to those who do not preach the Gospel ("1 Corinthians" 9:16).

4. Church

The word "church" is derived from the Greek word ἐκκλησία (transliteration ekklesía), which means "called out to gather". It refers to a group of Christians who believe in Jesus and were called by God to come together in one place. If Christ is considered the head, then the "church" is like his "body". Christians in the church have a close relationship with each other and with God. The church is not a physical building, but rather a group of Christians who have a vital connection with God and each other. Most Christians gather in church on Sunday, which is also called "the Lord's Day" or the first day of the week, to commemorate the resurrection of Jesus. During church services, they worship God by singing hymns, praying, listening to teachings from the Bible, making offerings, and fellowshipping with each other to worship and honor God.

5. Saying Grace

Before eating, Christians will pray and give thanks for the food they are about to eat. This practice is called "saying grace". Saying grace is a concrete expression of faith for Christians to express gratitude to God for the food on the table. They thank God for creating and providing all things, including the sunshine, rain, and various foods, that sustain human life. They also pray for clean and safe food and for those who suffer from hunger.

6. Lord's Supper

"Holy Communion" or "Lord's Supper" is an important sacrament in Christianity. In a narrow sense, there are two sacraments in Christianity, "baptism" and "communion," which signify joining the church, entering the grace of God, and receiving the power of the Holy Spirit. The Holy Communion is established to commemorate the sacrifice of Jesus, represented by the bread and the cup. Through Holy Communion, Christians experience an intimate and lasting relationship with Jesus Christ. Unleavened bread and wine are traditionally used for communion, but some churches may use grape juice instead. Jesus said, "I am the bread of life that came down from heaven. If anyone eats this bread, he will live forever. The bread I will give is my flesh, which is given for the life of the world. Indeed, my blood is drinkable. He who eats my flesh and drinks my blood abides in me, and I abide in him." (John 6:51, 55-56). Holy Communion is usually conducted during the worship ceremony, and only baptized Christians can receive it. It helps believers become one with the Lord and their fellow brothers and sisters in Christ, strengthens their faith, and reminds them of the love and sacrifice of the Lord Jesus. The apostle Paul said, "On the night when the Lord Jesus was betrayed, he took bread, and after giving thanks, he broke it and said, 'This is my body, which is given for you. Do this in remembrance of me.' After the meal, he took the cup in the same way and said, 'This cup is the new covenant in my blood. Do this every time you drink it, in remembrance of me." (Corinthians 11:24-25).

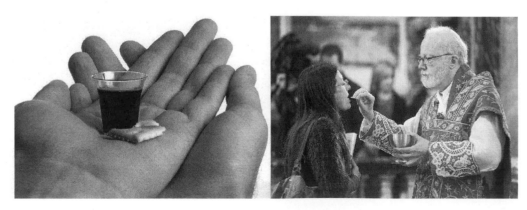

Communion

Image source: Taiwan Church Press

II. Questions and answers about the Christian diet

Q : Is vegetarianism common among Christians?

A : Some Christians, such as those in the Seventh-day Adventist Church, practice vegetarianism. They observe the Sabbath on Saturday and rest, refraining from work.

Q : Do some Christians not eat blood products ?

A : Some Christians choose not to consume blood products because of their interpretation of biblical teachings. Leviticus 17:11 states that "the life of the creature is in the blood," and in Genesis 1:29, God provides plants and fruit as food. In chapter 9, verses 3-4, it is stated that while animals can be consumed, meat with blood, which contains its life, should not be eaten. However, there are varying interpretations of the Bible, and some Christians believe they are free to eat any food, including blood products.

Q : Christians do not eat worshipped food

A : The Christian faith inherits from Judaism and regards eating as a ritual. Christians believe that when they gather for a meal, God is present, and that the focus is on the relationship between God and each other, rather than on what is being eaten. Therefore, a meal is often referred to as a "love feast," where believers eat together with joy and sincerity. The food that has been worshipped is also considered edible, as Christians believe that everything on earth belongs to the Lord, and that giving thanks (saying grace) makes the food clean. The guiding principle is to glorify God and to love others as oneself. "Loving God" and "loving people" are at the core of the Christian faith. While a nutritious, balanced, and satisfying diet is encouraged, there are no strict restrictions on what foods to eat and appetite is not emphasized.

 Islam

Islam, also known as Islamism or Muslimism, means "submission" and "peace" in Arabic, and those who follow the will of Allah are called Muslims. The Qur'an is the foundation of Islam. Muslims believe that the Qur'an is the language of Allah. Believers need to recite the Qur'an frequently. In Islamic countries, mosques and prayer rooms are established in major public places such as shopping malls to facilitate Muslims to perform their daily prayers five times a day. The "Five Pillars" of Islam are the fundamental practices that must be observed in Islamic belief. These include "Declaration of Faith, Prayer, Fasting, Alms-giving, and Pilgrimage".

I. The "Five Pillars" of Islam

1.Shahadah (Recite)

Shahadah, which means "recite", refers to the Islamic declaration of faith that involves testifying and taking an oath. Muslims are required to recite the statement "There is no god but Allah, and Muhammad is the messenger of Allah", which attests to the belief in the oneness of God and the prophethood of Muhammad. By reciting this declaration, one becomes a Muslim, and it is incumbent upon others to acknowledge their newly acquired identity. Additionally, the Muslim who recites Shahadah must also undertake all the obligations and responsibilities that come with practicing the religion.

2. Salat (Worship)

Salat, which means worship or prayer, is an essential religious practice in Islam. Muslims perform five daily prayers, known as Fajr, Dhuhr, Asr, Maghrib, and Isha. Through this act of worship, Muslims demonstrate their obedience to Allah and express gratitude for His blessings. As stated in the Qur'an, "If you are truly grateful, I will definitely grow wisdom for you; but if you deny, indeed, my punishment is severe. "(14:7). Muslims face the Kaaba, a cuboid structure in the holy city of Mecca, during their prayers. The pilgrimage to Mecca and the time of the pilgrimage are in the following:

Fajr	Dhuhr	Asr	Maghrib	Isha
Before dawn	Afternoon	Late afternoon	After sunset	Nighttime

Mecca- Kaaba

Image Source: National Religious Information Website

3. Siyam (fasting)

Siyam, which refers to fasting, is a significant religious practice for Muslims. Similar to how Chinese celebrate Lunar New Year and Westerners celebrate Christmas, Muslims celebrate Eid al-Fitr, also known as the Feast of Breaking the Fast. Before Eid al-Fitr, Muslims observe a month-long fast during the ninth month of the Islamic calendar, known as Ramadan. According to Islamic tradition, Ramadan is the month when Allah revealed the Qur'an to Prophet Muhammad. This month is considered the most sacred time of the year for Muslims, during which they strive to purify their hearts and souls. Through fasting and other acts of worship, Muslims aim to gain a deeper understanding of their faith and strengthen their relationship with Allah.

4. Zakat

Zakat, which means purification, is a form of religious donation that is an essential aspect of Islam. Failure to practice Zakat is viewed as a violation of Islamic principles and results in one's income being regarded as ill-gotten. By giving Zakat, Muslims purify their wealth and fulfill their obligation to support the less fortunate members of their community. The Zakat system is rooted in the principle of social justice and serves as a means of social welfare. Muslims are required to give 2.5% of their annual net income to relevant Islamic institutions, which use these funds to support those in need within the Muslim community. In addition to compulsory Zakat, Muslims are encouraged to donate at any time, with the proceeds often used for the upkeep and affairs of the mosque.

5. Hajj

Hajj, the pilgrimage to Mecca, is a mandatory religious obligation for Muslims who are physically and financially capable of undertaking the journey. This spiritual journey is a significant undertaking that requires a substantial financial investment. During the pilgrimage, pilgrims must overcome the challenges of inconvenient transportation, potential dangers, and other difficulties while constantly testing their faith in Allah. The Ka'bah, located in Mecca, is believed to be the dwelling place of Allah and the center of the universe. Hajj serves as a powerful symbol of Muslim unity, with Muslims from all walks of life and from around the world coming together to worship Allah equally. Upon completing the pilgrimage, Muslims are given the honorific title "Hajji," indicating that they have completed the five pillars of Islam and that their body, mind, and spirit have been renewed.

II. Ramadan

Islam requires female Muslims over the age of 9, and male Muslims over the age of 12 to fast for one month during Ramadan, with some exceptions made for individuals such as the elderly, weak, disabled, pregnant women, lactating mothers, menstruating women, children and travelers. All Muslims who are able to fast must begin their fast before the first dawn until sunset. Muslims abstain from eating, drinking, smoking, and sexual activity, during which time they should remain respectful and devoutly repent to Allah while reciting the Qur'an. If one is unable to fast during Ramadan for valid reasons, the missed days can be made up in the future. Alternatively, they could pay a ransom to help the poor, which is considered a meritorious act in the eyes of Allah.

1. Muslim do not eat pork

Muslims abstain from consuming pork, as it is forbidden in their religion. Following religious principles not only demonstrates obedience to God's instructions but also provides spiritual fulfillment. In 2:173 Qur'an outlines specific restrictions on permissible foods, which includes abstaining from consuming dead animals, blood, pork, and animals slaughtered without invoking the name of Allah. Additionally, Muslims consider pigs to be unclean animals, which may be related to their living conditions during that time. Therefore, abstaining from pork is both an act of obedience to God's instructions and a means of avoiding meat that is considered unclean.

2. Muslim do not drink alcohol

In 2:219 Qur'an, it is mentioned that both drinking and gambling are grave sins, and their harms outweigh their benefits. In 5:90 Qur'an also prohibits believers from engaging in impure activities such as drinking, gambling, idol worship, and lottery, labeling them as the behavior of demons. By avoiding alcohol, Muslims follow the teachings of the Qur'an and strive for spiritual purity.

III. Muslim Women's Clothing

The practice of Muslim women wearing headscarves is derived from the Islamic concept of "awrah". The Qur'an has records and requirements for modesty, such as in 24:31 Qur'an, which states "And say to the believing women that they should lower their gaze and guard their modesty; that they should not display their beauty and ornaments. In 33:59 Qur'an, which suggest woman to cover her body with a burqa, so that people can recognize her religious identity and avoid being violated. These are all considered important for women to wear hijab.

> ### Muslim female wear headscarves
>
> While the hijab is considered daily wear for Muslim women in Islamic countries, the number of Muslims in Taiwan is relatively small. Therefore, some Muslim women in Taiwan choose not to wear the hijab, except when going to the mosque or for other occasions when it is necessary. However, there are also Muslim women who are accustomed to wearing the hijab and feel uncomfortable or guilty when taking it off to go out in public.

However, Islam believes that men and women are different. The part that men need to cover is mainly the area above the knees, and they should not wear shorts that are too short. Adult women wear loose clothing or robes (jilbab), except for the face and hands, which can be exposed. Hair, ears, and neck are covered with a hood, but a veil is not required. The headscarf (hijab) conveys certain symbolic values for Muslim women, such as identity, holiness, and respect, so it has become a symbol for Muslim women to wear. Although hijab has different forms and styles, it can be roughly summarized into 5 main points:

- The clothing should not be form-fitting, and the body curve should not be revealed.
- The material should be opaque.
- The purpose of dressing is not to attract the opposite sex.
- The style must be different for men and women (men wear a small hat that is close to the hair, commonly known as taqiyah).
- Islamic clothing should be different from clothing worn by followers of other religions.

IV. Muslim men's clothing

Muslim men's clothing includes the taqiyah, a traditional headgear that is worn for religious purposes. This head covering is believed to have been worn by the Prophet

Muhammad, and imitating his example has become an important practice for Muslim men during the five daily prayers.

V. Jihad

Although terrorist organizations have used the term "jihad" to justify their actions, in Islam, the term means "struggle in the way of Allah". It is a concept that encompasses various forms of striving and exerting oneself for the betterment of oneself and society, such as resisting temptation, doing good deeds, and standing up for justice. The word "jihad" does not exclusively refer to warfare or violence.

VI. Mosque

A mosque is a place of worship for Muslims, and the word "mosque" is derived from the Arabic word "masjid," meaning "place of prostration." Before entering the worship hall, Muslims must perform a ritual of purification known as "wudu" or "ghusl." Mosques play an important role in the social and religious life of Muslims. They serve as centers for worship, education, and community activities. Visitors are welcome to mosques, but they should be respectful and follow the rules, such as speaking quietly and refraining from taking photos without permission. In Taiwan, there are nine mosques

Mosque in Daan District, Taipei

located in various cities and counties, including the earliest one built in Taipei in 1947. Mosques are closed during prayer time, and Friday is considered the holy day, similar to Sunday for Christians.

Hinduism

Hinduism is considered the "oldest religion" in the world and has over one billion followers, with 900 million living in India. Despite having a larger number of adherents than Buddhism, Hinduism is considered an exclusive religion due to restrictions on joining the Hindu community. As a result, Buddhism has taken its place as the third-largest religion in the world.

I. About Hinduism

- Hinduism is known for its closed characteristics. Being born as an Indian automatically makes one a Hindu, while non-Indians are not considered Hindus. The religion has no concept of conversion and apostasy. To that, any claims to Hinduism are often seen as provocative acts.

- Hinduism encompasses religion, belief, and lifestyle. Hindus believe in the concept of "karma" and "reincarnation," where every life is determined by the actions of the previous life. Hindus must practice and accumulate merit to attain the highest goal of life, which is recognizing "Brahman," the ultimate reality that transcends the universe. Hindus view life as a self-repeating cycle.

- Hindu religious customs involve taking a bath in a nearby river or at home in the morning to purify oneself. Before eating, Hindus prepare flowers and offerings to their local gods at a temple. Many families in India reserve a corner or a room for worshiping their favorite deity. Lord Ganesh, the elephant-headed God, is widely worshiped in India as the god of wisdom and wealth. In daily life, Hindus worship Lord Ganesh before important events such as the opening of a company, before marriage, before pilgrimage, and before starting a new business, among

India celebrates the festival of the elephant-headed god, which means the introduction of wealth, wisdom and good fortune

Image source: m.xuite.net

Varanasi

Image retrieved from Phoenix Travel website

others. The Ganesh festival, which lasts for about ten days between August and September in the Hindu calendar, is celebrated throughout India.

- Varanasi is considered to be the only holy city in the Hindu faith, much like Jerusalem is to Jews. It is believed that Varanasi not only belongs to Lord Shiva, but also that the River Ganges serves as the final resting place for the soul. The city boasts over 1,500 temples, which attract between two to three million worshippers and visitors from around the globe every year. Hindus believe that bathing in the Ganges River once in their lifetime will absolve them of their sins. Many hope to pass away in Varanasi, as it is believed that being buried in or having one's ashes scattered into the Ganges will release the soul. This is why Varanasi is also referred to as "the entrance to heaven"

- Take off the shoes when entering the temple. In India, cleanliness is considered to be of great importance, not just on a physical level, but also on a spiritual level. The four castes, known as the Caste System, are believed to be a reflection of people's cleanliness. The Brahman, who is considered the most religiously and morally pure, is believed to be the closest to God, followed by the Kshatriya,

Vaishya, and Sudra. Outside of these four castes, the Dalits are considered to be the least clean, and are often relegated to jobs such as garbage collection, sewage cleaning, corpse burning, and excrement removal. This explains why Indians are often required to remove their shoes before entering certain places. For instance, it is customary to remove one's shoes before entering a temple, as shoes are believed to carry many impurities. Bringing them into the temple is seen as disrespectful to the gods.

- Indians respect cows like gods. In Hinduism, cows hold a special and sacred status. One can often find statues or images of Lord Shiva and his mount, the bull "Nandi," outside and inside Indian temples. This is because cows are considered to be sacred animals. In addition to their religious significance, cows also play an essential role in Indian agriculture, serving as labor animals for plowing and transportation. Milk and dairy products are a crucial source of nutrition in a predominantly vegetarian society. Cow dung can be used as fuel, fertilizer, and building materials, and cow urine is one of the medicinal substances used in traditional Indian therapy. Due to various cultural, religious, and practical factors, killing cows is considered taboo in Indian culture, and they are neither eaten, whipped nor harmed. Cows are allowed to roam freely on the streets of India, enjoying the respect and reverence of the people.

II. Hindu diet

- Vegetarianism is widely practiced in India among devout Buddhists, Hindus, and especially strict for Jains, with more than half of the country's population abstaining from meat. As a result, many foreign restaurants operating in India have adapted their menus to cater to the vegetarian population. For instance, McDonald's in India offers vegetarian burgers and separates the kitchens for vegetarian and non-vegetarian food preparation. This is because Hindus do not eat beef, and Muslims avoid pork, but chicken and vegetarian food are acceptable. McDonald's Big Mac in India only contains mutton, and if one wants to consume beef, they must purchase it from a store and cook it themselves.

- Only allowed to eat with the right hand. Indian customs and traditions continue to be upheld. Despite on formal occasions where cutlery may be used, it is customary for Indians, both adults and children, to eat with their right hand and to pass food and

Hand Washing Pot

Image: From the Internet by Chris Martino

tableware with their right hand as well. This is because the right hand is deemed to be clean, while the left hand is considered dirty since Indians do not use toilet paper to wipe after using the bathroom; instead, they flush with water and use their left hand. At an Indian restaurant, warm water with lemon is provided in a small bowl towards the end of the meal for washing hands, and a plate of green wheat grains in the form of spices is served for everyone to chew on, to eliminate the odor in the mouth.

Shake your head indicate "OK" ?

Shaking one's head to indicate agreement or understanding is a common practice in India. When Indians express agreement or affirmation, they often tilt their heads slightly to the left and right, which can appear as if they are shaking their heads. They will then return their heads to the original position, signifying "OK," "Yes," or "I understood." This gesture is different from nodding, which is more common in Western cultures.

 Buddhism

I. About Buddhism

Buddhism originated in the sixth century BC and was practiced by Sakyamuni's disciples. It taught the principles of enlightenment and has spread to become one of the world's religions today. More than 90% of Buddhist believers are in the Asia-Pacific region, including Bhutan, Myanmar, Cambodia, Laos, Mongolia, Sri Lanka, and Thailand. Buddhism is divided into three traditions: Indian Buddhism, Chinese Buddhism, and Tibetan Buddhism. Chinese Buddhism covers China, Taiwan, Hong Kong, Japan, and Korea, as well as other cultural circles of Chinese characters

During the primitive times of Buddhism in India, Buddhists did not have special eating habits or regulations. Monks and nuns begged for alms and did not choose the object of begging, as they believed in forming good karma. Donors would offer whatever they could, including fish and other food. This is why Theravada Buddhism does not stipulate their adherent to be vegetarian.

Thousands of monks hold a bowl for charity at the Buddha's Birthday Cultural Festival in New Taipei

Image source : www.taiwanhot.net

Mahayana Buddhism emphasizes cultivating Bodhisattva fruit and having great compassion. In Mahayana Buddhism, all living beings are equal, and animals are a part of that. Therefore, meat is not eaten. In addition, eggs are also considered "meat", so monks who have accepted the Three Refuges and Five Precepts do not eat eggs or meat.

II. Buddhist diet

1. Being Vegetarian on the First and Fifteenth Day of the Lunar New Year

During the first and fifteenth day of the Lunar New Year, Buddhist who are vegetarians may choose to fast and meditate. This practice not only increases blessings but also creates merit and prayers for those within the community.

2. The Distinction Between "Hun Xing"

It is important to differentiate between "Hun" and "Xing" dishes. "Hun cai 葷菜" refers to vegetables with a strong aroma, such as garlic, shallots, leeks, and onions. The Shurangama Sutra states that eating "Hun cai" in raw provoke anger, while cooked one promote promiscuity. Before chanting, it is best to avoid Hun cai to prevent anger and greed from ghosts and gods listening to the scriptures. "Xing 腥" indicate meaty food. Other spices, such as chili, pepper, five spices, star anise, toon, fennel, and cinnamon, are not considered Hun cai and are not subject to precepts.

3. Abstaining from Alcohol

Buddhism values wisdom and abstaining from alcohol is crucial for practicing diligently and staying alert. At home Buddhist disciples are required to follow the Five Precepts, which prohibit killing, stealing, sexual misconduct, lying, and consuming alcohol or drugs.

III. General etiquette and taboos in Buddhism

- When you encounter monks in the temple, it's important to show respect by folding your palms together and saying "Amituofo" or "Hello".

- When greeting the monks in the temple, it is appropriate to use respectful titles such as "Master", "Monk " or "Shifu" to show reverence and honor towards them

- When inside the Buddha Hall, it is appropriate to perform a circumambulation around the Buddhist altar. This practice is said to bring many merits, but it is important to follow the correct direction of rotation, which should be from left to right, or "clockwise," as it is a sign of respect. The direction of rotation is derived from the traditional etiquette and customs of the Indians.

- In the Buddhist Hall, it is important to maintain a solemn atmosphere and avoid laughing or speaking loudly. These behaviors may be considered disrespectful and reflect poorly on one's character. The hall is a sacred space for worshiping Buddhas and Bodhisattvas, and should be treated with great care and reverence.

- When listening to the scriptures, you may take a seat with the crowd. When the master ascends to the Buddha, it is proper to bow to the Buddha and then to the master as a sign of respect. In the situation you must leave early, you should bow with holding hands and excuse yourself quietly.

- When offering incense at the temple, it is customary to enter temple from the left and exit from the right. Fruits and flowers are often offered during worship, but it is important to select appropriate fruits. Fruits with many seeds, such as tomatoes and guavas, should be avoided as they can be excreted and regrown after being

Devout follower praying for blessing

consumed, which is considered disrespectful to the gods. Sugar apples, which resemble the head of the Shakyamuni Buddha, should also not be used as an offering as it is not considered respectful.

- Believers can often be seen holding incense and worshiping in temples. The purpose of burning incense and worshiping Buddha is to show respect for the deities. However, offerings such as clear water, flowers, and fruits can also be used instead of burning incense. Burning incense is not mandatory. In recent years, due to increased environmental awareness, more and more temples have stopped using incense burners and banned the burning of gold paper. Regardless of the method, true sincerity can lead to spiritual peace.

Class activities 6

1. Ask students about their religious beliefs in class and encourage students to share their religion and activities. What are the taboos?
2. Ask students to discuss the activities of various religions, such as Easter in Christianity, Ulambana in Buddhism, Eid al-Adha in Islam, and Diwali in Hinduism. Additional resources for further reading may also be provided.

延伸閱讀

中華佛學研究所。《中華佛學研究》，第3期，頁175-206，http://www.chibs.edu.tw/ch_html/chbs/03/chbs0307.htm

全國宗教資訊網，https://religion.moi.gov.tw/Knowledge/Content?ci=2&cid=85

李在哲（2020）。《最重要的事──初信造就10堂課》（初版）。校園。

林長寬（2009）。五功。文化部台灣大百科全書，https://nrch.culture.tw/twpedia.aspx?id=1949

法鼓山全球資訊網，https://www.ddm.org.tw/

探索歷史之謎會（2008）。《一本讀懂世界三大宗教》。商周出版。

黃國煜（2015）。《圖解世界宗教》（新版）。好讀出版。

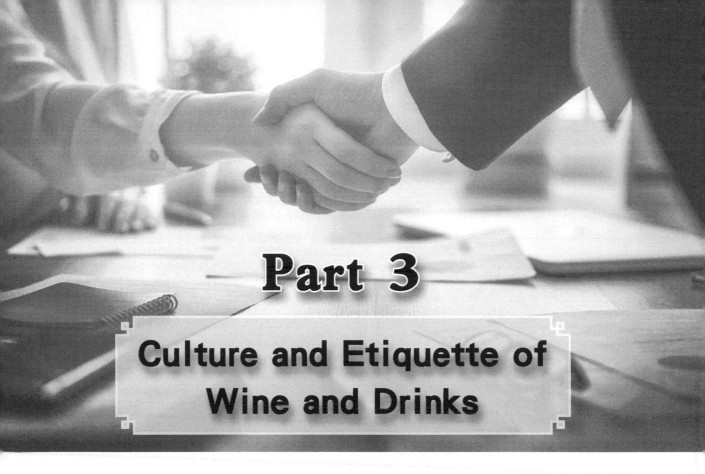

Part 3
Culture and Etiquette of Wine and Drinks

In previous chapters, we discussed dining etiquette in detail. In this chapter, we will focus on another essential element of dining etiquette - table wine. Table wine plays a crucial role in dining and is an essential element of the dining experience. It's not just a supporting character; it's a necessity that completes the dining experience. A feast would feel incomplete without the presence of table wine. Therefore, to have a comprehensive understanding of dining etiquette, it is essential to understand table wines and the diverse wine cultures in different parts of the world.

In the past, Taiwan's drinking culture was characterized by toasting and drinking competitions, with beer, brandy, and whiskey being the popular choices. Serving high-end alcohol during dining was also seen as a status symbol. Typically, social gatherings would involve multiple rounds of drinking, fail to bottom up the drink shows that you don't give face to the person who raised the glass. Who can drinks not drunk would be seen as bold, and make business deal with no troubles. However, drinking culture among the 25 to 40-year-old group has been influenced by the West, and their focus has shifted towards pairing alcohol with different types of food and lifestyle rather than business motives. Additionally, due to the high number of drunk driving accidents in Taiwan, more and more people are advocating "Don't drink and drive" and "Get a designated driver if you are going to drink". On January 24, 2022, the third reading of Taiwan's "Heavy Penalty for Drunk Driving" was passed. Among which, for repeat offenders who drink and drive twice within 10 years, their names, photos and the violations will be published publicly. Additionally, those who are also in the car together with the drunk drivers are subjected to fines of up to 6000–15000 NTD. If unfortunate events like the death of others were involved, a fine of less than 2 million NTD will be issued, while a fine of less than 1 million NTD is issued if the drunk driver caused a serious injury towards the victim.

Source: Workforce development agency, Ministry of labor

The binge drinking culture is prevalent in many Asian countries, including China, Japan, and Korea. In 2017, the Soongsil University Student Union in South Korea launched the "No Pressured Drinking Bracelet" campaign with the words "Respect Human Rights" to prevent potential incidents caused by drinking. Although it was only an advocacy campaign, it was embraced by all the students on campus. South Korea has had a "bad drinking culture" for a long time, as people would rather drink to death than reject a senior or boss's offer to drink. In 2019, three-color bracelets were introduced on campus. Yellow bracelets represent "I don't want to drink," and those wearing them cannot be pressured to drink. Pink bracelets signify "drink until your cheeks blush," meaning the person wants to drink a certain amount based on their physical condition. Black bracelets indicate "drink until the end," meaning the wearer has no limit for the night. These bracelets visually demonstrate one's drinking capacity and can help people avoid peer pressure. However, there may still be some individuals who disregard the purpose of the bracelets. Ultimately, it depends on the individual's willingness to participate.

Stop bad drinking culture

Source: theinitium.com

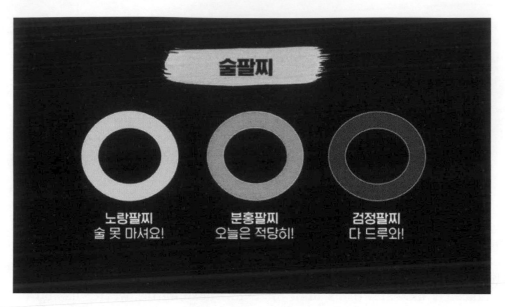

Three colors bracelets
Source: NAVER

In Taiwan, western bistros are gaining popularity compared to drinking in restaurants, bars, and nightclubs. Bistros not only focus on their food, but also emphasize matching the right wine to the food. This approach slows down the dining experience, creates a better drinking atmosphere, and reduces the pressure to drink excessively. Originating in Paris, France, bistros are small and affordable restaurants that serve alcohol. Many bistros feature their menus on small blackboards and have more casual service than formal restaurants. For women, a la carte ordering allows them to control meal portions more easily. As a result, more people in Japan, Korea, and Taiwan prefer to dine in bistros. While most bistros in Taiwan serve Italian or French cuisine, some pricier range restaurants also refer to themselves as bistros, implying they offer other foreign cuisine.

When traveling abroad, restaurant names can often be confusing and misleading. Even when you are able to dine or drink at these establishments, there may be significant differences between them. Understanding these differences can help you choose the best restaurant for your needs. Whether you are looking for a specific type of cuisine or a particular dining experience, knowing what sets these places apart can make all the difference.

French bistro

- Restaurant : Restaurants typically serve meals during lunch and dinner periods, with a break in between. Prices can vary widely, and the atmosphere can range from casual to formal and elegant.

- Bistro: Bistros are small French restaurants that typically serve lunch and dinner with a break in between. The menus feature simpler, traditional French dishes, and the service is not premium

- Brasserie: The term "brasserie" originally referred to restaurants with their own brewery, but now it generally refers to restaurants with a more casual atmosphere and longer operating hours. Customers can dine anytime throughout the day.

- Café: Cafés serve a variety of food, such as sandwiches, salads, and cheese platters, but they place greater emphasis on beverages. Customers can spend time with friends or alone, making cafés a popular spot for socializing.

Chapter

7

Scene of Food and Wine

- Different types of alcohol beverages

- Exotic food and wine culture

- Michelin Guides rating system

When dining in a foreign country, it's common for the waiter to ask for your drink order before taking your food order since meals and wines are often considered inseparable. In Europe, where food culture has a long history, wine is a beloved beverage. In France, having wine on the dining table is considered normal and classic. In Italy, it's common to have a glass of Grappa after the meal, as it's believed to aid in digestion.

Italy Grappa

Source: montemaggio.com

When it comes to pairing food with alcohol, different cultures have their own preferences. In Japan, for example, Sake is a popular choice as its acidity complements seafood dishes. Meanwhile, Koreans have a strong soju culture, with Jinro being the top-selling distilled spirit in the world for 16 consecutive years. However, despite its seemingly harmless appearance, with its little green bottle, Jinro has an alcohol content as high as 25%.

While beer and local wines typically dominate alcohol markets around the world, Taiwanese consumers have a preference for imported wines, with domestic market share decreasing annually. According to data analysis from the Financial Information Centre and the Customs Administration of the Ministry of Finance, beer is the most popular alcoholic beverage in Taiwan, followed by whiskey, sorghum (Kao Liang) and wine. In

Korean Jinro soju in Korean Drama "Descendants of the Sun"

recent years, whiskey has overtaken Brandy in popularity. Following the abolition of the government monopoly system in January 2002, private investment in alcohol and tobacco production was allowed to be in line with the trend of free trade. The tax on imported whiskey in Taiwan is lower than in other Asian countries such as Hong Kong and India, leading to a thriving whiskey import market and successful breweries in Taiwan such as the King Car Group, which established the first Kavalan Distillery and has won numerous awards.

Kavalan Distillery

Source: King Car Group

On the other hand, in China, Chinese Baijiu is the most popular alcoholic beverage. Kweichow Moutai holds the top spot, followed closely by Wuliangye Yibin, while snow beer takes the third place. Chinese baijiu accounted for 77.5% of the total alcohol sales turnover in China in 2020. Unlike western wine glasses, Chinese baijiu is typically consumed in small cups. This is because the alcohol content of Chinese baijiu is generally around 53%, which is too strong for most people to consume in large quantities, not to mention that it is also expensive. For instance, a 500ml bottle of Kweichow Moutai costs around RMB 1,499 in 2021.

In Spain, the concept of "Happy Hour" is represented by a pre-meal drink. It is common for Spanish restaurants to be named after Tapas, which are snacks or appetizers traditionally served with wine or beer before the main meal. The dining culture of a country is closely linked to its geography and cultural heritage. Understanding a country's food and wine culture can be a fascinating way to learn about the places we visit.

Kweichow Moutai

Source: item.m.jd.com

🤝 Different types of alcohol beverages

In addition to enjoying delicious meals, the quality of table wine is also an important consideration. A typical table wine often includes a range of beverages such as water, alcohol, soft drinks, coffee, and tea. While many restaurants in Taiwan provide

Spanish tapas

Source: tastespirit.com

free drinking water, it's important to note that water quality and standards vary across different countries. When traveling to a foreign country, it's common for people to experience some discomfort or difficulty adjusting to the new environment, including the food and drinks. Therefore, it's important to be mindful of the potential impact on our digestive system. Water itself also has much to offer in terms of its unique characteristics and qualities, making it a fascinating subject to explore.

I. Portable water

Foreign travelers often have different standards and expectations for water quality when traveling, especially those from developed countries visiting places with lower living standards. In many restaurants, portable or mineral water is offered as a standard. Portable water refers to water that can be consumed directly without any additional filtration or boiling. Some hotels provide complimentary bottles of water, which are also portable or mineral water. In some European countries, it is safe to drink tap water directly, but this may not be the case in other parts of the world. In Taiwan, tap water has been certified and regularly inspected to meet drinking water standards. It does not contain chemical pollutants, harmful metals, or pathogenic microorganisms, making it safe to drink directly from the tap. However, the water company does not recommend this practice due to concerns about older, rusty water pipes and unclean water tanks that could impact water quality. In countries with lower sanitary conditions, hotels often remind guests with signs that "Tap water is not portable" and provide free mineral water in the room for consumption.

1. Alkaline water

Often called alkaline ionized water or electrolyte water due to its slightly higher pH value of 8-9 compared to the general drinking water with a pH of 7. Water from natural sources such as mountain springs and sea water typically contain minerals. Alkaline water is produced by electrolysis, but its alkalinity is not very strong and does not react violently with stomach acid. Therefore, drinking alkaline water has a limited impact on our health and does not change our body's pH.

2. Still water

It refers to consumable water that may not come from tap water. This could be pure water such as reverse osmosis, qualified mountain spring water, or even deep-sea mineral water that is advertised as pollution-free. These waters contain traces of minerals, and Evian mineral water is a commonly seen imported still water brand.

3. Sparkling water

Both domestic and imported brands add carbon dioxide to mineral water to create carbonation. Perrier, a natural carbonated spring from Gard in southern France, is the most common imported brand of sparkling water. The water is purified, and carbon dioxide is added again to create the carbonation effect.

Mineral water Cape Grim from Australia. The dark blue cap is non-sparkling, and the gray cap is sparkling water

II. Apéritif

The word "aperitif" comes from the Latin verb "aperire", meaning "to open", and it is a pre-meal alcoholic drink that is meant to stimulate the appetite. Aperitifs are selected to relax oneself and to whet the appetite, and it is recommended to choose a dry alcohol with a lower sugar content and low alcohol percentage to avoid getting drunk before the meal.

1. Champagne

The name of sparkling wine varies from country to country, the most famous is Champagne from the Champagne region of France, and there is another sparkling wine called Crémant in France, such as Crémant di Alsace. The difference between the Champagne and Crémant is that Champagne must be produced from the Champagne region of France and its bottle pressure is 6 atm. On the other hand, Crémant means creamy and has a pressure of 3.6 atm, its bubbles are as smooth as cream and are less intense.

2. Dry white wine

Dry white wines usually taste sour but pleasant, and have an excellent appetizer effect. Few examples for the white wines that are not put into oak barrels are: Chardonnay, Sauvignon Blanc, Riesling, Pinot Grigio and Gruner Veltliner. These white wines are refreshing, sour and light-bodied, suitable for drinking before meals.

3.Pink wine

Rosé wine is very popular among females. A glass of rosé wine before a meal, whether dry or slightly sweet, is a good choice. The taste is refreshing, and the color is likable, which is perfect for creating a good dining atmosphere.

4. Dry Vermouth

Vermouth is a fortified wine containing anise and has an aromatic flavor. It tastes light and has a hint of bitterness. It is recommended to serve with ice as an aperitif

5. Dry Martini

Martini is known as the "King of Cocktails." It is made up of gin and vermouth. Dry Martini is a classic aperitif. There is a red-hearted olive in the wine to enhance the taste and whet the appetite.

6. Dry Sherry

Both Fino Sherry and Manzanilla Sherry is a good choice, it goes particularly well with ham and nuts.

7. Light-bodied beer

It is also common to drink a chilled beer before the meal, such as Corona Extra. Remember to avoid heavy wine or alcohol with a lot of bubbles to avoid feeling bloated before the actual meals.

III. Table wine

Just as red flowers complement green leaves, table wine complements a meal. As long as the host and guests enjoy the meal together, a single glass of table wine can enhance the dining experience without overwhelming the guest. Common table wines include Champagne, red wine, and white wine, each of which is matched with certain foods to bring out the best flavor. Generally, red wine pairs well with red meat while white wine is best with white meat, but the selection should also consider the sauces used in the dish. When there is no particular preference, it is recommended to choose regional wine that is matched with the regional food, based on the terroir theory. In chapter 9, this theory will be further elaborated.

IV. Digestif/ After dinner drink

Echoing Aperitifs to whet the appetizer and relax dinning mood, Digestif is to prolong the dining period for communication and friendship. In the stream of drinking process, it's nice to consume high alcohol and rich body Digestif at the end, sweet wine choice is perfect to announce the end of dining as well. The common Digestif are: Fortified Winc, Brandy/Cognac, Liqueur.

1. Fortified Wine

Portugal's Port wine or Madeira and Spain's Sherry wine are both popular Digestifs, with an alcohol concentration between 15 and 20 percent.

2. Liquor

Brandy is a classic after-dinner drink that is distilled from fruit juices, such as grape juice, and then matured in oak barrels. Other popular liquors include Cognac and Armagnac, which are also consumed in a brandy glass. Italians often enjoy Grappa, a clear liquor made from wine residues and aged in oak barrels. Grappa is transparent and colorless, but the alcohol content is quite high, about 35~60. Most of these spirits are consumed neat, without any dilution from ice.

3. Liqueur

Liqueurs are sweetened or flavored liquors that can be enjoyed on their own or used as mixers in cocktails. Some common examples of liqueurs include Bailey's Irish Cream, Kahlua, Grand Marnier, and Amaretto.

V. After meals coffee or tea

Hot beverages, such as coffee and tea, are often served after the meal. However, caffeine-sensitive individuals may prefer decaffeinated options to avoid disrupting their sleep. Popular choices for calming hot beverages include comfort tea and chrysanthemum tea. Specific types of tea may also be paired with certain cuisines, such as green tea with Japanese food, oolong tea with Chinese cuisine, and Pu-erh tea with Hong Kongese dishes, which is believed to help remove excess oil. In Korean restaurants, citron tea is often served at the end of the meal as a refreshing and fragrant option.

🤝 Exotic food and wine culture

Food and wine are a perfect pairing and each country itself has their own unique wine culture. In addition to enjoying wine on its own, many cultures have developed corresponding food pairings that result in fascinating culinary and wine experiences.

I. Taiwan

In the past, the older generation in Taiwan would often bring out local wines like sorghum, Zhuyeqing, Wujiapi, and Daqu when socializing with friends. Women would serve the guests and then quietly leave so that the men could enjoy their drinks and socialize. However, the younger generation nowadays prefers beer, especially After the abolition of retail distribution monoply, the variety of beer became more diverse. While wine has become increasingly popular in recent years, whiskey remains the most commonly consumed alcohol. According to the Scotch Whiskey Association, Taiwan consumes over 50 billion NTD worth of whiskey annually, ranking fourth in the world behind the United States, France, and Singapore.

In Taiwan, it is customary to pair stir-fried dishes with beer or whiskey during meals. Popular street foods include San Bei Ji, salted pork with garlic sprouts, Scallion beef, Basil fried clams, Preserved radish omelets, and freshly boiled seafood and sliced cold chicken. Taiwanese people often cheer with each other while drinking, and consuming an entire glass of alcohol in one go is considered impressive and shows approachability. Even those with low alcohol tolerance often follow suit to show sincerity. Bonding with friends over food and drinks in a small group is a common

Stir-fried restaurant in Taiwan

Source: jasminelady.pixnet.net

practice in Taiwan, and heartfelt conversations often ensue. However, one has to be aware that the legal drinking age in Taiwan is 18.

II. Spain

Europeans have a long-standing tradition of combining food and wine. Spanish cuisine is well-known and loved worldwide, with dishes like Paella, made with saffron, and Tapas being some of the most popular. Tapas, meaning "cover" in Spanish, originated from the practice of placing a piece of bread on top of a drink to keep flies away. Over time, olives, seafood, and ham were added to the bread, creating the delicious and diverse tapas we know today.

Eating habits in Spain are unique, with lunch starting at around 2 o'clock and dinner starting at 8 o'clock in the evening. However, tapas can be enjoyed at any time of the day, can be served either cold or hot, can be made upon order, as well as can be a buffet-style. Spaniards enjoy gathering to engage in lively conversations about current events, the economy, and their personal lives. The legal drinking age is 18 in Spain.

III. Japan

When it comes to Japanese dining culture, the first thing that often comes to mind is "izakaya." These bars can be found all over Japan, and the price of alcoholic drinks is relatively cheaper than in other countries. Many izakaya establishments also offer free refills. Thanks to the country's convenient transportation options, it is easy for people to enjoy a drink at an izakaya after work, and then take public transportation home, avoiding potential drunk driving accidents. Japan has a wide variety of sake, which makes it a paradise for alcohol enthusiasts. It is common for izakaya restaurants to serve side dishes that customers did not order, which will be charged for separately. Unlike Taiwanese culture, the Japanese only say cheers once at the beginning of a drinking session. Edamame is the most popular side dish served with alcohol, followed by seasoned bean sprouts, grilled meat, and fried foods. Sashimi also pairs well with beer or sake. The legal drinking age in Japan is 20.

IV. The United State of America

To gain an understanding of American culture, one could begin by exploring American bars and the wide variety of alcoholic beverages they offer. It is important to note that the legal drinking age in the United States is 21 years old. Many bars in the US also offer a special time period called "Happy Hour," during which they provide discounted prices on alcoholic drinks or small dishes. These discounts can often be as much as 50%, but some states have expressed opposition to Happy Hour, citing concerns about encouraging excessive alcohol consumption.

Types of American Bars:

- Sports Bar: Sports events like basketball, American football, European football, and baseball are highly popular among Americans, and they often gather at bars to cheer for their teams while forming social bonds with each other.
- Music Bar: Bars in America often invite bands to perform, featuring a variety of music genres such as rock, jazz, country, and more.

- Beer Pub: Beer is a beloved drink in America, and classic American beer brands like Budweiser and Corona are commonly consumed in pubs.

In the United States, the usual choice of snacks for drinking is often French fries, potato grids, onion rings, fried shrimp, Buffalo chicken wings, potato chips, tortilla and so on.

V. Korea

South Korea is known for its specialty table wine made from sweet potatoes, which has an alcohol content of about 20 degrees. The most famous brand of soju in Korea is "Jinro", which is widely available in street food stalls and restaurants. In Korean culture, pouring alcohol for each other is a sign of respect and friendship. When pouring a drink, the bottle should be held with the right hand, and the wrist of the right hand should be lightly held with the left hand as a sign of respect. The receiver should then use both hands to receive the drink to show gratitude. When drinking with elders, the younger

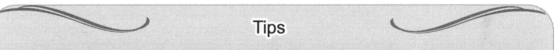

Tips

Tipping is a common practice in both European and American countries. In some places, waiters earn as little to no basic salary, and thus, rely on tips as a means of making a living. Tipping culture is an essential part of dining etiquette in Western countries. Although in Taiwan, we may not be accustomed to leaving tips for waiters, when traveling abroad, it is important to adapt to the local culture. Otherwise, it can be an awkward and embarrassing situation to be in when waiters have to approach you for tips. What do you do if you feel that the service provided is poor? Do you still have to tip? The answer is yes. In most cases, the restaurant and waiters do not intentionally provide bad service; it could be due to a bad day. Everyone deserves a second chance to make things right. When the meal is almost finished, the waiter will typically ask, "Is everything ok?" This is an opportunity to provide feedback to help improve the service. Not tipping is not the right approach to resolve any dissatisfaction.

generation should pour drinks for the elders first, and only drink after the elders do. They should not face the elders directly and cover their mouth when drinking. In addition to the famous Korean appetizer "Korean Fried Chicken", there are many other classic Korean appetizers, such as raw octopus, grilled sausage, grilled pork skin, grilled meat, pancakes, and kimchi soup.

Michelin Guides rating system

What is a Michelin meal? What are the different levels and their differences

The Michelin Guide has its origins in 1900 and was established by André Michelin, the founder of Michelin tires. Initially, the guide aimed to encourage drivers to take to the road using a small red guidebook and only recommended places based on the principle that "man only truly respects what he pays for," winning the trust of consumers. It has now evolved into an authoritative French institution specializing in evaluating the catering industry. Michelin-starred restaurants are considered some of the best restaurants in the world. Achieving Michelin star status, particularly three stars, is a significant recognition for chefs, as it affirms their exceptional cooking skills. It also attracts more customers to dine in these restaurants, ultimately creating more business opportunities. Notably, not only the food, but the service and overall experience are evaluated, and only those deemed to be exceptional in all aspects receive a Michelin star.

Michelin rating standards:

- Quality of products
- Mastery of flavor and cooking techniques
- The personality of the chef represented in the dining experience
- Value for money
- Consistency between inspectors' visits

The Michelin Guide is highly coveted by chefs and can have a significant impact on the fate of a restaurant. One star being a very good restaurant in its category, two stars being excellent cooking and worth a detour and lastly three stars being exceptional cuisine and definitely worth a special journey.

According to the Michelin Guide, there are 132 three-star restaurants in the world in 2021, one of which being the Le Palais in Taipei, Taiwan and is awarded for 5 consecutive years (2008-2022). Additionally, there are 8 restaurants in Taiwan that are awarded as Michelin two-stars restaurants, namely Logy, RAW, RyuGin Taipei, Omakase, Taïrroir, Guest House Sheraton Grand Taipei Hotel, JL Studio and L' ATELIER de Joël Robuchon. Lastly, there are 25 restaurants in Taiwan that are awarded as Michelin one-star restaurants, they are Top Cap Steakhouse, Da-wan, A Cut, Golden Formosa Taiwanese Cuisine, Impromptu by Paul Lee, Ken Anho, Kitcho, Longtail, Mingfu Restaurant, Mountain & Sea House Restaurant, Sushi Nomura, Sushi Ryu, Tien Hsiang Lo, Ya Ge, Fleur de Sel, Molino de Urdániz, Sushi Akira, Forchetta and Oretachi No Nikuya. In addition, the newly selected ones are, De Nuit, Fujin Tree, Mixiang Tai Cai Restaurant, Mudan , T+T and Sur-.

In addition to the Michelin-starred restaurants, the Michelin Guide also includes a list of Michelin Plate restaurants and Michelin Bib Gourmand recommended foods. The guide is highly respected and coveted in the culinary industry and can greatly impact a restaurant's business and reputation.

- Michelin Plate Rating: Restaurant environment (comfort and quality), expressed in five grades with crossed spoon and fork symbols, namely: moderately comfortable, comfortable, very comfortable, top-notch comfort, traditional style luxury
- Bib Gourmand: Since 1955, the guide featured the corporate logo "Bibendum" has also highlighted restaurants offering exceptionally good food at moderate prices. The restaurants must offer menu items priced below a maximum determined by local standards. These prices are within a fixed price range, for example European cities are within 36 euros, 40 USD in American cities, 400 Hong Kong dollars in Hong Kong, 5,000 yen in Tokyo, and 1,000 Taiwan dollars in Taipei, which can enjoy three dishes of a high standard.

Additional denotation:

price friendly notable wine list sustainable gastronomy

Michelin star

source: guide.michelin.com

延伸閱讀

Demi Monde半上流社會。米其林完全指南，https://demimondetw.com/2015-06-18-134/

Mao. Y., Tien. X., & Wang. X., (2021). I will empty it, Be my guest: A pragmatic study of toasting in Chines Culture. *Journal of Pragmatics, 180*, 77-88.

什麼是餐前酒？哪些酒適合做餐前酒？。紅酒百科全書的博客，http://blog.sina.com.cn/s/blog_8cad55d90102xmh6.html

防制酒駕專區——內政部警政署全球資訊網，https://www.npa.gov.tw/ch/app/folder/619

洪昌維編著（2019）。《葡萄酒侍酒師》。全華圖書。

菸酒產製進口統計資料——財政部國庫署，https://www.nta.gov.tw/multiplehtml/121

歐子豪、渡邊人美（2019）。《日本餐酒誌——跟著SSI酒匠與日本料理專家尋訪地酒美食》。積木文化。

Chapter

8

The Art of Wine

- Wine introduction
- Wine Varieties and Brewing

As trends and practices evolve, wine has gained popularity among Chinese consumers, becoming an essential component of many social occasions. Learning about wine is like mastering another language; it breaks down language barriers and expands one's social network. Wine is not only a form of art but also a cultural tradition that has been present in Europe for centuries. In this chapter, we will delve into the world of wine, exploring its fundamentals and embracing it as a part of our lives.

Wine introduction

I. History of wine

The earliest evidence of wine dates back to Mesopotamia in Central Asia, where large vineyards were planted. The wine culture then spread westward to Egypt, where the wine-making process was depicted in Egyptian murals. By 2000 BC, the cultivation of grapes had made its way to Greece, making it the first country in Europe to plant grapes and make wine. Epic poems like "Iliad" and "Odyssey" by Homer featured stories related to grape cultivation and winemaking. Greeks held wine celebrations to worship Dionysus, the god of wine and pleasure. The Romans adopted viticulture techniques from the Greeks and promoted wine in the Italian peninsula, creating their own Dionysian culture known as "Bacchus." In the 6th century BC, the Greeks brought grapes to France through the port of Marseilles, passing on viticulture and brewing techniques to the French. The expansion of the Roman Empire helped grapes and wine to spread rapidly throughout Eastern Europe, including France, Spain, southern England, and the Rhine and Danube River regions in Germany. After the fall of the Roman Empire in the 5th century AD, the church took over the development of wine, and Christians around the world regarded it as the holy blood of Christ.

1. Father of Oenology

The French wine industry has a reputation for excellence, but winemakers have

Wine making in ancient Egypt

Source: www.gourmet.com

faced the challenge of wine spoilage over time. To address this problem, they sought the expertise of Dr. Louis Pasteur, a microbiology specialist. In his research, Pasteur initially focused on the fermentation process of wine. He extracted grape juice using a glass needle and placed it in a sealed flask to observe the results. His experiment revealed that the interaction of grape juice with air and yeast from grape skins leads to fermentation. When grape juice is sealed without exposure to air or yeast, fermentation is impeded. Pasteur then shared his findings with winemakers, concluding that wine sourness is caused by lactic acid, which is a byproduct of fermentation. He advised winemakers to exercise greater caution during the wine-making

Louis Pasteur-French chemist and microbiologist

process to prevent bacteria from causing the wine to become acidic.

2. Wine-making formula

In 1857, Pasteur unveiled the principle of alcohol fermentation, which suggests that alcohol is a byproduct of yeast and carbon dioxide generated during yeast respiration.

However, the production of wine is not as straightforward as just mixing yeast and grape juice. To qualify as wine, the beverage must be made from fermented grape juice and contain alcohol. The grapes used must be in their natural form, and the natural yeast used must come from the grape skins. If the beverage is made from concentrated grape juice, it cannot be deemed as wine. Hence, the process of making wine is stringent and demands meticulous attention to detail to ensure that the final product meets the standards for being classified as wine.

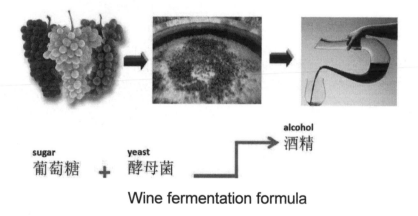

alcohol
酒精

sugar
葡萄糖 ＋ yeast
酵母菌

Wine fermentation formula

II. Important vocabulary for wine

This book compiles the most crucial and frequently used wine vocabulary. It is a valuable resource for beginners who are just entering the world of wine. Familiarizing oneself with these terms is not only beneficial for comprehending wine-related literature but also for confidently participating in conversations at wine events.

1. Old / New world

The majority of wine-producing regions are located in two geographic bands that encircle the earth between 30 and 50 degrees north and south latitude, where the climate is ideal for growing wine grapes. The northern latitude is home to the "Old World" of wine, where wine was first originated. Countries such as France, Germany, Italy, Spain, Portugal, Austria, Hungary, and others have a long history of winemaking. On the other

Betty Wu and her red wine endorsement for Pandorla : Is the red wine you drink real?

According to an article in Apple Daily, a study was conducted by the Institute of Food Industry Development at Kaohsiung University of Hospitality and Tourism, as well as several renowned wineries, to test 12 of the most popular and inexpensive red wines on the market. The results revealed that the Pandorla red wine, which is endorsed by Betty Wu, may not have undergone proper fermentation. There were suspicions that the wine was produced by mixing water, fruit juice, and alcohol. Chen Chien Hao, a wine expert, claimed that some commercially available wines are made with alcohol, essence, saccharin, and distilled water. For that it was clear that none of these ingredients underwent proper wine fermentation.

Celerbrity endorsement

Source: EBC News dated 2015/10/11

hand, the term "New World" refers to countries such as the United States, Australia, New Zealand, Chile, Argentina, Canada, South Africa, and others. The history of winemaking in the New World began in the 16th century, and many of the techniques used today originated in the Old World.

◆Differences between old world and new world

The wine-making process in the Old World is steeped in tradition, encompassing everything from brewing to bottle labeling. Brewing methods are strictly regulated by laws that govern every stage, from planting to aging the wine. For instance, in Europe,

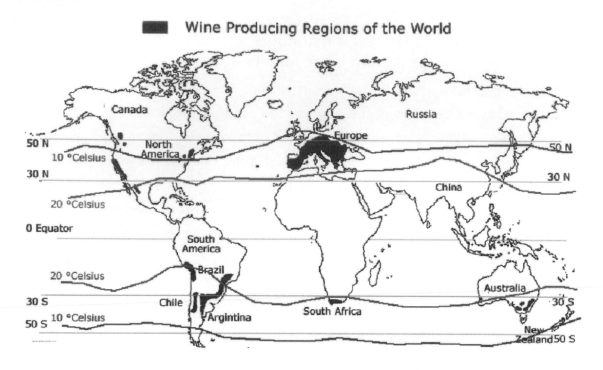

Source: researchgate.net

irrigation of vineyards is prohibited due to the belief that such human intervention affects wine quality, even though it may boost grape production. However, this regulation has been relaxed in Spain in recent years. In the Old World, wine labels highlight their regions and wineries, reflecting their geographical location and territorialism. Conversely, New World wine labels primarily indicate the grape variety used, and they tend to be more diverse and creative.

◆Flavors of the Old World and the New World

Old World wines are typically known for their refreshing and conservative style, with a lower alcohol content. In contrast, New World wines are often characterized by their rich fruit aromas, modern approach, and relatively higher alcohol content. In terms of packaging and marketing, New World wines tend to have a more consumer-oriented culture and are constantly promoting various wine varieties. They offer a diverse range of flavors, which is why many consumers prefer them. When opening a bottle of New World wine, the strong fruity aroma can be overpowering. Ultimately, consumers can choose between Old World and New World wines based on their personal preferences.

2. Characteristics of making wine

◆Grapes for wine

It is important to note that grapes used for winemaking are distinct from table grapes. Table grapes tend to have thinner skins, smaller seeds or even be seedless, larger pulps, and are juicier. Wine grapes, on the other hand, have thicker skins, larger seeds, smaller pulps, and are relatively sweeter. These differences are significant because the rich flavors in wine are derived from the grape pulps, skins, seeds, and other components. This means that the process of extracting these flavors is crucial to the winemaking process.

◆Terroir for wine

A good bottle of wine depends on Terroir and its conditions including four elements, namely climate, soil, and tradition

- Climate: It refers to the weather, rainfall and sunshine
- Soil: Soil texture, quality, nutrients and its drainage condition
- Terrain: A stretch of land , elevation/altitude
- Tradition: Inheritance of winemaking techniques, talent and experience of winemakers

Bordeaux, France, is renowned for its exceptional terroir. The region is situated at 45 degrees north latitude in the southwest of France and has a typical

Old World wine label on the left and New World wine label on the right.

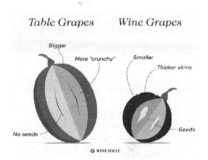

Comparison of table grape and wine grape

Source: winefuture.net

Different wine glasses

Source: winefolly.com

oceanic climate. In winter, there is minimal frost, while summer and autumn provide ample sunshine, creating ideal conditions for grape growth and ripening. The soil in Bordeaux is composed of gravel, clay, and well-drained sandy stone, making it perfect for grape cultivation. The three main rivers in the region, Gironde, Garonne, and Dordogne, offer sufficient moisture for the grapes to absorb, resulting in the production of world-class wines.

◆Types of wine

4 types of wine:

- Still Wine：Red wine, White wine and Rose
- Sparkling Wine： Champagne and Sparkling wine
- Fortified Wine： Port wine and Sherry
- Aromatic Wine：Refers to aromatic wine, for example, Gewürztraminer and Mustcat

3. Wine Region

While France may be the most famous wine-producing country, there are many other regions around the world that also produce wine, such as Italy, Spain, the United

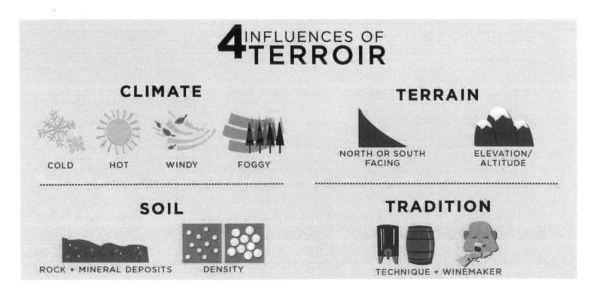

Source: https://smallaxepeppers.com/what-is-terroir/

States, and Australia, to name just a few. Taiwan is a relatively new player in the world of wine production, and while its production levels are still quite low, its wines have gained recognition on the international stage for their quality and unique characteristics.

◆Bordeaux and Burgundy

France is widely regarded as one of the world's best wine-producing countries, and two of its most well-known regions are Bordeaux and Burgundy. These regions have unique terroirs that have given rise to many world-renowned wineries and wines. Bordeaux wine labels often use the term "Chateau" to indicate that the grapes used come from specific vineyards, while Burgundy labels often use the term "Domaine." Some of the most famous wineries in Bordeaux include Chateau Lafite Rothschild, Chateau Latour, Chateau Margaux, Chateau Haut-Brion, and Chateau Mouton Rothschild. Meanwhile, in Burgundy, Domaine Romanée-Conti (DRC) is considered the most expensive winery in the world.

First-Growth Châteaux

	Chateau Latour	Chateau Lafite Rothschild	Chateau Margaux	Chateau Haut-brion	Chateau Mouton Rothschild
Appellation	Pauillac, Medoc	Pauillac, Medoc	Margaux, Medoc	Pessac-leognan, Graves	Pauillac, Medoc
Area	78 Hectares	112 Hectares	99 Hectares	52 Hectares	90 Hectares
Annual Production	16-18,000 Cases	15-25,000 Cases	10,000 Cases	11,000 Cases	20,000 Cases
Average price (grand vin)	$855	$1,007	$774	$659	$720
Aging potential	20-60+ Years	20-50+ Years	20-50+ Years	15-30+ Years	30+ Years
Second wine	Les Fortes de la tour	Carruades de lafite	Pavillon rouge du chateau margaux	Le clarence de haut brion	Le petit mouton

Source: https://www.vinovest.co

DRC（Domaine Romanée-Conti）

◆Taiwanese wine

Changhua Erlin, located in Taiwan, is often referred to as the "Taiwanese version of Bordeaux." In the past, both Golden Muscat and Black Queen grapes were planted for winemaking, and the irrigation from the Zhuoshui River allowed the grapes to grow in better quality and become sweeter. Currently, there are 16 wineries in Changhua Erlin, and it is considered the hometown of red wine in Taiwan, producing around 20,000 bottles of wine each year. Unlike European grapes that are harvested once a year, Taiwanese grapes can be harvested twice a year. Another winery in Taichung, Shusheng Winery in Houli, uses the fertile soil from Houli and moisture from the nearby Dajia River to produce the award-winning "Moscato Oro Vino Fortificato NV."

4. Wine Bottles & Glasses

◆Shapes of wine bottles

There are four common wine bottle shapes used for different types of wine.

- Champagne: The champagne bottle itself is relatively thick, because it has to withstand the force of about 6 atm.

Shapes of wine bottles

- Bordeaux: Bordeaux bottles have shoulders and are commonly used for Cabernet Sauvignon and Sauvignon Blanc from the Bordeaux region of France.
- Burgundy: Burgundy bottles have a sloping shoulder and are often used for Pinot Noir and Chardonnay from the Burgundy region of France.
- Hock: Hock bottles, named after the ancient German wine, are used for white wines in the Rhine Valley of Germany and the Alsace region near France. These wines do not require long-term storage and do not have pomace in the wine, resulting in a slimmer and longer bottle shape.

◆An introduction to wine glasses

The shape of wine glasses is carefully crafted to enhance the experience of drinking wine. Each glass is designed to bring out the unique characteristics and flavors of the wine it is intended for. Ultimately, choosing the right wine glass comes down to personal preference and the occasion. Whether it's a formal dinner or a casual night in, the right wine glass can elevate the experience of enjoying a good bottle of wine.

- Champagne glass: The traditional champagne and sparkling wine glasses are designed with a long flute shape that is slender and elegant. This design allows the drinker to watch the delicate bubbles rise to the surface and appreciate the flavor and aroma of the wine. The combination of taste and visual effect makes for a truly enjoyable drinking experience.

- Bordeaux glass: In the Bordeaux region of France, Cabernet Sauvignon is the most common type of red wine. To enhance the drinking experience, the glass for this type of wine typically has a wider opening rim. This design allows the wine to flow directly to the back of the mouth, reducing direct contact of tannins with the tongue. As a result, the strong tannin taste is smoothed out, providing a full and tactile experience of the wine.

- Burgundy glass: The Burgundy region of France is known for its Pinot Noir grape variety, which has a lower tannin content and higher acidity compared to other red wines. Burgundy wine glasses typically have a shorter but larger bowl. This design allows the wine to flow towards the tip of the tongue, increasing the contact between the wine and both sides of the mouth wall. This enhances the sophisticated flavors of the tannins while also toning down the acidity of the wine, resulting in a well-balanced and enjoyable drinking experience.

- ISO glass: ISO also known as the International Standard Organization, it has a capacity of only 215ml and is mainly used in professional wine tasting competitions.

- All purpose glass: Shaped like a mini version of a Bordeaux glass. It has no specific purpose and is suitable for red wine, white wine and various types of wine

- Brandy glass: Also known as a snifter or a balloon glass, is characterized by its relatively short stature and wide bowl shape. When holding the glass, the palm is typically facing upwards with the index finger and middle finger gripping the cup handle, while the remaining fingers hold onto the bottom of the bowl. This method allows the warmth of the palm to gradually release the complex aromas of the brandy, creating a more aromatic experience.

From left to right : Brandy glass, Champagne glass, ISO glass, Universal glass, Bordeaux glass, Burgundy glass and larger Burgundy glass.

◆Ways of holding onto wine glass

Wine glasses are typically designed with long leg. This is to allow the drinker to hold onto the leg or base of the glass, rather than the bowl, while consuming the wine. There are two reasons for this:

- Social etiquette: Holding the bowl of the glass can leave unsightly fingerprints and smudges, detracting from the visual appeal of the wine and the glass.
- Temperature control: Holding the bowl of the glass can increase the temperature

different ways of holding onto wine glass

of the wine, which can negatively affect its taste and quality. By holding the leg or base, the drinker can maintain the wine's ideal temperature and flavor.

5. Sommelier

The origins of the sommelier role can be traced back to the French Sommelier Association, which was initially responsible for the supply and transportation of food and beverages. Over time, the role evolved into that of a server in a palace, responsible for providing drinks to the King. In modern times, the sommelier's main responsibility is to recommend suitable food and wine pairings in restaurants, as well as manage the wine selection. To achieve the title of sommelier, individuals must undergo various forms of education and training, including the following...

- Wine knowledge: Wine is extensive and profound. As a sommelier, to provide relevant information and suggestions for guests, they must be able to identify the variety of grapes, production regions, and harvest year. Sommeliers are also responsible for managing wine in the restaurant, which includes designing menus

Sommelier at Le Cote LM

and wine lists and storing wine within the restaurant's budget.

- Food culture literacy: In addition to wine knowledge, sommeliers must have an understanding of food cultures and cooking ingredients from various countries, as well as differences in cooking techniques. This enables them to match the appropriate wine with the food.

- Ability to operate and manage: Sommeliers must also have sales ability, as their role in a restaurant is to bring business and revenue to the company.

- Multilingual: Multilingualism is crucial for sommeliers, as they deal with wine-producing countries such as France, Germany, Italy, and Spain. Being able to deliver information about the wine label in different languages is important, as sommeliers interact with people from all over the world.

- Professional service: A sommelier's professional image, observation skills, and communication skills are essential to maintain great service. They should be able to identify a customer's wine preference on the spot to provide the best recommendations.

6. Wine Tasting Party

Wine tasting parties have gained popularity in recent years, with different types of events catering to different tastes. These parties can either be food-based and wine-assisted or wine-based and food-assisted. Wine-based food-assisted parties can be further categorized by country or region, such as Spanish wine, a Burgundy-themed event, or wine dinner featuring exclusive wines from Domaine de la Romanée-Conti. Additionally, La Paulée is a popular wine tasting party where attendees bring their own fine wines to share with like-minded wine enthusiasts and enjoy good food together.

7. Beaujolais Nouveau

Beaujolais is located in the southern part of Burgundy, France. Its soil is rich in minerals, making it an ideal location for growing the Gamay grape variety. Beaujolais Nouveau is a young wine made from grapes harvested from the latest batch. Since it has not been aged in oak barrels, it lacks the sophisticated texture of aged wine. However, its

Types of wine tasting party

Types of wine tasting party	Description
Food-based	The focus of this type of party is on the meal, and the sommelier works closely with the chef to select the best wine to pair with the food. Factors such as the ingredients, cooking method, and sauce selections are all carefully considered.
Wine-based	The primary objective of this party is to enjoy wine, and it is typically not a formal gathering. The chef creates dishes that complement the wine being served.
Wine-based tasting party	
Wines from different countries	These types of wine tasting parties are centered around a particular country, such as a Spanish or Argentinean wine tasting party. Wineries often organize such events, and only wine from the designated country is consumed.
Different wine variation	This type of wine tasting party is focused on one specific type of wine, such as red wine, white wine, or a particular grape variety like Grenache or Pinot Noir.
A vertical wine tasting	A vertical wine tasting, such as for Chardonnay, allows guests to focus on one type of wine over several years.
A horizontal wine tasting	A horizontal wine tasting, Drink Sauvignon Blanc from different regions in different countries to understand the characteristics of each region
Aged wine	For example: In a Spanish old wine party, only aged Spanish wine is consumed, and the host must be experienced and attentive to the state of the wine being served.
Expensive wine	DRC wine tasting parties exclusively consume the luxurious DRC from the Burgundy region of France.
La Paulée	La Paulée is a wine tasting party that brings together like-minded wine enthusiasts, with each attendee bringing a good wine to share with the group, creating a gathering of fine wine and food.

fruity flavor makes it ready to drink without decanting. Every year, on the third Thursday of November, people from all over the world celebrate the release of Beaujolais Nouveau, which was barreled in September of that year. This celebration is known as the Beaujolais Nouveau Festival, and it attracts a large number of tourists who gather in Beaujolais to taste the new wine of the year and join in the festivities.

Source: www.beaujolaisnouveau.fr

8. *Le Nez Du Vin*

Le Nez Du Vin is a set of tools designed to train the sense of smell to recognize the different aromas of wine. Invented by Frenchman Jean Lenoir, the aim was to help people differentiate the scents or aromas released by wine, as he believed that this was an important way to understand and appreciate wine. However, it can be challenging to find the right words to describe a specific aroma, which is why Le Nez Du Vin can be especially useful. It can help you develop the sensitivity of your nose and describe the

Le Nes Du Vin

flavors you smell, which is beneficial for wine tasting. A complete set of Le Nez Du Vin includes 54 bottles, covering all the flavors found in wine.

Wine Varieties and Brewing

The vast and profound nature of wine knowledge means that a comprehensive understanding cannot be achieved overnight. Without fundamental knowledge of wine, it is difficult to truly appreciate its beauty. As a result, we will be introducing basic wine knowledge, covering wine varieties, characteristics, and production methods.

I. Wine varieties

To truly grasp the essence of wine, it is essential to first understand the grape varieties, much like knowing a person's background and identity. Just like the various types of mangoes in Taiwan such as Aiwen, Yujing, and Jinhuang or Taiwan authentic mango, there are a plethora of grape varieties to explore. It is recommended to learn the different names in English or their original language, as the Chinese translations can differ between Taiwan and China. For example, Sauvignon Blanc is translated to "Bei Shu Wei Ong" in Taiwan, but "Chang Xiang Si" in Mainland China, while Gewürztraminer is called "Ge Wen Zi Te Ming Na" in Taiwan and "Qiong Yao Jiang" in China. Taiwan uses transliteration for the wine names, while China derives names using stories and sense. Therefore, it is best to learn the wine variety's name using its original name to avoid confusion.

1. White wine variety

◆Chardonnay

Chardonnay is a grape variety that grows in the Burgundy region of France, but it is now cultivated in many different parts of the world due to its adaptability. However, Chardonnay grapes grown in different regions may exhibit different characteristics. This grape variety is known for its versatility and can be used to produce a wide range of wine styles, therefore is recommended and loved by sommelier. Chardonnay is one of the few white grape varieties that can be aged in oak barrels, which imparts unique flavors and aromas to the wine.

◆Sauvignon Blanc

One of the most popular white wine varieties, which originated from Bordeaux, France, is widely produced in various regions around the world including New Zealand, USA, Australia, and others. Among those, New Zealand Sauvignon Blanc is popular worldwide.

◆Pinot Gris

Pinot Gris is a white and pink wine grape variety that is thought to be a mutation of the Pinot Noir red wine grape. In France, Pinot Gris produces wines that are rich in flavor with larger grape pulps, while in Italy, where it is known as Pinot Grigio, it produces wines with a much more refreshing taste.

◆Riesling

Riesling is Germany's most representative wine. It thrives in cooler climates and has a distinct acidic taste with a subtle hint of honey flavor. Unlike other wines, Riesling is rarely aged in oak barrels. Some people describe Riesling as having a gasoline taste, which scientists believe is caused by the hydrolysis reaction of two polysaccharides during the aging process. However, this flavor is less likely to be present in younger Riesling.

◆Gewürztraminer

This is a German word that can be difficult to pronounce due to its length. However, it is well worth the effort to learn as it describes a unique and rich fruity aroma, similar to lychee or candied fruit. It is particularly well-suited for pairing with Chinese cuisine.

2. Red wine variety

◆Cabernet Sauvignon

Cabernet Sauvignon is currently the most popular and highly rated red grape variety in the world. The grapes have small, thick-skinned, dark purple pulp. In China, it is called "Chi Xia Zhu" because of its thick skin, high phenolic substances, and strong tannin. Despite its astringent taste, Cabernet Sauvignon is delicate and elegant, especially after aging. It is highly suitable for aging.

◆Grenache/ Garnacha

Originally from Spain, this grape variety is locally known as Garnacha. It has a high sugar content, which contributes to the elevated alcohol levels in the resulting wine. However, the tannin content in Garnacha is relatively low. In Spain, Garnacha is a crucial grape variety and is often blended with Tempranillo.

◆Merlot

Merlot is a great wine for beginners due to its subtle tannin content and lower acidity. It is also commonly blended with Cabernet Sauvignon; each has its own characteristics to come out a favored wine to the public.

◆Pinot Noir

Pinot Noir is originally produced in the Burgundy region of France and is an exquisite variety with a thinner skin, making it challenging to grow. Pinot Noir is also the main type of grape used to make Champagne. It has a complex flavor profile and a silky texture, and many are produced as single-variety wines.

◆Syrah/ Shiraz

Shiraz, originally produced in the Rhône region of France, is known for its dark color, rich aroma, high tannin content, and suitability for aging. In addition to France, Australia is also known for producing high-quality Shiraz wines.

II. Wine making procedures

The process of making wine largely depends on the natural gifts of the grape, including its sugar content and the yeast present on its skin when it ripens. During the fermentation process, carbon dioxide and alcohol are produced. The basic steps of winemaking are:

- Harvesting: In Taiwan, grapes are typically grown using the Pergola training method, while in Western countries, Vertical Shoot Positioning (VSP) is more common. Harvesting can be done by hand or using machines. However, for noble rot grapes, winemakers prefer to harvest them manually due to their delicate nature. The grapes undergo screening to ensure their quality.

- Crushing and Pressing: The grape skins are torn during this process, allowing the pulp to come into contact with the yeast on the skins. The juice is then pressed out of the grapes, with care taken to ensure that the pressure is not too intense. To extract more color, flavor, and tannins during fermentation, the grapes are repeatedly pushed down and pumped over.

- Fermentation: The grape juice is placed in stainless steel tanks for fermentation, during which the sugar is converted into carbon dioxide and alcohol.

Vertical Shoot Positioning (VSP) used in France

Source: winetaste.com

Pergola Training method used in Taiwan.

Source: Emily's vineyard

Fermentation stops when all the saccharides have been converted, the temperature exceeds 45° C, or the alcohol content reaches 16%. The wine typically has an alcohol content under 14-15%.

- Clarification: The pomace, or solid matter, is removed from the wine, and the red wine is aged in oak barrels to integrate the aroma of the oak into the wine and add flavor.

- Aging and Bottling: The wine is stored in a wine cellar after bottling until it is stable enough for release into the market.

1. The making of white wine

After the harvesting and screening process, the winemaker quickly crushes the grapes to separate the juice from the skins, seeds, and stems to avoid bitterness. Then, the grape juice is put into stainless steel tanks for fermentation. Once the wine has matured, clarification is conducted before proceeding to bottling. Some winemakers also choose to mature their white wine in oak barrels to add flavor.

2. The making of red wine

After the red grapes are harvested and screened, the skins are typically crushed or broken down to release the juice and allow it to be in contact with the skins. This contact time, which can last from a few days to two weeks or more, is what determines the resulting color and tannin content of the wine during fermentation. Once the fermentation is complete, the solid material, or pomace, is removed to improve the clarity and quality of the wine during clarification. Red wines are often then matured in oak barrels to enhance their flavor before they are bottled and released into the market.

3. The making of pink wine

The process of making rosé wine involves pressing the red grapes after they have been harvested. The juice is left in contact with the skins for a shorter period of time, typically a few hours to three days, compared to red wine production. This is to extract only the color from the grape skins and not the tannins. The fermentation process continues after removing the skin.

4. The making of Sparkling wine

The first round of fermentation for sparkling wine is the same as that for white wine. Most sparkling wines do not have a vintage as they are made by blending various grape varieties or grapes from different vineyards. After blending, a mixture of grape juice and yeast is added to start a second fermentation. The wine is then bottled and sealed. During this second fermentation in the bottle, carbon dioxide is produced and dissolved into the wine. After aging, the yeast sediment is removed, the wine is topped up, and corked for bottling.

III. Understanding Wine Labels

1. Wine brand - wine label

The wine label on a bottle of wine can be likened to a name tag worn on a shirt; it serves as the identification of the wine and contains important information. Generally, wine labels include details such as the winery or production area, the type of grape used, the vintage year, the country of origin, and the alcohol content of the wine.

2. Wine sticker

Some wine bottles feature competition awards or excellent appraisals, and there are many such labels available on the market. These labels can serve as a helpful guide for consumers when selecting their preferred wine. The most famous appraisal system is the PP (Parker Points), which was created by the American wine critic, Robert M. Parker Jr. He is regarded as the most influential wine critic globally, and his appraisals are widely

This Cawarra series comes from Lindemans winery in Australia in 2002.
It was blended with Shiraz and Cabernet Sauvignon, with an alcohol
content of 13.5%

Robert Parker and the magazines " Wine Advocates", Source: robertparker.com

THE 100-POINT SYSTEM

100 – 96	Incredible!
95 – 90	Great!
89 – 85	Very Good!
84 – 80	Good
79 – 70	Average
69 – 60	Below Average
59 – 50	Not Recommended

Robert Parker rating system

respected. He scores red wines based on the Parker Points system, with a maximum score of 100 points.

The Wine Advocate is a bimonthly magazine founded by Robert Parker that provides regular reviews and the latest information on wine. In addition to the PP Point, there are many associations, institutions, or competitions in the market that evaluate wine. These serve as references for consumers when purchasing wine.

3. What does "Good Year" mean?

There is a common misconception that the year on the wine bottle refers to the year of packaging, when in reality it denotes the year of harvest. For wine enthusiasts, the year of harvest can be a crucial factor in selecting a wine. Grapes are an agricultural crop, and their growth is heavily influenced by factors such as light, temperature, and

Figure 8-21 The golden label on the top "SA WOMAN's WINE & SPIRITS AWARDS 2018" is the winner of the gold medal in the wine competition judged by women. The copper label below "CHINA WINE & SPIRITS AWARDS 2018" is awarded with a bronze medal award by China Wine and Spirits Awards.

rainfall, which in turn can impact the yield, quality, and style of the wine. It is often said that wine quality depends 70% on the quality of the grapes and 30% on the winemaker's technique, so it's clear that weather conditions can have a significant impact on wine quality. If the weather is unfavorable during harvest time, it can affect the grape's quality and yield. However, consumers need not be overly concerned with specific harvest years, as a bad year does not necessarily mean there is no good wine produced. Excellent wineries can still produce top-quality wine using their unique techniques and terroir, even in challenging harvest years

4. Does wine get better with age?

Aging wine can improve its quality, but it depends on various factors. Certain grape varieties are more suitable for aging, and the aging process requires both nature and nurture conditions. Proper nurturing conditions, such as the right temperature, humidity, and sunlight exposure, are crucial for wine aging. If these conditions are not favorable, then the storage of the wine should be carefully considered to maintain its quality. Ultimately, the age of wine does not always determine its quality, and the best approach is to enjoy wine at its peak, whether young or aged.

Class activities 8

1. Prepare the different types of wine glasses. Allows the students to elaborate their functions and match these glasses to a specific wine.
2. Prepare the different types of wine glasses. Let the students to identify the difference in shapes
3. Prepare a set of Le Nez Du Vin and split the 54 bottles among the groups. Let the students practice their sense of smell and elaborate.
4. Please ask students to search on the Internet and find out which large-scale wineries are in Taiwan.

延伸閱讀

WSET Level 1, Level 2教材。

王淑儀譯（2016）。佐藤陽一著。《葡萄酒餐酒誌》。積木文化。

王鵬、吳郁芸譯（2020）。葛瑞格・克拉克、蒙特・畢爾普著。《文豪們的私房酒單》。麥浩斯。

林裕森（2007）。《葡萄酒全書》。積木文化。

林裕森（2013）。《弱滋味》。水滴文化。

黃雅慧譯（2020）。渡辺順子著。《商業人士必備的紅酒素養2：頂級葡萄酒的知識與故事》。大是文化。

Chapter

9

Wine Tasting

- Wine tools
- Wine Tasting

A wine tasting experience is a form of art that engages all five senses and provides enjoyment for both the body and mind. The process of wine tasting relies heavily on our sensations, including the environment, physical and mental state, and the wine itself. All of these factors contribute to our overall enjoyment of the wine tasting experience. It is important to prepare oneself when attending a wine tasting event, by relaxing, being in a good mood, and dressing appropriately for the occasion. This allows us to radiate confidence and be more receptive to the ever-changing world, as claimed by psychologists. While drinking alone can be enjoyable, sharing a few bottles of good wine with close friends provides a different level of appreciation for the wine. However, it is the responsibility of the host to ensure the setup and wines are in place to achieve true wine tasting enjoyment. This chapter will discuss the necessary preparations for a successful wine tasting event.

Wine tools

Wine tasting parties are gaining popularity in Taiwan, but it's important to keep in mind certain etiquette when attending such events. One of the most overlooked aspects of wine etiquette is refraining from wearing perfume, as it can interfere with one's ability to fully appreciate the wine's aroma. Imagine being seated next to someone who has applied an excessive amount of perfume, it would be disappointing and unpleasant as it disrupts one's sense of smell. Wine is a form of beauty in life, and the sensory evaluation process involves all of our senses, including sight, hearing, smell, taste, and touch. If one is hosting a wine party, it's essential to prepare the necessary tools and utensils and possess basic knowledge, from opening and pouring the wine to tasting and serving it at the table.

I. Wine tasting preparation

1. Temperature

To properly enjoy wine, preparation is essential. The first step is to ensure the

The author teaches wine etiquette at National Chung Hsing University

wine is at the appropriate drinking temperature. For white wine, it should be chilled to between 9 and 12 degrees Celsius, while champagne or sweet wine should be chilled to between 6 and 8 degrees Celsius. Most wine cellars offer suitable storing conditions, including temperature and humidity control. If you don't have such equipment at home, you can chill white wine by placing it in a bucket of ice or in the fridge. Red wine, on the other hand, should be served at room temperature or about 18 degrees Celsius. In hot weather, you can refrigerate the red wine and take it out of the fridge before serving. Conversely, in cold weather, warm the red wine to the ideal drinking temperature. It's important to decant red wine before drinking to allow it to interact with the air and become smoother. This process also reduces the harshness of tannins, making the wine more drinkable.

2. Cork

To open a bottle of wine, it is important to first understand the type of closure it has. Wine bottles are typically sealed with a cork, but sometimes they may also have a metal cap. Here are some of the different types of closures used to seal wine bottles:

◆Natural Cork

Natural Cork: Made from the bark of the cork oak tree, natural cork is a biodegradable and renewable wine closure. To ensure quality, the bark is peeled every 9

White wine needs to be pre-chilled and placed in the ice bucket after opening.

years from a tree, that is at least 25-years-old, and 1/3 of the skin must be left for each peeling. The lifespan of a cork oak tree is typically 170 to 180 years.

◆Agglomerate Corks

Agglomerate Corks: These are made by grinding up off-cuts of natural cork to form granules, which are then glued together to form a compressed block. This method

Agglomerate Corks

reduces waste. Another compound method is the 1+1 or 2+2, which wraps a disc cork on a compound stopper so that the wine remains in contact with the natural cork.

◆Synthetic Corks

Synthetic Corks: Made using modern technology and traditional cork-making methods, synthetic corks resemble natural cork but are made from plastic compounds or processed wood chips. They come in various colors.

◆Sparkling Wine Corks

Sparkling Wine Corks: Champagne and sparkling wine corks are designed to withstand the air pressure in the bottle, which can reach 4.5-6 atm. These corks have a wider lower end to prevent bursting.

◆Screwcaps

Screw Caps: Screw caps are a popular wine closure option due to their lower cost and convenience. However, they do not allow the wine to breathe as well as cork stoppers, which can impact the wine's taste. While some wineries are shifting to screw caps for white wines, cork stoppers are still the preferred closure for many high-end wines.

Synthetic Corks

Source: Kaola.com

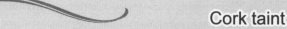

Cork taint

The quality of wine is closely related to the condition of the cork used for sealing the wine bottle. Proper wine storage requires specific humidity and temperature to prevent the cork from drying and cracking, which could allow air to enter and oxidize the wine. However, changes in cork quality can occur due to various factors, such as the use of low-quality cork, poor storage conditions, or contamination by a chemical called TCA (Trichloroanisole). TCA is a bacteria found in the air that can cause the wine to develop an unpleasant and moldy taste, known as cork taint.

II. Wine bottle opener

1. Opener

◆Foil Cutter

A foil cutter is used to remove the foil from the top of the wine bottle, ensuring a clean and flat cut.

◆Bottle opener

The professional bottle opener known as the Sommelier's knife, is commonly used. With this tool, there is no need for a foil cutter as the sommelier's knife can neatly cut the foil and use pigtail to drill into the cork before pulling it out.

◆Other bottle opener

For older wines, an Ah-So bottle opener is used. This tool has two prongs that gently clamp the cork, allowing it to be extracted without damaging it. Additionally, there are more stylish bottle openers such as the rabbit corkscrew and butterfly corkscrew.

Wine openers

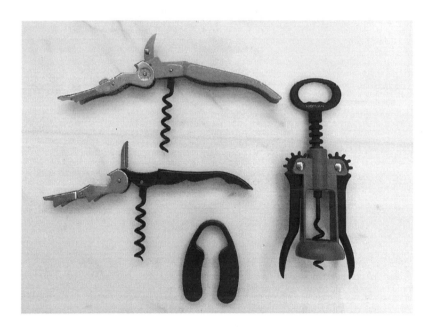

On the left showing 2 Sommelier's knives while on the right showing a
butterfly corkscrew. On the bottom showing an foil cutter.

2. Decanter

Typically, white wine does not require decanting, but there are a few special
decanters suitable for aged white wine. On the other hand, decanting is recommended
for aged red wine or full-bodied red wine as it makes the wine more enjoyable to drink.
An aged red wine can even be decanted twice. The tool used to decant wine is called a
decanter, and the act of decanting is simply referred to as "decanting." There are various

decanting

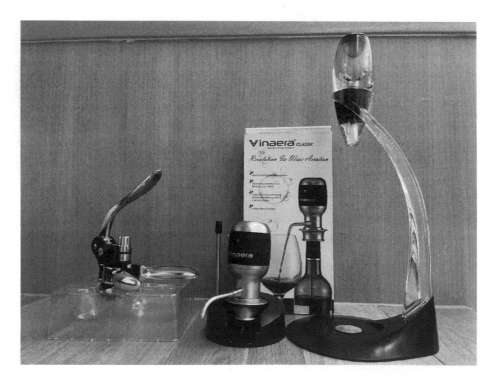

Left: Rabbit opener, Middle: Electric wine aeration, Right: Magic decanter

Different types of decanters

types of decanters available in the market. For instance, an electronic decanter can be set with a decanting time between 0 to 180 minutes. Another example is the Magic Decanter, which is also useful for aerating wine. However, if you're drinking your favorite wine, it's recommended to decant it in the most traditional way possible to enjoy the wine at its finest.

III. Preparations prior to drinking wine

1. Wine glasses

To fully appreciate the aroma of the wine, it is essential to choose the right wine glass. In Chapter 8, we provided information about which wine glass to use for each type of wine. When holding a wine glass, maintain an elegant and professional posture to present both yourself and the wine in the best light.

2. Pouring the wine

Overpouring wine into a glass is considered poor etiquette. To ensure the ideal amount, carefully observe the shape of the glass and pour the wine to the widest horizontal line. This not only helps maintain the wine's temperature but also provides enough space for swirling to release the wine's aroma.

3. Other wine tools

Wine tools are essential for enjoying wine, and make excellent gifts for wine lovers. With such a variety of wine tools available, everyone can find something that suits their personal taste in wine. Gift-giving of wine tools is practical, yet affordable.

◆Wine Pourers

Wine pourers come in various designs, some with an internal sieve to filter out residues, while others are silver wine pourer discs that prevent spills and can be disposed of after use for hygiene purposes. When choosing a wine pourer for home use, it's important to prioritize convenience and avoid staining the wine label. However, sommeliers, who are experienced in wine service, may not require such tools as it adds to the overall dining experience with the professionalism of the sommelier.

◆Wine Rings

Similar to"Lord of the Rings", wine rings are designed with a piece of cotton cloth in the middle to absorb any spilled wine. They can be placed at the mouth of the wine bottle during pouring to prevent staining of the wine label. This accessory is particularly helpful for those who are not experienced in pouring wine.

◆Wine Stoppers

If the wine is unfinished and the cork cannot be replaced, a wine stopper is a good option. You can choose a stopper based on your preferences, such as one with a vacuum function to remove air from the bottle for better storage. Unfinished wine should be stored in the fridge and consumed as soon as possible or used for cooking to prevent oxidation.

Wine accessories

Wine Tasting

When it comes to drinking, there are three main aspects to consider: visual, smell, and taste. While many people might assume that taste is the most important, visual and smell play a significant role as well. In fact, the sense of smell is particularly important in distinguishing different aromas, and taste serves as a tool to confirm your sensory judgment. Students interested in wine can benefit from practicing their visual and olfactory skills. For those who may not have many opportunities to taste wine, using tools such as Le Nez Du Vin can enhance their sense of smell and expand their wine vocabulary. When tasting wine, it's important to take note of the appearance, taste, and distinct features of the wine. Apps such as Vivino or Wine Searcher can be used to scan wine labels and read notes from other wine enthusiasts. In summary, drinking, writing, and reading more about wine can help individuals become more familiar with wine.

Source originated from the Korean Drama
"Descendants of the Sun"

I. The sequence of tasting wine

Drinking wine in a certain order can help to ensure that your taste buds are in the best condition. For example, if you eat chocolates before fruit, the fruit may not taste as flavorful because the chocolate has already overwhelmed your palate. Similarly, when tasting wine, it's important to consider the order in which you consume it. In general, sparkling wine should be consumed before white, pink, and red wine, and then distilled wine or fortified wine. When drinking wine, whether it's white or red, the following principles can be applied:

- Light-body wine before heavy-body wine
- White wine before red wine
- Younger wine before aged wine
- Sauce should be considered

II. The 4S in wine tasting

Drinking wine can be a simple yet enjoyable experience, as long as the taste is to your liking. However, when it comes to wine tasting, it's important to follow the 4S rules in order to fully appreciate the wine. While there are different versions of the 4S rules available online, the core message is essentially the same. Tasting wine is ultimately about making judgments based on your sensory experiences, from your eyes, to your nose, to your mouth.

1. Swirl

The first step is to swirl the wine gently in your glass, which allows for better oxygenation and the release of its flavors and aromas. When swirling, hold the glass with your dominant hand and move it in a counterclockwise direction if using your right hand, or clockwise if using your left. If the glass is on a table, place your fingers through the stem and swirl in either direction. When observing the color, place the glass in the direction of light or against a white background.

2. Smell

The second step is to smell the wine by placing your nose close to the glass and taking in its aroma. Be careful not to exhale into the glass when sniffing. Swirling the wine helps to release more of its aroma, and you can identify notes of fruit, herbs, or oak barrels.

Swirling the glass on the table or hold it in hand but be cautious not to spill it over

3. Slurp

The third step is to take a small sip, hold it in your mouth, and stir it with your tongue to ensure it reaches all areas of your mouth. Alternatively, you can drink it like mouthwash or inhale the wine with an "O" shaped mouth to release its aromas.

4. Spit/ Swallow

The final step is to either spit or swallow the wine. When dining, it's appropriate to swallow the wine, but when tasting multiple wines, spitting is acceptable and professional. It allows you to better appreciate the characteristics of the wine and avoid getting drunk. Sommeliers regularly spit out wine to refine their judgment and taste, demonstrating their specialized techniques and high proficiency.

A spitting bucket is provided during wine tasting

To fully appreciate the different flavors of wine, it is recommended to use multiple wine glasses when tasting different types of wine. This will allow you to better observe the color and differentiate the taste. To avoid mixing flavors, you should rinse your mouth between different types of wine with plain or sparkling mineral water. This will help to cleanse your palate and reset your taste buds so that you can fully appreciate the unique characteristics of each wine.

III. Aroma of wine

The aroma of wine is divided into three categories of aroma:

- The primary aroma of wine is derived from the grape variety itself and varies between different types of grapes. This aroma is characterized by scents of fruits, flowers, and herbs.
- The secondary aroma comes from the fermentation process and is a result of the interaction between the grape, yeast, and oak barrels.
- Tertiary aromas are developed during the wine aging process and are a result of the wine's exposure to air, oak, and time. These aromas can include notes of spices, earth, leather, and tobacco, among others.

By identifying and distinguishing these three types of aromas, we can gain insights into the possible grape varieties used in a particular wine, as well as whether the wine has been aged or fermented in oak barrels.

IV. Balance in a wine

A fine wine should exhibit coordination and balance in all its aspects. When we talk about balance in wine, we are referring to the harmony between tannins, acidity,

---

Wine aroma categories

- Fruit flavor: For example, there are white fruit aromas in white wine, such as apples and pears; red wine has berry aromas, such as strawberry, cherry and other aromas.
- Floral flavors: such as roses, violets, etc.
- Herbal and spice flavors: e.g., pepper, truffle etc.
- Animal-like smells: such as leather
- Baked flavors: such as toast

sweetness, alcohol content, fruity aroma, and aftertaste. These elements serve as the foundation for a well-balanced wine. To illustrate, think of sweet and sour pork dish, it loses its balance if it lacks sugar. Similarly, if any of the components is lacking in a wine, it will not be balanced. Here are the five main components of a wine:

1. Acidity

Acidity is a crucial component of wine, and there are three main acids found in grapes: tartaric acid, malic acid, and citric acid. It provides the backbone of a bottle of wine, and without it, the wine can become flat and lifeless. However, too much acidity can make a wine undrinkable. Therefore, achieving balance is key. Acidity triggers the salivary glands to produce saliva, which helps to enhance the wine's flavors. Wines from colder regions tend to be more acidic than those from tropical areas. Additionally, white wines tend to be more acidic than red wines, giving them a refreshing and crisp taste. In the wine world, acidity is often described as "crispy."

2. Sweetness

Sweetness in wine comes from the unfermented portion of the grapes. However, a wine with only sweetness can be bland and monotonous. To achieve balance, the remaining wines with higher sugar content must also have a corresponding alcohol content. Sometimes, wine may release a sweet aroma of fruit or flowers, but this doesn't necessarily mean that the wine is sweet. If a wine has a very small residual sugar content, it is considered dry. The European Union defines wines with less than 4g of sugar as dry, followed by semi-dry, semi-sweet, and sweet.

It is important to understand that dry wine is not the same as wine that gives you a very dry taste. Dry taste typically refers to the sensation on the tongue when tasting high-tannin wines. It is worth noting that when people describe a wine as "dry," it does not necessarily indicate that it lacks sweetness. Additionally, in Champagne, the term "Dry" actually means sweet, while "Brut" indicates a lack of sweetness.

3. Abv (Alcohol by volume)

The level of burning sensation in the throat can help to judge the alcohol content of a wine. Grapes grown in colder European climates tend to be less sweet and have lower alcohol content compared to those grown in warmer regions like the USA and South America. The sweetness in alcohol creates a warm and subtle taste in the mouth. A skilled winemaker aims to achieve a delicate balance between sugar and alcohol in a wine. Wines with higher residual sugar content require a higher alcohol content to achieve a well-balanced flavor profile.

4. Tannin

Tannins are present in grape skins, stalks, seeds, and oak barrels, which is why white wine lacks tannins. Tannins create a dry sensation in the mouth, similar to drinking overnight tea, by reacting with proteins. A refreshing red wine should not be too tannic, as tannins reduce fruity aroma. Red wine aging is affected by tannins and acidity; higher levels of these components impede oxidation, while wines with lower tannin levels have shorter storage lives. Tannins are also considered beneficial for heart health, as they protect the arterial wall, prevent arteriosclerosis, and control cholesterol levels.

5. Body

The weight or consistency of wine in the mouth is referred to as body. Similar to the difference between full-fat milk and sugar-free green tea, wines can have light, medium, or heavy body. The body of a wine is influenced by factors such as tannins, alcohol, and sugar content. Wines with high alcohol content and residual sugar tend to have a heavier body. A full-bodied wine is often described as bold and is becoming increasingly popular. In fact, many wines today have an alcohol content of 14% or higher, reflecting this shift in preference.

6. After Taste/ Finish

A good bottle of wine is usually complex in textures and has a lasting aftertaste.

The finish refers to the flavors that remain in the mouth after the wine has been swallowed, described as being a long, medium or short finish.

V. Systematic Approach to Tasting

The systematic approach to wine tasting is a method used in the WSET British Wine and Spirits Foundation certification course, developed by master sommelier Tim Gaiser. This method involves a step-by-step process of evaluating wine, beginning with visual assessment, followed by olfactory examination, and concluding with tasting and interpretation.

Systematic Approach to Wine Tasting

1. Visual Appearance

Begin by observing and appreciating the color of the wine. If the lighting is insufficient, use a white paper or tablecloth to improve visibility. Use descriptive words such as light, medium, and dark to characterize the color of the wine. For instance, a white wine may be described as having a medium gold hue. The following words can be used to describe the color of wine:

- White wine colors are:
    ①Lemon: younger wine
    ②Gold
    ③Amber: aged wine.

White wine gets darker with age

- Red wine colors are:

①Purple: Young red wine

②Ruby

③Garnett

④Tawny: an aged red wine

Red wine gets lighter with age

2. Nose

While the taste sensation can only identify sour, sweet, bitter, salty, and umami flavors, the human nose is capable of distinguishing over 100,000 different scents. If the

Wine tears / legs: Wine tears or legs refer to the droplets that form and stream down the inside of the glass when it's swirled. They are related to the sugar and alcohol content of the wine. Wines with lower sugar and alcohol content, such as German white wines, tend to have thinner and faster-moving tears. Conversely, wines with higher sugar and alcohol content, like Australian Shiraz, have thicker and slower-moving tears that are more obvious.

Wine tears/legs

taster is in good physical and mental condition, they should be able to detect the nuances in the wine's flavor. To fully appreciate the wine's aroma, one should bring the glass to their nose and inhale deeply, then slightly open their mouth to perceive the wine's bouquet and flavor. Generally, youthful wines have a fruitier aroma, while mature wines have a more complex, mellow aroma. Initially, it may be difficult to distinguish between different aromas, as our brains have limited databases of scent memories. However, with practice and experience, our vocabulary and ability to identify different aromas will improve.

3. Palate

While drinking wine, it is important to pay attention to its acidity, body, aroma, alcohol content, and aftertaste. Simply drinking and forgetting the details of a particular

Wrong ways of drinking the wine

Excessive swirling of the wine glass: Swirling the wine glass excessively may not be necessary for all wines. Some wines, such as Beaujolais Nouveau, are ready to be enjoyed straight out of the bottle without the need for decanting. In fact, excessive swirling may cause the wine to lose its flavor and become flat. Therefore, it is best to avoid excessive swirling and simply savor the wine as is.

Overpouring the wine: Overpouring the wine can be problematic for a few reasons. Firstly, if the glass is filled to the rim, it can be difficult to swirl the wine effectively. Additionally, pouring too much wine may lead to wastage if you are unable to finish it within a reasonable time. This is especially important during the summer months when the heat can cause white wine and champagne to quickly warm up, making it difficult to maintain their ideal drinking temperature. To avoid these issues, it's best to pour an appropriate amount of wine and drink it at a leisurely pace.

Put it for too long: Leaving wine for too long can have a negative impact on its quality. If the wine is not finished and is left for an extended period of time, it may become acidified, and its overall quality can deteriorate. To ensure that your wine retains its optimal taste and quality, it is best to consume it within a reasonable time frame and store it properly.

wine would be a waste. It is recommended to take notes and record observations to help develop a better understanding of the wine's characteristics.

III. Food Wine Pairing

According to the French, a perfect food and wine pairing is like a marriage - both complement and enhance each other's flavors, bringing out the unique qualities of each other beautifully. If you are not familiar with pairing food and wine, a safer approach is to match regional wines with regional foods. This concept is similar to pairing Oolong tea with Chinese food, Puer Tea with dim sum, Taiwanese stir-fried food with beer, and sake with Japanese cuisine. Following this approach, you can achieve successful pairings about 90% of the time. For instance, Burgundy Pinot Noir is a great match for Burgundy red wine beef, while California Cabernet Sauvignon pairs well with American steak. However, it's essential to note that the general rule of pairing red wine with red meat and white wine with white meat is just a reference point. To achieve a truly successful pairing, extra attention should be paid to the sauce used. Western dishes tend to focus on ingredients, while Chinese dishes often incorporate soy sauce or spicy condiments like ginger, garlic, and chili, which can significantly affect the final flavor profile. Therefore, it's crucial to consider the changes in taste brought on by the ingredients and select the right wine accordingly.

5 principles to follow for food-wine pairing:

- Which is the main focus? In a dining experience, sometimes the food takes center stage, and other times it's the wine. As a supporting character, the wine should complement the food without overpowering it. If the wine is the main focus of the meal, then the food should bring out the unique characteristics of the wine, and vice versa. A well-matched meal and wine can create a magical effect, making each element shine and enhancing the overall experience.
- Acidity: Acidity in wine can complement sour foods and help balance out their flavors. This is because the acidity in the wine can make the food taste less sour for the consumer. For example, Sauvignon Blanc's refreshing taste makes it a

good pairing for sourer foods. Meanwhile, Chardonnay can pair well with fish dishes with stronger seasonings. By pairing wine with the appropriate level of acidity, you can elevate the flavors of your meal and create a more enjoyable dining experience.

- Sweetness: The sweetness in wine can help reduce the spiciness and saltiness in certain dishes, making it a suitable pairing for hot stir-fry and Taiwanese cuisine. Sweet white wine can also complement fruity desserts.

- Tannins: Red wine contains tannins, which bind with and remove salivary proteins, creating a dry sensation in the mouth. This makes it an ideal pairing for red meats that are rich in protein, fats, and salt, as the tannins can help relieve the grease of the meat. Additionally, the mineral taste of tannins makes them a good pairing for grilled food.

- Alcohol content: Spicy food can intensify the effects of alcohol, so when choosing a wine to pair with spicy food, it's best to opt for a lower alcohol content. Sweeter wines can also help balance out the spiciness and reduce the intensity of the alcohol.

Things to avoid in food-wine pairing

- To avoid enhancing the fishiness taste in seafood, it's recommended to steer clear of wines with heavy tannins or oak barrel flavors when pairing them with seafood.
- It's important to pair sweet foods with wines that are sweeter than the food to prevent one flavor from overpowering the other.
- For spicy dishes like Thai cuisine, consider pairing them with white wines that are both sweet and rich in acidity, such as Riesling. Keep in mind to choose a wine with lower alcohol content as higher alcohol content can intensify the spiciness of the dish.

Class activities 9

1. Arrange a wine tasting session in class and make use of the 4S rule in wine to appreciate and evaluate the taste.
2. Practice using different kinds of bottle opener
3. Practice various decanters and pouring of the wine

延伸閱讀

何信緯（2014）。《旅途中的侍酒師》。麥浩斯。

洪昌維（2019）。《葡萄酒侍酒師》。全華。

張一喬譯（2016）。瑪德琳·帕克特、 賈斯汀·哈馬克著。《Wine Folly：看圖學葡萄酒》。積木文化。

葉姿伶等譯（2014）。歐菲莉·奈曼著。《我的葡萄酒生活提案》。三采文化。

劉永智（2015）。《頂級酒莊傳奇》。積木文化。

矗汎勳（2017）。《酒瓶裡的品飲美學》。日日幸福。

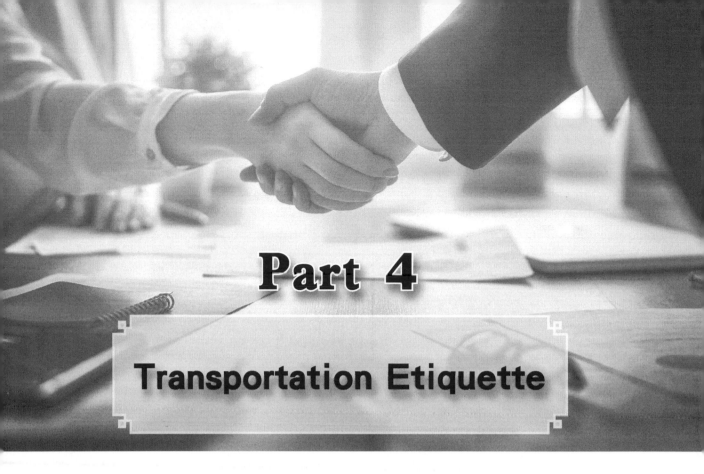

Part 4

Transportation Etiquette

Transportation has become an integral part of modern life, and the development of automobile technology has made it more convenient than ever before. Electric vehicles have become a trend, thanks to the efforts of innovators like Tesla founder Elon Musk, and these vehicles are now expanding beyond personal use to public transportation. While electric cars are still in the experimental stage, they will soon become a common sight on the roads. Although autonomous airplanes are technically possible, there is still much discussion and review required regarding the ethics of artificial intelligence by experts. Space flight is also making strides, with Virgin Atlantic announcing its private space travel plans in 2021, which send founder Richard Branson into space. While these trips are expensive and primarily accessible to the wealthy, it is clear that the modes of transportation will continue to evolve and change beyond our imagination. This is why it is important to constantly remind ourselves of transportation etiquette, as it remains relevant to our lives.

Space tourism becoming a reality

Source: ntdtv.com.tw

Chapter 10

Public transportation Etiquette

- Car ride etiquette
- Etiquette for new form of transportation
- Travel Etiquette

Public transportation is defined as the means of transportation used by humans to replace walking or to transport goods. This includes bicycles, motorcycles, cars, trains, ships, and aircraft, as well as moving vehicles driven by man or animals such as horse-drawn carriages, bullock carts, or human-powered sedans. Technological advancements have led to the rise of shared rides, with companies like Ubike and Uber becoming increasingly popular due to their accessible and easy-to-use ride-sharing systems. However, it is important to remember the potential for interactions when using these forms of transportation and to cultivate respect and tolerance for others. This section will discuss transportation etiquette in more detail.

Car ride etiquette

There are few things one should be aware of when taking a car ride, such as paying attention to the traffic rules and regulations, mannerism, and seating etiquette. For the regulations, one can refer to the Directorate General of Highways MOTC of the Republic of China. The general etiquette in car ride usually revolves around the safety considerations and mutual respects of the passengers and the driver. As for the seating etiquette, one should have the courtesy to offer their seats to those in need.

I. Car ride etiquette in general

- When driving a car, it is essential to follow traffic rules and prioritize safety. Avoid excessive honking, maintain a safe distance from the car in front, and refrain from flashing headlights unnecessarily to prevent accidents.
- Passengers riding in a car should always respect the driver by refraining from smoking, consuming strongly flavored food, or drinking coffee or milk to avoid spilling and dirtying the owner's car.
- All passengers, including the driver, should fasten their seatbelts while riding in a car. Failure to comply with regulations could result in fines for the driver. According to the law, children should sit in a designated child seat. Additionally,

children should not stick their heads or hands out of the car or open the car's roof as it could potentially put them in danger.

- Avoid using mobile phones while driving. Instead, utilize a Bluetooth device in the car. Navigation or phone conversations should not distract the driver. Passengers should also avoid speaking loudly to prevent agitating the driver.

- Never drink and drive. As of January 2022, the third reading for traffic regulations has approved an increase in penalties for drunk driving. Passengers involved in drunk driving are subject to a fine of 6000-15000NTD. If an innocent person dies in a drunk driving incident, the driver is subject to a fine of up to 2 million NTD. In the case of serious injury, the driver is subject to a fine of less than 1 million NTD. It is your responsibility to find a substitute driver if you plan on drinking. Remember, safety is the only way home.

- To maximize comfort in the car seats, luggage should be placed in the trunk. However, ensure that the size and weight of the luggage are within the recommended range to avoid obstructing the driver's view.

- It is gentlemanly behavior for men to allow ladies to enter the car first, and when

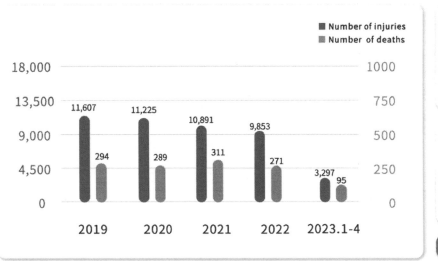

Statistic of drunk driving accidents during 2019-2023

Source: Road Traffic Safety Portal. https://168.motc.gov.tw/

alighting, men should open the door for the ladies. The same courtesy should also be extended to the elderly and seniors.

- Always park your car in a designated area and avoid parking in areas that could potentially cause danger to others. If you need to park temporarily, ensure that you do not block the entrance or exit and leave your contact number for others to reach you if they need you to move your car. If someone notifies you to move your car, remember to remain respectful and avoid showing attitude.

II. Car Seat Etiquette

Passengers should be mindful of seating etiquette when taking a car ride, as there are guidelines for car seat positioning. It is important to consider the seniority and relationships of other passengers and the driver to avoid unintentional impoliteness. There are two situations to consider when it comes to car seat etiquette: Chauffeured driving, and host driving.

1. When the Chauffeur is driving

When taking a business-related car ride, it is important to pay attention to the seating arrangement. If the host is unable to pick up the person, they may arrange for a chauffeur or agency to do so. In such cases, it is important to be mindful of proper etiquette, including:

- In a car with the steering wheel on the left, the right side of the rear seat is considered the main passenger seat, followed by the left side of the rear seat, and then the front passenger seat. If there are four passengers, the third most important person should sit in the middle seat at the back, and the fourth person will take the front passenger seat. It is generally considered international etiquette for female guests not to sit in the front seat.
- In a car with the steering wheel on the right, the left side of the rear seat is the main passenger seat, followed by the right rear seat for the second person. However, in Japan, the main passenger should take the right rear seat even though

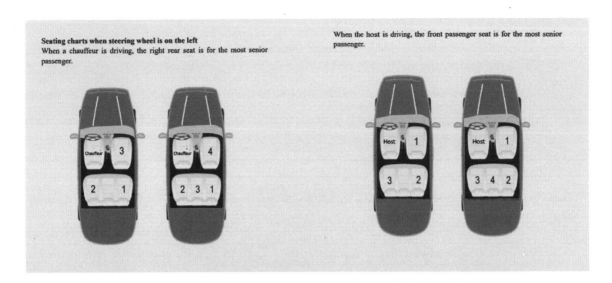

Seating charts when steering wheel is on the left
When a chauffeur is driving, the right rear seat is for the most senior passenger.

When the host is driving, the front passenger seat is for the most senior passenger.

Seat arrangement in the car

the steering wheel is on the right.

- In the car with three passengers while driving on the right side, the first passenger should enter the car through the left rear door. In crowded areas where it may not be convenient to enter through the left side, the first passenger can enter through the right rear door and move to the left rear seat. The person in the most humble position or the driver should help to close the door and then return to their seat.

- When getting out of the car, the person of the most humble position should exit first and open the door for the passengers at the back. The rear seat passengers should then get off from the right side according to their priority.

- When men and women are riding together, the woman should get on the vehicle first, and the man should occupy the seat on the right. When getting off the vehicle, the man should open the door and get off first, then assist the woman to get off.

2. When the host is driving

When the host personally drives for the passenger, it indicates that the passenger is viewed as an important customer or friend. As a result, passengers should not treat the host solely as a driver, and instead consider the seating arrangement based on the social interaction between the guests and the driver.

- The first seat is the front seat next to the driver, which is reserved for the guest of honor. It allows for easy interaction between the host and the guest. It is impolite to regard the host as a driver and sit directly in the rear seat.

- The second seat is the right side of the rear seat, followed by the position behind the driver's seat.

- When the host couple drive to pick up their friends couple, the host's partner should take the front seat, while the friends couple should take the back seat.

- When the host sends the guests off, they should follow the order of seniority. When the main passenger gets off, the next passengers in the rear seats should fill the front empty seat, making it easy for the host to send them off in turn.

- Nowadays, with more businesswomen and people in higher positions, if the first honorary seat is occupied by a female officer, she should still sit in the honorary seat next to the host driver. This rule is not affected by any international conventions. When getting off the car, the passengers in the back should get off first and open the door for the person seated at the front.

To ensure maximum comfort and maintain a safe distance between passengers, it is advisable to avoid having people sitting in the middle seat, especially when male and female passengers are sharing the ride.

3. Seating order in other means of transportation

- When taking public transportation, the window seat is considered the priority seat, while the aisle seat is considered the humble seat. Subordinates should allow superior or the elderly to take the window seat first and assist with placing luggage before sitting in the aisle seat. When disembarking, subordinates should get up first to retrieve luggage and wait for superior or the elderly to get up before disembarking themselves.

- When taking a jeep, the seat next to the driver is considered the primary seat, followed by the rear right, then the rear left. When traveling on a nine-seater bus, the row behind the driver is considered the priority row, then the row behind, until the last row. When considering seat priority, it should be arranged in order from right to left and front to back. The last two passengers sat in the front row with the driver. The middle seat next to the driver is the unassuming one.

- When traveling in large vehicle such as a tour bus, the most honorable person should be accorded the highest level of respect. When enter the bus, it should be in reverse order of seniority, and exit bus follow the priority, unless the primary person has other seating preferences.

Etiquette for new form of transportation

The emergence of U-bike and Uber as new forms of transportation has provided added convenience to people. However, it is important to be mindful of certain etiquette when using these services.

I. U-bike

Taiwan is globally recognized for its advanced bicycle technology, and the U-bike service offered by the Taipei City Department of Transportation in partnership with local manufacturer Giant Bicycle is a prime example of this. Since its inception in March 2009, the service has become incredibly popular, with close to 600 million U-bike rides and over 2.8 million monthly users across Taiwan, making it the most successful public bicycle service in the world. Its success has inspired many countries to learn from and emulate its model. Liu Jinbiao, the founder of Giant Bicycle, highlights some of the key advantages of the U-bike service, which include:

- The U-bike system is a subsystem of the MRT, providing convenient connectivity between destinations at both ends.
- Borrowing a U-bike is hassle-free, as users can rent a bike from one location and return it to another. The system accepts various forms of payment, including

EasyCard, credit card, and mobile phone, making it easy for users to rent a bike. This system has gained global recognition for its high borrowing rate, being the most popular public bike rental service worldwide.

- The U-bike system promotes a more aesthetically pleasing environment in cities. In the past, many scooters and bicycles were often parked for extended periods in front of main stations, leading to cluttered and disorganized surroundings. With the U-bike system, a neat and tidy environment is advocated, reducing the number of parked bikes, and improving the overall landscape of the city.

- The U-bike system's rental rotation policy has led to increased turnovers, enabling people to travel to their destinations with greater ease. This policy also helps reduce the space occupied by parked bikes, making it more convenient for pedestrians and motorists to navigate the city.

The U-bike system provides a bicycle sharing service, promoting "green transportation" that offers people convenient, eco-friendly travel options while reducing the need for cars and public transportation. However, as cycling becomes more popular, conflicts between cyclists and pedestrians are increasing, often due to the lack of etiquette guidelines. In response, U-bike has implemented a penalty system for rule violators, although currently, the system prioritizes warnings over penalties to encourage greater usage. Adherence to rules is essential to avoid road chaos. The Taipei City

Polite and friendly cyclist etiquette advocated by Taipei City Department

Source: tw.news.yahoo.com

Department of Transportation is leading an initiative to promote a friendly and courteous bicycle culture, advocating for cyclists to avoid trespassing on others' property, saying "sorry, excuse me, and thank you," and ringing the bell when passing pedestrians. Other cycling etiquette guidelines include:

- It is important to treat U-bikes with care and respect as they are public property. Misusing or damaging the bicycles not only shortens their lifespan but also creates a negative personal image. It is strictly prohibited to use U-bike parts to fix personal bicycles.

- Riders should ensure that the U-bike is clean and ready for the next user. Garbage should not be left in the basket, and spills should be cleaned up.

- When riding with pets, they should be leashed and secured to prevent accidents. It is recommended to clean the bicycle with alcohol before and after use, even though there are no laws against pets on bicycles.

- It is not allowed to ride U-bikes on zebra crossings, sidewalks, or in parks. Violators will face consequences.

- U-bikes have a code of conduct, violated users could be reported. Drunk riding, trespassing, speeding on sidewalks, and running red lights result in penalty points. Accumulating three points will result in a two-week account suspension, while reaching seven points leads to membership cancellation.

Bicycle traffic signals

Source: news.tvbs.com.tw

The increase in the number of cyclists on the road has prompted the City Department of Transportation in Tainan to launch specific signs for cyclists. This initiative has since inspired many other cities to adopt similar signage, providing a safer and more peaceful cycling experience for riders.

II. Uber

Founded in 2009, Uber is headquartered in San Francisco USA, and is a transportation network company that uses mobile applications to connect passengers with drivers to provide car sharing services. One of the benefits of Uber is its ability to reduce the overall number of vehicles on the road, which contributes to the concept of low carbon footprint and green development. Uber drivers can also work part-time to supplement their income. The Ministry of Transportation categorizes Uber as a "multi-taxi" because it has a similar appearance to a private car and does not require a yellow, taxi-labeled sticker or hire signal on its body. Payment for fares is made through the mobile app rather than with cash, and the car plate number on an Uber is red. People prefer Uber over traditional taxis because it provides a more pleasant ride experience with better drivers, vehicle conditions, real-time fare previews, and safer protection mechanisms.

In the United States, strict regulations are in place for private car services like Uber. For instance, minors under the age of 18 are not permitted to ride without a parent or guardian, and parents must bring their own child car seats when traveling with young children. Failure to comply with these regulations can result in fines for the driver and even lead to their termination. To address this issue, Uber has introduced "Uber Baby" services in many countries to provide child seats. Moreover, Uber's evaluation system allows both drivers and passengers to rate each other, giving drivers the option to decline a ride based on the passenger's rating. In contrast to taxi services, there are varying practices and regulations for Uber.

- When taking an Uber, it's important to be considerate and ensure that the driver can safely stop, especially in areas with traffic or narrow lanes. Failure to do so can result in fines. Unlike traditional taxis, Uber drivers do not stop automatically when hailed, so it's important to be mindful of the driver's safety and the traffic around you.

- To avoid delays and confusion, it's important to enter the correct pick-up location when using the Uber app. The app uses an automatic positioning function, but this can sometimes be inaccurate, leading to delays or incorrect pick-up locations. Double-checking your address before requesting a ride can save time and frustration.

- As a courtesy to other passengers, it's best not to eat in the car. This helps maintain a comfortable and clean environment for everyone to enjoy.

- To ensure a comfortable ride for all passengers, it's best to avoid entering the car with strong smells, such as pungent food, excessive sweat, or heavy perfumes. These scents can be unpleasant and make the ride uncomfortable for others.

- It is important to treat Uber drivers with respect, acknowledging their presence and greeting them when entering and exiting the car. Even if you don't want to engage in conversation, a simple greeting can go a long way in creating a positive experience for both the driver and passengers. Additionally, it's best to open and close the door gently, as the small, shared space can amplify any loud or abrupt movements.

Options for Multi-taxi riding

Taiwan boasts a highly convenient transportation system, with taxis easily accessible in urban areas. However, in remote regions, it can be challenging to hail a taxi. Uber's arrival in Taiwan has sparked a wave of new, innovative ride-hailing apps, including LINE TAXI, Yoxi, 55688 Taiwan Taxi, Find Taxi, TaxiGo, and more. Similar services have also emerged globally, such as Lyft in the United States, Didi Chuxing in China, Grab in Southeast Asia, and Ola Cabs in India.

III. Ride-Sharing

Some multi-taxis also offer shared ride services, and Uber provides two types of shared ride services. The first allows friends to board at different locations, while the other is known as "Uber Share," where passengers share a ride with strangers. While some find the idea of sharing a ride with strangers socially challenging, the attraction is the lower fare. However, due to the Covid pandemic, Uber has temporarily suspended its shared ride services. Nevertheless, the concept of multi-taxi and shared rides remains relevant as they can reduce traffic congestion, pollution, and parking demand, addressing modern societal problems.

Travel Etiquette

Tourism heavily relies on transportation, and in Taiwan, flying is often the go-to option for traveling abroad due to its island geography. Domestic tourism, such as visiting islands like Penghu, Kinmen, and Matsu, is also popular among locals. Accessibility is a crucial factor for travel considerations, according to the statistics from Taiwan EasyCard Company. In addition to having easy access to destinations, practicing good manners while traveling can enhance the overall experience.

I. Domestic travel transportation etiquette

The domestic tourism industry in Taiwan has experienced a significant decline since the decrease in mainland tourists. In recent years, the Covid-19 pandemic has further restricted travel, leading to changes in people's travel habits. As a result, domestic tourism has become a popular alternative, creating new business opportunities. The domestic tourists' considerations when planning their trips include several key factors according to the tourism industry statistics.

The primary consideration for the majority of the population, regardless of age or income, is the accessibility of public transportation. The petty bourgeoisie and the younger generation tend to prefer travel destinations with lower prices, while the elderly group likes to stay away from crowded areas. Traffic jams are a common annoyance among people, but younger and senior travelers find it more troublesome to arrange their itineraries, while middle-aged individuals are more concerned about natural disasters and accidents.

When it comes to transportation options, travelers can choose between public transportation for the entire journey, public transportation combined with a car rental service, or self-driving for the entire trip. Out of these options, 44% of people prefer to drive themselves, citing the cost-effectiveness of driving, particularly when traveling in a group.

1. General etiquette for public transport

Taking public transportation is no less than driving by yourself. Taking public transportation requires more physical strength, patience and time. One has to be rather conservative when packing his travel luggage in order to make his travel experience a more pleasant one. What are some of the things we should be aware of when taking public transportation?

◆Pay attention to physical hygiene

When traveling alone, you may need to walk a lot to find your way or catch transportation. When taking public transportation, it's important to maintain personal hygiene since you'll likely have close contact with others. Avoid being someone people want to avoid.

◆Prepare what you need for your trip in advance

While some prefer to travel without stress, preparing in advance can make the journey smoother. This includes having necessary documents, coupons, or paperwork ready to avoid long wait times or lost items that can affect the holiday mood.

◆Pay attention to queuing etiquette

Respect queuing etiquette when taking public transportation to avoid cutting the line. Avoid being called out on social media or disturbing others.

◆Luggage Placement Etiquette

There are space limitations on public transportation, and as luggage increases with trip length, it's best to place luggage vertically on the luggage rack or in the space next to the seat to avoid hindering others' movement. Once placed, sit down quickly to avoid disrupting other passengers. Avoid placing luggage in the aisle as it can cause others to trip.

◆A show of public comity

Offering seats to those in need, especially if the seats are not designated as priority seats, is a way to show kindness. Helping those who have difficulty moving or placing their luggage is another way to be helpful.

◆Seat belt etiquette

Fasten your seatbelt as soon as you are settled. This is especially important for passengers in certain seats, such as the middle seat in the last row. If a passenger in this seat does not fasten their seatbelt, an emergency brake could cause them to be thrown forward and seriously injured.

◆Be mindful of talking or music volume

Silence your phone during the journey and be mindful of the volume of your conversations or music. Loud music can damage your hearing and disturb other passengers.

◆Avoid inappropriate behavior

It's important to be considerate of others when using public transportation. Avoid doing activities that produce strong smells, such as applying nail polish or cutting nails, as well as activities that may make others uncomfortable, such as displaying affection or putting feet on seats. Smoking is also prohibited in public areas in Taiwan, and chewing betel nuts is not allowed on high-speed rail carriages. Additionally, littering and eating food with a strong smell are considered inappropriate behaviors.

◆Be mindful of travel time

Planning ahead and arriving on time can prevent the need to rush when boarding public transportation. Making sure to leave enough time before departure to gather documents, coupons, or other relevant paperwork can help ensure a smoother journey.

◆Seat according to your reservation

When traveling on public transportation with reserved seating, it's important to sit in the designated seats according to the ticket purchased. Avoid occupying seats that belong to others, and if you need to switch seats with someone, make sure that both parties are traveling to the same destination.

2. Self-driving

Self-driving offers a higher level of autonomy than other forms of transportation. You do not have to carry your belongings around during the journey, making it more convenient and easier to navigate. However, there are still driving etiquettes that one must pay attention to during the trip to ensure a smooth and enjoyable journey.

◆Check vehicle equipment before traveling

To ensure a pleasant travel experience, it is important to check your vehicle before embarking on a long journey that may span several days. While Taiwan is known for its convenience, any unforeseen breakdown can disrupt traffic and spoil the mood for everyone involved.

◆Make good use of the App to avoid traffic jams

Travel delays caused by traffic are often frustrating. To avoid such situations, it is advisable to use traffic apps to stay informed about traffic conditions. For passengers such as the elderly, children, or pregnant women, frequent bathroom breaks can be inconvenient. In case of heavy traffic, alternate routes can be explored.

◆Road Manners

Take national highway as an example:

- When driving, it is essential to choose the correct lane based on the type of vehicle and the situation. The inner lane is for overtaking, while the outer lane is suitable for larger vehicles. While overtaking, it is advisable to return to the original lane as soon as possible.
- Safety should be a top priority while driving. Maintaining a safe distance from the vehicle ahead is important. Additionally, always use the light signal when changing lanes, and avoid crossing the trough line when entering or exiting interchanges to prevent accidents and penalties.
- It is crucial to be respectful and considerate of other drivers on the road. Pressuring others or misusing light signals can endanger everyone's safety. Therefore, it is essential to practice caution and ensure that your actions do not cause any harm.

3. *Various public transport vehicles in Taiwan*

◆High-speed rail

When taking the high-speed rail, it's important to arrive at the station early and board on time. Make sure to check your train's direction and number to avoid getting on the wrong one. If you're not eligible for discounted tickets, don't purchase them as

Tatala boat in Lanyu, Taiwan

Special means of transportation - The jigsaw boat, known as Tatala in the Dawu language, is a traditional means of transportation used by the Dawu people residing in Orchid Island, Taitung County, Taiwan. Unlike a canoe, a jigsaw boat is constructed by joining planks one by one, while a small canoe is made of 21 pieces of wood and a large canoe is made of 27 pieces. The canoe holds great significance to the Dawu people, and therefore, there are several taboos associated with it.

- Photography of jigsaw boats should be done with permission: Since ancient times, taking pictures of these boats without permission has been prohibited. However, due to increased tourism, the tribe has become less sensitive to this taboo. The tatala is considered sacred to the tribe, as each carved pattern on it represents their tribe's God. These patterns are believed to ward off evil spirits, provide guidance, and represent ancestor spirits. It is important to seek permission before photographing these sacred boats.

- Women should not touch tatala: In the past, women were not allowed to canoe at all, particularly during flying fishing season. Women were not even permitted to approach the beach. Thankfully, this prohibition is gradually being lifted. Female tourists should be aware of such taboos because the older generation of the Dawu people still strictly adheres to tradition.

Tatala boat in Lanyu

Source: travelerlux.com

it could result in a penalty of 50% on top of the ticket price. If you have a non-reserved seat ticket, avoid occupying reserved seats to avoid additional charges. It's also important to refrain from eating strong-smelling food, polishing nails, chewing betel nuts, or bringing pets onboard. Finally, make sure to place your luggage in the designated area.

◆Taiwan Railway

When traveling on Taiwan Railway, be sure to follow their guidelines on luggage size and number. Pets should be placed in specified pet boxes or bags, and only purchase tickets that you are entitled to. The child ticket regulations for Taiwan Railway are as follows: children below 115cm are free; those over 150cm and below 150cm must purchase a child ticket; those over 150cm must purchase a full ticket. Children above 150cm but under 6 years old do not require a ticket if they present their ID, and children over 150cm but under 12 years old can purchase child tickets with their ID.

◆MRT

Currently, MRT is only available in Taipei, Kaohsiung, Taoyuan Airport, and Taichung, but it's becoming more common in other cities. Children below 115cm or over 115cm but under 6 years old are exempt from purchasing tickets if they present their ID and are accompanied by a passenger who has already purchased a ticket. A passenger who has purchased a ticket can accompany up to 4 children who are exempt from purchasing tickets. It's prohibited to eat or drink on the MRT, and offenders may be fined between 1500 to 7500 NTD. Balloons are not allowed in the station and should be deflated before boarding the MRT. Passengers carrying foldable bicycles should use the barrier-free elevator when entering and exiting the station to ensure the safety of other passengers.

II. International travel etiquette

There are various methods of transportation for traveling abroad. Generally, Chinese travelers prefer to join tour groups for a more relaxed traveling experience, particularly due to language barriers and unfamiliarity with the location. If you are traveling solo, it is recommended to plan ahead and research local transportation and regulations. This can help you avoid unintentionally violating local laws or disrespecting the local culture.

1. Join a tour group

When participating in a tour group, various modes of transportation may be involved in the itinerary, depending on the specific group of participants. Since the group may include elderly individuals, pregnant women, and children, it is essential to arrange appropriate means of transportation that can accommodate their needs. Additionally, there may be individuals in the group whose behavior could be considered inappropriate, and it's important to be aware of what behavior is considered unacceptable in a tour group setting.

- Being late repeatedly: When traveling with a tour group, one of the biggest challenges is dealing with people who are consistently late. Despite agreeing to a set gathering time, there are always a few individuals who fail to arrive on time, causing delays and frustration for the rest of the group.

- Picky people: Some travelers can be picky about choosing their seats, insisting on a particular spot and refusing to settle down until they get it. It's important to treat fellow group members with courtesy and avoid making things difficult for the tour guide. Flexibility and willingness to compromise can help create a more pleasant and cooperative atmosphere during group travel.

- Nonchalant: Nonchalant behavior can cause disruptions during the tour. Some people may ignore the instructions of the tour guide and end up getting lost, losing their belongings, or delaying the whole group's schedule. It is important to listen and follow the tour guide's instructions to avoid any unnecessary delays or complications.

- Being noisy in the bus: When traveling in a tour bus, it's important to be considerate of others. If you want to talk, try to keep your voice down so as not to disturb fellow passengers. If you tend to snore, it's best to try and get a good night's sleep before the trip. If you bring kids along, make sure they are well-behaved and under your control to avoid disrupting the journey for others. Remember, everyone has different needs, so let's all be mindful of one another's comfort.

- Singing: If there's karaoke equipment in the vehicle, it can be enjoyable to sing during the trip, but it's important to avoid monopolizing the microphone. Be considerate of others who may want to rest or enjoy the scenery in silence. Control the duration and volume of the singing to ensure everyone has a pleasant experience.

- Be polite: You should remain respectful and care for one another. Always try to put yourself into other people's shoes to maintain a harmonious atmosphere.

- Tipping etiquette: Tipping requirements are typically communicated in advance if necessary. Even if you have tipped, it is important not to treat staff like servants.

2. Self-guided tour

In addition to language fluency, self-guided tour tests your problem-solving and planning skills. Transportation is a crucial aspect of your trip, and with advance planning, you can enjoy various local transportation options. It's important to follow local regulations and understand your rights and responsibilities. Here are some examples of transportation methods you may encounter during your travels:

- Gondola in Venice, Italy: The gondola is an iconic and traditional rowing boat of Venice, Italy. Typically painted in black, a boatman stands at the end to maneuver the vessel. Historically, gondolas were exclusively owned by nobles and were meticulously handcrafted. Today, due to their high cost, water buses are the primary mode of transportation in Venice. However, gondolas continue to attract tourists seeking a more authentic experience. When boarding a gondola, it is important to be mindful not to cause any damage to the hull. If planning to take pictures during the ride, it is advisable to ask for permission beforehand to avoid any infringement. Overall, riding a gondola is the perfect way for tourists to admire the beautiful scenery of Venice.

- Hong Kong sailing boat Agua Luna: Agua Luna is an antique sailing boat that sails across Victoria Harbor in Hong Kong. With its nostalgic exterior and modern interior design, this 28-meter-long vessel consists of two floors. Passengers can take in the beautiful night view of Victoria Harbor from the Hong Kong River. However, it's important to note that bringing outside food and drinks is prohibited and seats are not reserved.

- Japanese Human-Pulled Rickshaws: Rickshaws are an integral part of Japan's cultural heritage, dating back to the 19th century. They can be found in various scenic locations throughout Japan, such as at the Kaminarimon of Sensoji Temple in Asakusa. Tourists interested in Japanese history can follow the rickshaw driver, who can often speak fluent English, Chinese, French, and other foreign languages. Since pulling a rickshaw is a physically demanding job and drivers may pick up several trips per day, it is important to communicate clearly with the driver before boarding.

- British DUKW: The British DUKW, also known as the "duck boat," is an amphibious vehicle similar to the Dutch Amfibus. Tourists can enjoy the street views of Britain and the scenic Thames River by taking this yellow vehicle, which can be driven on both land and water. However, it's important to ensure that there are enough life vests on board and to avoid excessive movement when the DUKW is in water for safety reasons.

- San Francisco Cable Car: The cable car is not only a form of transportation for residents in San Francisco USA, but has also become a popular tourist attraction. It has three routes that cover many tourist attractions and shopping centers such as Fisherman's Wharf, China Town, and Union Square. As seats are limited, it's important to hold on to the handles for safety. With plenty of hills in San Francisco, passengers should also pay attention to their safety in case of emergency brakes. When getting off, passengers should exit quickly to avoid delaying others.

- Thailand Tuk Tuk: Thailand's Tuk Tuk is a popular mode of transportation with a roof that can protect passengers from the sun and rain. Tuk Tuk rides offer a unique opportunity to enjoy the local scenery and lifestyle. However, it's important for passengers to be aware of their surroundings and avoid wearing expensive jewelry or accessories that could attract pickpockets.

- Philippine Jeepney: In the Philippines, jeepneys are a beloved and widely-used form of public transportation. Many jeepneys are decorated with vibrant colors and designs, making them especially popular among riders. However, due to their popularity, these jeepneys can become extremely crowded. It's important to keep a close eye on your belongings to prevent theft.

Class activities 10

1. Discuss your pleasant or unpleasant encounters you have when taking public transportation
2. Let students discuss the situation they have encountered in domestic and foreign countries when taking public transportation
3. Let students discuss their experiences with U-bike and Uber

延伸閱讀

台北捷運官網，travel.taipei

台灣高鐵官網，thsrc.com.tw

台灣鐵路官網，railway.gov.tw

交通部：愛上安心期——自行車生活禮儀與安全騎乘指南，http://168.motc.gov.tw/TC/index.aspx

交通部觀光局電子書，taiwan.net.tw

唐受衡、林雨荻、何旻娟（2021）。《國際禮儀：韓商業禮儀及領隊導遊禮儀》（第三版）。華立圖書。

Chapter

11

Airplane Etiquette

- The process of taking a plane
- Boarding etiquette

Traveling abroad and domestically can be very different. The reasons for traveling abroad may vary, from leisure to business or diplomatic reasons. It is important to consider our identities and the purpose of our trip when traveling abroad. Are we representing ourselves as individuals, or as part of a family, school, team, or even our country? The example of Taipei Mayor Ko Wen-je's visit to Israel in February 2019 highlights the importance of being mindful of our actions while representing our country abroad. When traveling overseas, we are not only representing ourselves but also our country. For instance, during his visit to Israel for a conference, Mayor Ko Wen-je was not just an individual, but a public figure. Consequently, it was expected that he would behave appropriately. It is essential to remember that our action abroad can reflect on our country, and as such, it is necessary to be mindful of our behavior.

Taipei mayor being criticised for sitting on
the floor to charge his phone in Israel airport

Source: news.ltn.com.tw

International airports and flights provide us with ample opportunities to interact with people from diverse backgrounds. As individuals, our behavior and actions shape the perception of our group as a whole. Stereotypes are often based on the behavior and conduct of certain races or nationalities. Therefore, when traveling, it is essential to display good manners to promote a positive national image. Boarding etiquette begins at the check-in counter and extends all the way to arrival at our destination. It is crucial to be mindful of the procedures and etiquette along the way. What are some of the procedures that we should follow, and what are some of the etiquettes we should bear in mind to ensure a smooth and pleasant travel experience?

The process of taking a plane

I. Packing

Preparing for a trip abroad can be a challenging yet critical task, especially when it comes to packing. Different countries have varying regulations on what can and cannot be brought into the country. Therefore, it is essential to plan ahead and pay close attention to the following details:

1. The preparation

- Familiarizing yourself with the travel details, such as the airport, terminal, and reporting time.
- Checking the number of pieces and weight restrictions for your flight, which varies for domestic, Asian, European, and American routes, as well as different cabin classes.
- Knowing the items and quantities that are permitted or prohibited in the destination country, such as animal and plant commodities, tobacco, and alcohol.
- Adhering to relevant measures during the epidemic, such as vaccination, nucleic acid test certificates, and quarantine regulations. It's also crucial to keep track of the destination country's epidemic situation and make necessary quarntine hotel reservations.
- Complying with the regulations on 3C products, such as mobile phones, laptops, power banks, or spare batteries, which cannot be checked-in and must be placed in carry-on luggage.

2. Items that can be checked in but cannot be carried on the plane

- All kinds of knives (fruit knives, nail clippers, etc.).
- Sharp items (bow and arrow, darts, compasses, needles, etc.).
- Sticks and tools (hoes, mallets, screwdrivers, ice picks, camera tripods folded over 60 cm, selfie sticks, etc.).
- Sport equipment that can be transformed into offensive weapons (golf clubs, pool sticks, skateboards, nunchakus etc.)
- Liquids, gels, and sprays (not to exceed 100ml when carried on the plane, and must be packed in a resealable transparent plastic zipper bag not exceeding one liter (20*20cm) in size, and others should be placed in the checked baggage in luggage.

3. Prohibited items in all baggage

- Explosive: Grenades of all types, blasting caps, detonator, fuse, explosives device
- Oxidizer: bleaching powder, peroxides
- Flammable liquids / solids: industrial alcohol and flammable accessories
- Action suppression equipment: pepper spray cans and other irritating substances.
- Poisonous drugs, corrosive substances, etc.

II. Check in

It is recommended to arrive at your terminal early before your scheduled departure time. The terminals are usually arranged alphabetically, so if you are flying with United Airlines, which starts with the letter "U", it may be located at the far end of the terminal. To avoid unnecessary hassle, locate your boarding gate based on the alphabetical order, so you don't have to make an additional round around the terminal.

1. Luggage trolley

Upon arriving at the airport, locate a luggage trolley to transport your luggage. In Taiwan, luggage trolleys are free for both arrival and departure, but in some countries, they may require a fee. In the US, for example, most cities do not charge for luggage trolleys upon arrival but may charge upon departure, so be prepared with local currency or a credit card. Remember that luggage trolleys are designed for luggage only, and children should not ride on them to avoid accidents.

2. Check-in counter

Look for your check-in counter on the TV screen upon entering the airport. The check-in counter is usually located near or in front of the airline counter, but if multiple flights are departing at the same time, it may be farther away. Always check the TV screen to ensure you go to the correct counter, which is divided into business, economy class, and group passenger check-in counters. While in line, prepare your passport, relevant documents, such as nucleic acid test certificates, and pack your luggage for a smoother check-in process. Cooperate with the ground crew and place your luggage on the weighing scale for the X-ray inspection before leaving. Lastly, make sure to have your boarding pass, passport, and luggage tag before heading to your departure gate.

3. Security Check and CIQ (Custom-Immigration-Quarantine)

- Security check: Have your passport and boarding pass ready to speed up the security check process. Empty any drinking water before going through customs. Place your carry-on luggage on the conveyor belt for X-ray inspection and remove any personal belongings, such as loose change and belts, placing them in the inspection basket. Wait for the previous person to finish before proceeding, and only go when the detection light turns green.

- Immigration Inspection: Have your passport and boarding pass ready and wait in line for the immigration officer to inspect your documents. If you're traveling with children, kindly ask for permission to clear immigration together. Be honest and respectful when answering any questions asked by the immigration officer.

- Custom and Quarantine: If you need to declare or carry agricultural products, make sure you comply with local regulations for their entry. If you're unsure, you can confirm with the quarantine office.

III. VIP Lounge

Each airline or airline alliance typically sets up VIP lounges in airports, with some credit card companies also having their own lounges. These lounges are primarily reserved for first-class and business-class passengers, as well as members of frequent flyer programs. Credit card company lounges are typically accessible through credit card points or an additional payment. While in the lounge, passengers can relax, read, and enjoy various catering services. However, it's important to note that only first-class passengers will receive boarding time reminders, and business and economy class passengers should keep track of their own boarding times. To avoid missing a flight, travelers should always check for potential time differences.

Airline Alliance

There are three major airline alliances in total, including:

- Star Alliance: It is the first global airline alliance with the largest number of members. It currently has 26 members, including EVA Air.
- Sky Team: It has 19 members, including China Airlines, Air France, etc.
- One World: Composed of 14 airlines, including Cathay Pacific Airways, Japan Airlines, Qatar Airways, and other airlines

Benefits of airline alliance

- Alliance member airlines can provide a larger route network through code sharing.
- Shared maintenance, operation equipment and VIP lounges. The staff also support each other, reducing the cost of airport ground handling and catering operations.
- The cost is reduced, passengers can buy air tickets at a lower cost. Enabling the flight to have more flexibility

China Airline VIP lounge

Source: china-airlines.com

Eva Air lounge

Source: evaair.com

Airline Business Class Cabin Design

There is significant polarization between cabin classes on planes, with some airlines phasing out first class in favor of business class. While first class cabins typically have fewer passengers than business class, some airlines have responded by creating even higher standards for first class, including upgrades to suite-like accommodations. For instance, Emirates now offers a first-class cabin suite on its A-380 passenger plane, complete with flight attendants who convert seats into beds after takeoff. Singapore Airlines has introduced the "sky double bed" for couples or families to sleep together in one bed. In air travel, luxury knows no bounds.

A380 First Class Suit

Source: Singapore Airlines

The summarized etiquette for boarding before flight is as follows

- Know the airline luggage policy
- Prepare the correct travel documents, check the expiry date.
- Arrive at the airport early to ensure there is sufficient time for check-in.
- When using luggage carts, pay attention while pushing and avoid improper use.
- Line up to check-in according to the cabin class, and you should not jump the queue or skip the class to check-in.
- Be polite and respectful to ground crew assisting the check-in process for you.
- Before leaving the counter, double check that all documents have been retrieved and that the luggage has passed the inspection
- When passing through the security check, baggage and person will be checked separately.
- Be polite when clear CIQ, answer questions seriously.

IV. Boarding

To board your flight, make sure to locate the correct boarding gate and wait for your flight. If you have time, feel free to shop at the duty-free store, but be mindful of any time zone differences and avoid missing your boarding time. Prior to boarding, have your passport and boarding pass ready and follow the instructions of the ground crew. As soon as you board, stow your carry-on luggage promptly and take your seat, fastening your seat belt. If you need to change seats, wait for the passenger to arrive, and ask for permission before making any changes. Unauthorized seat changes should be avoided.

Boarding etiquette

Getting on plane is probably the most relaxing part of travel. The process of preparing for a flight, including packing luggage and navigating the airport, can be quite tiring. Similarly, tasks such as checking luggage documents, checking in, dropping off checked luggage, and clearing customs can also be a hassle. However, once you have boarded the plane, you can finally unwind and savor the remainder of your journey.

I. Boarding procedures

When boarding a large aircraft, typically both the first and second doors on the left side of the plane are opened. The first door is located between first and business class, while the second door is situated between business and economy class. First and business class passengers board through the first door, while economy class passengers board through the second door. In contrast, only one door is opened for boarding on a small aircraft. Boarding procedures are arranged to ensure a prompt and efficient boarding experience. The airline's boarding announcement typically includes:

- "Ladies and gentlemen, this is the ___ airline flight bound for ____. We are now beginning the boarding process, and would like to invite our first-class and business-class passengers to board. We kindly ask that pregnant women, children, and passengers requiring assistance also board at this time

- Thank you for your patience. We would now invite our economy class passengers to board. For a smooth boarding process, we kindly ask that passengers in zone _____ board first. All other passengers remain seated until your zone is called. Thank you for your cooperation.

- Thank you for your patience, all passengers are now invited to board the plane

Upon entering the boarding gate, the ground staff will check your passport and boarding pass again. Once you enter the air bridge, you may put away your passport as you will only require your boarding pass to locate your seat on the plane. It is important to note that the airline follows a specific boarding order, beginning with the last cabin (located at the tail of the aircraft). If passengers in the front section attempt to board simultaneously, this may block passengers in the back section from easily accessing their seats and stowing their luggage.

II. Placing luggage properly

- When placing your carry-on luggage, it is important to use the public space sparingly. This space includes overhead bin, the space underneath the seat in front of you, and the closet (if available for certain aircraft types or cabin classes).

- It is helpful to assist your passengers sitting next to you with placing their luggage, as this will not only foster better social interaction but also ensure everyone's safety. You will be spending time with your neighbors during the flight, so being friendly and helpful can make the journey more pleasant.

- If you are unable to find space for your luggage, you may ask the flight attendant for assistance, but please remember that they are not luggage service specialists. It is important to travel light and smart by packing only the essentials in your carry-on baggage. This may include:

① Travel documents, wallets, cards, and pens

② Necessary items such as: thermos, lotion, lip balm, socks, or paper slippers

③ A book or magazine to read on the go

④ Necessary Medicines

⑤ Warm clothing, etc.

III. Before and after takeoff

1. Passengers boarding

The boarding process is typically brief and busy for both passengers and flight attendants. Therefore, it is essential to settle into your seat quickly. If you require assistance, be sure to signal a flight attendant promptly.

- Use toilet if you are in need, as there may be a period of time during takeoff when passengers are refrain from using facilities.

- In economy class, drink service may not begin until after takeoff, but you can always request a glass of water or ask the flight attendant to refill your water bottle if you're thirsty.

- Flight attendants may provide headphones, blankets, and pillows to make your journey more comfortable. On long-distance flights, business class passengers may receive an overnight kit with essential items such as a toothbrush, toothpaste, mouthwash, comb, men's hair balm, eye mask, earplugs, hand cream, lip balm, and wool socks. Economy class passengers can also request additional pillows, blankets, or paper slippers for extra comfort, even if they do not have an overnight kit.

- If you wish to change seats on the plane, it is advisable to wait until after take-off. Airlines are under pressure to depart on time, which means boarding time is typically shorter. Situation, such as rearranging seating for tour groups or accommodating double bookings, can also arise during this period. If you are traveling with family, it is recommended that you reserve seats online or arrive at the airport early to secure seats together. When changing seats,

Overnight kit provide by EVA Air

Source: EVA Air

Blankets on plane

Blankets are not always provided by all airlines, with some budget airlines omitting the service for cost-saving purposes. In some cases, blankets are not provided on short-haul flights but are available on long-haul flights. Business and first-class passengers can usually expect to receive a blanket on all flights. However, on flights to remote locations without service stations, used blankets may not be swapped for new ones. It is worth noting that some airlines recycle used blankets, fold it for use on returning trips. Passengers should consider whether to use the blankets provided, for hygiene reason.

ensure that the other party does not have any special meal orders and that the seat is not a designated special seat, such as an emergency exit seat.

2. Before takeoff

Before the plane takes off, flight attendants perform certain safety checks, which include playing aviation safety videos, ensuring that passengers are aware of the location and operation of escape equipment, and checking the status of the cabin to ensure that everything is in position for takeoff.

Emergency Exit Row

This location is situated next to the emergency exit door, which requires passengers to be willing and able to assist flight attendants in evacuating passengers during an emergency. Therefore, they must be physically capable (i.e., an Able-Bodied Person) and have the necessary language skills to communicate with the flight attendants.

- As part of safety precautions before takeoff, flight attendants check that carry-on luggage is stowed properly, passengers have fastened their seatbelts, seats are upright, tray tables are put away, and window shades are opened, for better vision and more space for escape. Takeoff and landing are the most critical period of a flight, so these checks are crucial for passengers' safety.
- Cabin lighting is adjusted to match the outside environment to ensure passengers' pupils can adapt to the difference in light. This helps maintain good judgment and reaction times in case of an emergency.
- As part of safety procedures, all service items, including used trolleys and utensils, should be put away.
- Passengers must put away empty cups and ensure their hand luggage is properly stowed.

IV. After the takeoff

1. seat belt sign off

After takeoff, the aircraft will reach to the cruising altitude between 30,000 to 35,000 feet. Flight attendants will begin working after the aircraft reaches around 20,000 feet. When the "Fasten Seatbelt" sign is turned off, it indicates that it is safe to move around the cabin. However, in the situation of turbulence, the captain will turn on the "Fasten Seatbelt" sign, and passengers should return to their seats immediately and fasten their seatbelts securely to ensure their own safety. As the airline has fulfilled its obligation by cautioning passengers, failure to comply with safety instructions may result in consequences for passengers.

2. In-flight service

- For flights over three hours, meal service will be provided. Usually, drinks will be served first followed by meals. This is because passengers are not allowed to bring drinks during the CIQ check, plus 20-30 minutes takeoff time, hence, it is necessary to serve drinks first. On short-haul flights, there will be limited beverage choices, such as water, orange juice, cola, and soda, which will be provided on a tray by flight attendants. If you need a special drink, you can request it individually. After the beverage service, flight attendants will provide corresponding meals based on the departure time. For example, if the departure time is in the morning, breakfast will be served. Similarly, if the departure time is close to noon or evening, lunch or dinner will be served, respectively. The meals provided on planes are dependent on the departure time.
- Passengers who have ordered special meals will receive priority service before

Fight attendant on the aisle

the general catering begins. If a passenger who has ordered a special meal is dissatisfied and wishes to change their order, they will only be accommodated if there are additional meals available after all passengers have been served. Therefore, passengers should carefully consider their dietary needs before placing a special meal order, as changes may not be possible in flight. For instance, the airline does not accept orders for children's meals from adults. In the case a passenger desires a second meal, they may request one from a flight attendant, who will typically wait until all passengers have been served. Moreover, small buns are an alternative to offer to those passengers still hungry. Passengers are encouraged to communicate any special needs or preferences in advance to ensure a satisfactory dining experience.

- On international flights, drinks and alcohol are typically refillable. However, passengers should be aware that the reduced air pressure at high altitudes can decrease their alcohol tolerance. For instance, one may be able to consume a bottle of wine without getting drunk on the ground, but the opposite can occur on a plane. Passengers who cause trouble after drinking excessively may be reported to local police, causing unnecessary problems for themselves. Therefore, passengers should exercise restraint and not drink excessively just because alcohol is freely available. During meal service, passenger could decide their own meal preference, this could speed up the service, help flight attendant to provide a smooth and timely service. In such a confined space, mutual understanding is crucial for a pleasant and comfortable journey.

3. Descending and landing

When the plane begins to descend, you may have some time before the captain turns on the seat belt sign. During this time, you can use the lavatory or organize your luggage, but please be mindful of other passengers as there is usually a limited number of toilets on the plane. Avoid occupying the lavatory for too long to prevent long queues. Additionally, remember to follow proper lavatory etiquette, such as flushing the toilet after use and washing your hands thoroughly with soap and water.

In-flight seat preference and reasons

- The exit seat is typically located next to the emergency exit door or window (on small aircraft), providing more space and legroom. It is also easier to move in and out of these seats, making them a popular choice. However, not everyone is comfortable assisting with emergency evacuations or sitting opposite of the flight attendant, as it comes down to personal preference.

- The first row of each class usually has no seats in front, creating a more spacious environment with ample legroom and an unobstructed view of the screen. Many passengers prefer the bulkhead seat option for this reason. However, it's important to note that baby bassinet are often located in the first row, so passengers may encounter crying babies, which is difficult to control in a shared environment.

- Passengers who prefer window seats typically enjoy sleeping by the window or observing take-off and landing. The only drawback is the limited mobility.

- Aisle seats are a convenient choice for passengers who prefer to move around freely, such as accessing the toilet or stretching their legs. However, passengers should be aware of beverage and dining carts as well as duty-free sales carts that may block the aisle. Carelessness could lead to bumps or spills.

Inappropriate behaviors on board

- It is important that both flight attendants and passengers respect the privacy of politicians, businessmen, or celebrities who may be on the plane. It is inappropriate to disturb them or ask for pictures or autographs. Everyone on board should be treated with equal respect and given the space they need to feel comfortable.

- Excessive flatulence: If you are prone to bloating or stomach issue, it is recommended to watch your diet before boarding the flight. To avoid causing discomfort to nearby passengers, it is best to limit consumption of gas-producing foods, such as beans.

- During long flights, the body is confined to a narrow seat space, which can lead to poor circulation. To promote blood flow, it's important to stand up periodically.

However, it's not appropriate to put your legs on the chair in front of you, including the back and armrests, as this can be disruptive and disrespectful to other passengers.

- Constantly pressing the service bell and asking flight attendants to provide service
- Ask to take photos with stars and celebrities on the same flight.
- Roaming through the different class area
- Keep chatting with the beautiful stewardess and affecting their work
- Burst out laughing when using a headphone to watch movies or TV, disturbing your neighbors
- Borrowing a pen from the flight attendants to fill up your arrival card and not returning the pen

- The toilet on the plane, also known as the lavatory, should be used in the right manner. Always lock the door and follow the instructions for proper use, familiarize yourself with the features of the lavatory.
- Smoking is strictly prohibited in the lavatory, and cigarette butts should not be disposed of in the trash bin. The toilet paper in the bin is flammable and could cause a fire, which would be extremely dangerous in a plane.
- The lavatory uses a powerful vacuum system to flush waste and can make loud noises that may scare young children. It is advisable for children to use the lavatory with an adult, and passengers should not dispose of anything in the toilet bowl to avoid clogging it. Flight attendants may have to lock the lavatory if it becomes clogged, causing inconvenience for everyone.
- The lavatory usually has two oxygen masks for emergency use in case of high-altitude decompression. This is helpful for family members who may need to assist young children in the lavatory.
- The lavatory is stocked with essentials like toilet paper and women's hygiene products. Passengers should not take these items as souvenirs, as it could cause inconvenience for other passengers. Some airlines, such as Hello Kitty flights,

have had issues with passengers taking the Hello Kitty toilet paper as a keepsake.

V. Landing

The plane landing and reaching the destination does not signal the end of the flight. It is important to remain patient and prioritize safety by continuing to follow the instructions of the flight attendants.

- Do not retrieve your belongings when airplane is still taxing, there may be unexpected situations like emergencies or sudden brakes that can lead to accidents. If you get injured, seeking medical help in a foreign country can be challenging and expensive. Prioritize safety and be cautious.

- Double-check your belongings to avoid leaving anything behind. Any items left on the plane will be confiscated, and it can be very challenging to retrieve lost items.

- Ensure that you do not carry any prohibited items like meat or fruits that are not allowed in the designated country. Do not take unfinished food off the plane as it can spoil quickly and cause gastrointestinal issues.

- Leave your seat tidy before leaving the plane. Basic courtesy is to clean up after yourself and not leave a mess for others to handle.

- Show appreciation to the flight attendants for their hard work by thanking them as you leave the plane. Sometimes, the captain may show up to express gratitude to the passengers at the door. Your gratitude can make a significant impact on the crew and create a heartwarming atmosphere.

Class activities 11

1. Facilitate discussions about their flying experience among the students. Which part of the journey do they like the most and which part do they dislike the most?
2. Please ask students to list out the items that can and cannot be brought when traveling abroad
3. What are some of the convenient facilities in the VIP lounge?
4. How do one achieve both travel light and smart?

延伸閱讀

New A380 Suits，https://www.singaporeair.com/en_UK/us/flying-withus/cabins/suites/new-a380-suites/

呂江泉、郭名龍（2012）。《航空服務業管理》。華立圖書。

桃園機場長榮航空貴賓室EVA Air Lounge-The Infinity，http://www.evaair.com

張瑞奇（2020）。《航空客運與票務》（第五版）。揚智文化。

華航桃園機場第二航廈貴賓室啟用，https://www.china-airlines.com/tw/zh/discover/news/press-release/20180906

Chapter

12

Airlines Crew Preparation and Etiquette

- Preparation while schooling
- Aviation Interview Response

The aviation sector has always been a sought-after career path for young students who aspire to explore the world by flying high in the sky. Graduates from the department of hospitality are highly valued by airlines, as the hospitality industry offers numerous employment opportunities in aviation. Despite the department of hospitality having relatively low entrance requirements, the standards of hospitality in Taiwan have been on the rise in recent years. The students of the Hospitality and Tourism department are equipped with essential knowledge and service training, giving them a competitive edge in the aviation industry. In this chapter, we will provide a step-by-step guide for those interested in pursuing a career in aviation. Starting with academic preparation, graduates can then take the exam to enter the aviation industry. We will also discuss the etiquette and professionalism expected of aviation practitioners. This chapter will be useful for any students pursuing a career in any field, as it provides valuable insights into the workforce.

🤝 Preparation while schooling

As a university teacher, I am frequently asked by my students, "How should I prepare for the airline exam?" My response often depends on their current academic

Training and development for professional service personnel

level, and I hope to hear that they are either freshmen or sophomores. These students have more time to prepare for the exams, and the preparation during their time in school is crucial for their success. This preparation involves self-reflection and equipping oneself with the necessary skills and knowledge required in the industry, including language proficiency, and cultivating a professional image. Focusing on these aspects during their academic years is a form of internal preparation, which is essential for a successful career in the airline industry.

I. Language practice

The biggest challenge is not mastering the language but maintaining consistency in one's efforts. Generally, language proficiency requirements are based on the most commonly used languages in the world, followed by regional language preferences. For example, if you are applying for American Airlines, English and Spanish language abilities are usually required. Similarly, if you are applying for Korean or Japanese airlines, fluency in Korean and Japanese would be advantageous. For Thai or Vietnamese airlines, being able to speak Thai and Vietnamese would be beneficial. If an airline operates a wide and diverse range of routes, they are more likely to prioritize candidates with language skills. This is similar to applying for a position in a symphony orchestra, where the most beautiful and harmonious music is created when all instruments are involved. Therefore, it can be concluded that a candidate with strong language skills will have an edge in the airline industry recruitment process.

1. Mother tongue ability

Almost every student can speak their mother tongue well, but that does not guarantee fluency. Working in the airline industry provides numerous broadcasting opportunities, such as the captain broadcasting about the flight situation after takeoff, flight attendants informing passengers about safety regulations and available services, and ground crew announcing boarding information. Working in aviation means frequently speaking to the public, and this raises the question of whether your voice is pleasant to listen to. Public addressing, requires speaking to the public, and crew members often use a different speaking tone and language from their normal conversations, which is developed over time. If you have participated in a reading contest during your younger years, you may have already developed the fundamental skills required. However, most people lack the ability to articulate well, so early preparation is essential for those wishing to pursue a career in aviation.

2. Broadcasting Techniques

When it comes to broadcasting skills, whether it's public speaking or addressing a larger audience, it's important to pay attention to the following language skills and details:

◆Vocal

Broacasters do not usually show their presence, therefore clear and correct articulation is essential to ensure that the message is easily understood by listeners. As messages broadcasted are often important news or instructions that passengers need to follow, good articulation is critical.

◆Speed

If the airport broadcast is very hasty, and mere a formality, such broadcast can be very annoying to passengers, and will not be successful to delivering message to the public.

◆Tone and intonation

You may have noticed that Japanese people are full of smiles and respect when they talk on the phone until they hang up the phone. This is because mood and attitude will affect a person's tone and performance. Work from home (WFH) has become increasingly popular over the years. Although one is not physically required to be present in the office, one still has to dress appropriately during video meetings to show professionalism. Your professionalism will be discounted if you dress casually in your comfort space. Here are some things to keep in mind when broadcasting:

◆Content and nature

When making a public announcement, it's important to pay attention to the content and purpose. For instance, if it's a greeting announcement, the tone should be welcoming and excited. Use clear language to indicate the flight number and destination, like "Dear guests, welcome to XX airlines, flight number X, to..." A monotonous tone can make it seems like the crew is just doing his/her job, rather than genuinely welcoming passengers. To make a successful announcement, try to sound enthusiastic by imagining you are hosting important guests or an admirable idol. This will make your tone sound vibrant, energetic, and polite. Remember, passengers are the airline's source of income, so their long-term support is crucial for survival.

◆Timing

It's crucial to pay attention to the time of day when making public announcement. During the morning, the crew's voice should be energetic and enthusiastic, particularly for the first announcement. Even if some broadcasts are repeated, it's important to capture passengers' attention from the start, so subsequent broadcasts can be delivered in a more relaxed tone. On the other hand, if the announcement is made at night, the crew's voice should be calming and pleasant to avoid startling resting passengers or making others feel anxious.

◆Clarity

When broadcasting "important information" through a microphone, it is crucial to ensure clarity and easy comprehension. For instance:

- Let's take the boarding announcement in a waiting room as an example: "Ladies and gentlemen, we are about to begin boarding. We kindly ask passengers in "First and Business Class" to board first. Additionally, we would like to invite "pregnant women" and passengers "traveling with infants" to board at this time."
- Dear passengers, we are about to land at "Osaka International Airport", and the current time is "evening" "x o'clock x minutes" local time in Japan...
- Ladies and gentlemen, we are going to start our meal service in the cabin. Please help the flight attendant to "lower your table". For the convenience of "you"

and "rear" passengers, please turn your "seat back upright" Thank you for your cooperation

◆Friendly tone

Regardless of the language, the broadcasting tone should always be warm and welcoming. The choice of words must make passengers feel at home and comfortable. For instance, Chinese from different region may use different word choices to express warmth and hospitality. Paying attention to such details can make passengers feel cordial and valued. This is why airlines employ people of diverse nationalities, to make passengers feel at home when they hear accents or languages they are familiar with. To improve language level, one can practice listening to Taiwanese, Hakka, Indigenous languages, or seek guidance from the elderly at home. Being capable of speaking a variety of languages puts you at an advantage, especially in the airline industry.

◆Correct pronunciation

- Mandarin: Many students are aware that one part of the test is reading airline broadcast announcements. To excel in Mandarin broadcasting, it's crucial to pay attention to correct pronunciation, such as distinguishing between "ㄢ" and "ㄤ" or retroflex sounds like "ㄓ", "ㄔ", and "ㄕ". It's also important to differentiate between "ㄥ" and "ㄣ". Some people may pronounce "ㄒ" as "C" in English. Pronunciation is key in public speeches or broadcasts in Mandarin.

- Dialects: Taiwan has several dialects, including Taiwanese, Hakka, and aboriginal languages. According to the Executive Yuan in 2020, Mandarin is the most widely used language in Taiwan, also known as Taiwanese Chinese, spoken by 66.3% of the population. Taiwanese is spoken by 31.7% of the population, Hakka by 1.5%, and less than 1% speak other languages. In recent years, Taiwan has been actively promoting the inheritance of dialects, and various communities have been advocating for dialect certification tests. Having proficiency in these dialects can be a bonus point for certain companies. However, it's essential to prioritize good Chinese and English abilities first before pursuing other languages.

Taiwanese dialects.

Source: Executive Yuan

II. Foreign language practices

Many people tend to associate foreign languages with English, being able to speak it fluently is essential to exploring the world. It's never too late to start learning English, so don't be afraid to practice speaking it whenever you can. Take the example of Lei Jun, the founder of Xiaomi, who imitate Steve Jobs to promote products on stage in public, struggled conveying precise information about his products during a conference due to his limited language abilities. Thus, it's essential to develop proficiency in languages to effectively communicate and succeed in today's globalized world.

Different regions within China and English-speaking countries have distinct accents that can be recognized by experienced listeners. For example, it is easy to distinguish between British and Australian accents. In Taiwan, American English is widely adopted, and the vocabulary used by Taiwanese people is similar to that of Americans. American airlines tend to use American English, while British and Hong Kong airlines prefer British English. While accents may be important in some contexts, such as job interviews

Xiaomi Product Launch Conference

Source: Youtube

with British airlines, the most critical aspect of speaking a foreign language is the appropriate selection of words. It is often evident whether someone is proficient in a language based on their choice of vocabulary.

The so-called "good English" or good foreign language ability should be:

1. Correct pronunciation

When trying to speak English, it can be frustrating if other foreigners have trouble understanding you due to your Taiwanese accent affecting your pronunciation. Often, we rely on our way of pronouncing words, leading to the development of different accents across countries such as Japanese English, Chinese English, and Korean English. Adapting to a new accent can take time, especially if you have been taught in a local accent for a long time. However, it is not necessary to completely change your accent as your unique way of speaking can create a special connection with others. For example, James Bond's British accent in the 007 movies only added to his charismatic persona despite trying to adapt to an American accent for the films. Instead of being overly concerned about our accent, we should focus on listening, adapting, and adjusting our pronunciation. To speak good English, it is important to keep the following in mind:

- It is important to pronounce English words correctly and completely, especially when it comes to sounds such as "L" and "R", "TH", and "V", which are often challenging for Chinese speakers. Another important aspect is to ensure that you fully voice out the vowels, as failing to do so can make it seem like you are only saying half of the sentence. It can be frustrating when foreigners cannot understand your English, which can lead to a loss of confidence. By focusing on proper pronunciation and enunciation, you can increase your chances of being understood and feel more confident when speaking English.

- Basic grammar: When it comes to speaking, we need not worry too much about our grammar. In our daily lives, we often use Mandarin without adhering to the correct grammar. However, in formal settings, we must be more cautious with our words and expressions to ensure that we use proper grammar.

2. The right materials

When it comes to learning English, it's important to be selective about the materials you use. Traditional teaching materials tend to focus on reading and writing rather than oral skills, and may not reflect modern English usage. To improve your listening and speaking skills, it's best to listen to correct English from reliable sources such as CNN, BBC, and TED talks. However, be cautious about using casual English in formal settings. If you listen to English broadcasts to practice your listening skills, make sure to choose ones that use proper English. By being selective in your choice of materials, you can improve your English skills more effectively.

3. Speak elegant English

Regardless of whether you are speaking Mandarin, foreign languages, or dialects, the content of what you say is the most important thing. The choice of words used reveals how culture of an individual is. Do not become complacent and think that being able to communicate in a foreign language is enough. The next step is to speak the language elegantly and politely, so that people are impressed by your expressions. For example, the Japanese language tends to use honorifics, and people from well-educated families are accustomed to using them. It is important to pay attention to the nuances of language and the culture behind it, and strive to speak with elegance and grace.

III. How to learn a foreign language well

In fact, the strategies for learning any language are quite similar. It is generally more challenging to learn a foreign language later in life if you did not start at an early age. Learning a language involves a lot of imitation, just like learning an instrument. Good listening skills help you identify subtle differences in language, and good oral expression can help you achieve proficiency in English. Many students get stuck at their current level and are unsure of how to enhance their language ability. Here are some tips for acquiring a new language:

1. Talk more

speak out, speak out loud, speak out the English you know. Where can you practice? Here are several methods:

- On campus, there are many exchange students from various foreign countries. Although they may not come from English-speaking countries, they often communicate in English when living abroad. Therefore, it is a good idea to take the initiative to find them and practice speaking English together. Doing so can increase confidence and provide more opportunities to speak English. This can be a mutually beneficial arrangement for both parties. Exchange students can make local friends while local students get the chance to practice their English. To expand their social circle and practice their foreign language, students can look to foreign language centers, international offices, foreign students/overseas students associations, and other departments within the school.

- Participating in the school's English club or taking advantage of free foreign teacher consultations in the foreign language center can be another useful way to practice English. Many schools actively promote international teaching and have more and more professors coming from foreign countries. Courses are often taught in English, and students can also choose modules or apply to be a teaching assistant for particular courses to increase interaction with professors and practice their English.

- Consider joining events like Toastmasters, which organizes activities every month. Founded in 1924 in Colorado, USA, there are currently over 16,600 affiliated associations in 145 countries worldwide. Toastmasters can provide opportunities to make local friends and offers communication and speech courses that effectively improve one's English and foreign language skills.

- Join English classes: Taking English classes is another option. There are many tuition centers in Taiwan, and students can choose one that suits their preferences. Students should actively practice speaking English during class and avoid skipping classes, as it will be a waste of money.

2. Expanding Vocabulary

Expanding your vocabulary is essential for speaking a language fluently. It is similar to how you learned to speak as a baby, by mimicking your parents and gradually building your vocabulary. Having an adequate vocabulary is like having enough bullets in a battlefield; you won't run out of ammunition soon. To avoid getting stuck in your progress, it is best to split the studying load into smaller portions. Instead of trying to memorize the entire book at once, divide the time into four main parts. Spend the first three quarters memorizing new vocabulary and the last quarter on revision. This approach can help you to remember words more effectively and avoid overwhelming yourself with too much information.

◆Methods as below

- In half a year, which is equivalent to 24 weeks, it is recommended to divide the time into four equal parts of 6 weeks each. During the first three quarters of the time, focus on memorizing the content and context, and dedicate the last quarter to revision. For example, if you have a book with 180 pages, divide it into three portions of 60 pages each. Within a 6-week period, aim to memorize 60 pages, or 10 pages per week. This translates to just 2 pages a day, if you dedicate 5 days per week to reading. By following this approach, you can gradually build up your vocabulary without feeling overwhelmed.

Example of progress table

Goal: to read 180 pages of words in half a year (24 weeks)				
Progress	Pages	Per Week	Daily (week)	2 days in weekend
first quarter (0~6 weeks)	1~60	10pages	2 Pg / 24words	Revise 10 pages of words
Second quarter （7~12weeks）	61~120	10pages	2 Pg / 24words	Revise 10 pages of words
Third quarter （13~18weeks）	121~180	10pages	2 Pg / 24words	Revise 10 pages of words
Revision Period				
Progress	Pages	Per Week	Daily (week)	Weekend twice
Fourth quarter (19~24weeks)	Revision 1~180	30pages	5Pages	Take out the words you already know review those that you don' t

- The most common mistake when trying to memorize new words is to force yourself to remember them, which can result in fast forgetting. Instead, a more efficient approach is to take it easy and learn at a comfortable pace, such as by focusing on only two pages per day, which may contain around 10 to 15 new words each. In other words, learning about 24 new words daily. Sitting at a desk and trying to force yourself to remember words can be challenging. A better way to learn is:

①To effectively memorize new words, it is important to read them carefully and understand their meanings and usage. It is also recommended to practice reading them aloud several times. If there is an audio recording available, listening to the correct pronunciation can be helpful. In cases where there is no audio available, you can use resources like Google Translate to listen to the correct pronunciation and then practice reading the word aloud several times.

②After writing the words on flashcards, you can review them regularly to reinforce your memory. You can carry these flashcards with you wherever you go, so you can practice and review the words anytime, anywhere. This will help you to retain the new vocabulary and improve your language skills.

③On the following day, take advantage of your free time to review the flashcards. It's recommended to practice your pronunciation during the day to reinforce your memory.

④At night, it's helpful to review the two pages of new vocabulary before moving on to the next two pages.

⑤The next day, continue with your progress from the previous day and repeat the same steps outlined above.

⑥During the weekends, you have a buffer time of two days that can be used to catch up on any delayed progress from the week or to thoroughly review the vocabulary learned during the past five days.

◆Small tips

Using the above method to learn, here are a few tips:

- Utilize spare time during the day, such as waiting for appointments, using the restroom, or taking a break before class, to review and read the words.

- In addition to flashcards, use English-Chinese dictionary apps to input and listen to the pronunciation of the 24 new words learned each day. This method saves the hassle of carrying flashcards and drawing attention. However, it's important to avoid revising during work or lecture time. If learning in a high-profile environment suits you better, use that to your advantage.

- During the weekend, set aside time to review the 60 words accumulated over the course of the week. Follow these three steps to review the words:

  ①For flashcards users

   Step (1) Recite the 60 words sequentially several times.

   Step (2) Shuffle the flashcards and try to see if you still remember these words.

   Step (3) Take out the flashcards that you know each time, and continue to read the remaining flashcards to enhance your memory on these unfamiliar words

  ② For app users

   Step (1) Read these words according to your desired daily progress.

Step (2) Then try shuffling up the sequence to see if you can recall the words

Step (3) Delete the words you have already learned, so that the amount of words left in the search history can be reduced.

• After completing a week of learning new vocabulary, set aside those words and focus on the next week's progress. Avoid including the words you learned in the previous week as it can lead to unnecessary stress. If you have enough energy at the end of the week, you can revise the previous week's words. Alternatively, you can schedule a time at the end of the month to review all the words learned in the past four weeks.

• By the end of the 24 weeks, you will have 6 weeks left to review and recall all the 2160 words you have learned. You can use the same three-step method: memorize, shuffle, and remove, to help reinforce your memory of the words.

• To reduce pressure when memorizing vocabulary, remember that it's okay if you only manage to memorize half of the book. What's most important is to be consistent with your learning efforts. Don't put too much pressure on yourself when reciting words. Even if you can't memorize 100%, if you can remember 70%, there are already more than 1500 words. Even if it's only 50%, there are nearly 1100 words, what's most important is to be consistent with your learning efforts.

3. Practice listening

listening to native speakers is the most effective way to learn a foreign language. You can do this by watching videos, talks, or TV dramas. Another great way to pick up the language is to listen to the keynote speakers at graduation ceremonies. Try to capture whole sentences or paragraphs and commit them to memory. Don't worry too much about grammar when quoting these speakers, as their language is usually near-flawless.

4. Self-Questioning and Self-Answering

Practice recalling the words you have memorized at any time of the day without referring to your flashcards or app. Use these words to make sentences or questions for yourself to answer, as this is a great way to reinforce what you have learned. In fact, taking a bath is a very good time for self-asking practice.

5. Buying English Books or Magazines

Purchase English books or magazines that introduce Taiwan in English. Imagine how you would introduce Taiwan to a foreigner and talk about the beautiful scenery, people, food, snacks, and Taiwanese culture. These are common topics that foreigners are curious about.

6. Joining English-Language Clubs

Join English clubs in schools or public organizations like Toastmasters to increase opportunities to speak English. Additionally, there are many free podcasts and YouTube videos available that can help improve your English skills. In the beginning stages, choose a few snippets and memorize them. Once you have mastered them, you can then begin speaking practical English.

IV. Other preparations

1. Background knowledge preparation

- Aim to achieve a high score on the TOEIC exam, which is often considered by airline companies. You can take the exam multiple times until you feel that you have achieved your highest score. A score of 600 or above is typically required for aircrew positions, while captains may have a higher requirement.
- Join international clubs or organizations such as international youth ambassadors, volunteers, or diplomatic pioneers to gain a better understanding of global issues and opportunities to practice speaking English. To prepare for conversations about your culture, read books that introduce your country in English.
- Form a study group with classmates or friends who are also applying for airline positions. This group can provide support and supervision to help each other

improve. Consider collecting recruitment information, test materials, and interview questions from various airlines, role-playing exam scenarios, and practicing resume writing, choosing photos, and walking

①Collect recruitment information: Pay close attention to airline recruitment information and inform each other.

②Collect test materials: Gather test procedures, test content, and interview questions from various airlines.

③Role play: Stimulate the exam settings and allow one another to evaluate for advice and improvement.

④Check each other's resumes, choose photos, practice walking and more.

Broadcast practice

It is often required that airlines staff to make public announcement. To prepare for public announcements, both air and ground crew need to practice their Chinese, Taiwanese, and English regularly. Many broadcast practice resources are available online. It's essential to focus on clear articulation and maintain a friendly tone while broadcasting. Even though passengers may not see the broadcaster, they can still sense the level of professionalism, warmth, and welcoming attitude conveyed through the microphone.

Cabin announcement handbook

2. Skills preparations

It is commonly believed that the first impression is crucial, and you may not have a second chance to make it. In industries such as aviation, how you present yourself is of great importance. Therefore, it is essential to present yourself in the best possible way every day. School years provide an excellent opportunity to figure out what type of hairstyle, make-up, and clothing styles suit you best. Observe your peers and pay attention to what they wear, but focus on finding what makes you stand out, rather than blindly following trends.

◆Hairstyle

Hairstyle is an important aspect of personal grooming in the aviation industry. To keep your hair healthy and looking good, it's important to avoid over-cleansing, which can cause scalp allergies, oily hair, or dandruff.

- Male: For men, it's important to keep your hair clean, tidy, and find a hairstyle that suits you. You can refer to hairstyle samples recommended by the aviation industry or seek advice from a stylist. Practice styling your hair regularly and use hair products that work best for you.
- Female: For women, hair is often called the "second face" and can leave a lasting impression. It's essential to take good care of your hair by washing and treating it regularly. You can also experiment with different hairstyles and hair accessories to find what works best for you.

  ①Girls with short hair: To maintain a stylish short hairstyle, it's important to practice blow-drying. If you wash your hair at night, make sure to blow-dry it before bed to avoid a "Bad Hair Day" the next morning. When blow-drying, dry your hair in the opposite direction of the hair roots to add volume and prevent it from looking flat. Your fringe should not cover your eyebrows, and if your hair is over the shoulders, always tie it up during the interview.

  ②Girls with long hair: For females with long hair, hair health is crucial. Use suitable hair care products and dry your hair before bed if you wash it at night

Hairstyle for men

to avoid frizziness and deformation. Don't leave a towel wrapped around your hair for too long to let your scalp breathe properly. Practice tying your hair in buns or French twist for the airline exam, and watch online tutorials to improve your skills. Choose elegant hair accessories, such as pearls, and use no more than four hair clips to avoid an overwhelming look.

◆Makeup

Both boys and girls must care about self-presentation

- Boys should prioritize facial hygiene to keep their skin clean and healthy, especially when exposed to air pollution or when riding motorcycles. It's perfectly acceptable for males to use basic facial care products like lotions. They should exfoliate and moisturize their skin occasionally, as well as keep their eyebrows, nose hair, and beard trimmed. To prevent chapped lips during seasonal changes, it's a good idea to have a lip balm on hand. Boys should also maintain clean, short nails. In the summer, applying sunscreen in moderation can help prevent uneven skin tone, peeling, and dryness.

- Girls: Just like painting, the canvas basically needs to be clean. It is important to maintain good skin quality, neither too oily nor too dry. Choose facial care products that suit your skin type, and seek professional help from a dermatologist if needed. Avoid handling acne on your own to prevent scarring. By keeping your skin in good condition, it will be easier to apply makeup and enhance your natural beauty.

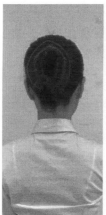 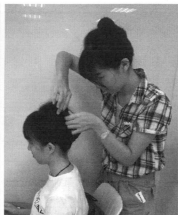 

Practice makes perfect

①Self-care routine: Start by choosing facial care products that are suitable for your skin type, including facial wash, toner, and lotion. It is important to keep your face moisturized, especially during seasonal changes. Regularly trimming your eyebrows is also recommended.

②Foundation application: After completing your self-care routine, apply primer before sunscreen/protector, liquid foundation, and powder in that order

③Make up

· Eyebrows are an important part of one's appearance. Pay attention to the color of your eyebrows and choose a shade that is slightly lighter than your hair color. This will give you a milder look and will not be too overbearing.

· Eye makeup: It's important to choose eyeliners that don't smudge easily. If you're just starting to learn makeup, it's recommended to choose earthy colors for eyeshadow, so that your makeup looks natural and not too bold.

3. Materials preparation

When applying for a job at an airline company, it is important to come prepared. This includes carefully selecting the attire and shoes worn to the interview. It is important to choose clothes that complement your body shape, and to maintain a healthy figure through regular exercise.

Learn and practice make-up

Which color tone suits you? Warm or cool?

Here are two simple ways to find out:

First, check if you look better in gold or silver jewelry and frames. If gold looks good on you, you likely have a warm undertone. If silver looks better, you may have a cool undertone.

Second, examine the color of your veins on your wrist. If your veins appear green, you likely have a warm undertone, and if they appear blue or purple, you may have a cool undertone.

For those with cool undertones, lipstick shades that work well include bright reds, pinks, and nudes. If you have warm undertones, on the other hand, go for lipsticks in shades of orange and coral.

Airlines favorite make-up

Makeup for airline applications: If you are interested in applying for a particular airline, you can take inspiration from the makeup worn by the airline's flight attendants. Their makeup is carefully selected to complement and accentuate the company uniform. By following the standard makeup guidelines of the airline, you can create a standout look that sets you apart from other candidates.

◆Men's Attire

When it comes to dressing up for an interview, boys should opt for a well-fitted suit that includes a suit jacket, white shirt, tie, belt, trousers, socks, and shoes. To look sharp and polished when in a suit, it's important to follow certain guidelines. For instance, always make sure that the collar, sleeve opening, and pocket square are visible. The tie should be long enough to touch the belt but not go lower than it. If you're on the slimmer and shorter side, go for slender ties to create the illusion of height. On the other hand, if you're tall and muscular, thicker ties can make you look more generous. The trousers should end at the heel, neither shorter nor longer. Lastly, choose dark-colored socks to complement the suit.

The 3 whites on suit

The so-called exposing 3 white parts of a suit: To achieve a sharp and polished look in a suit, it is important to follow the rule of exposing the three white parts. A well-fitting suit should complement your body size and shape. The first white part refers to the collar of the shirt which should be half an inch higher than the suit to be visible from the back. The second white part is the opening of the sleeves, which should be of the right length, neither too long nor too short. Lastly, the pocket square/puff fold should be shown to enhance your gentlemanly appearance.

Showing the "3 whites" while wearing a suit

Source: lookastic.com

◆Women's Attire

Preparation for Women: It's important for women to prepare their attire for an aviation industry interview well in advance to ensure a proper fit. Waiting until the last minute can lead to unnecessary stress and may result in not finding suitable clothing.

- Attire: It's important to plan your attire for an aviation industry interview in advance to ensure a proper fit. Consider a one-piece dress or a three-piece suit, with a skirt being the preferred option. However, some industries are more flexible, allowing for trousers as well. Skirt length should be kept about half an inch above the knee, avoiding anything too short or tight-fitting as it may send the wrong message to interviewers.

- Shoes: Opt for pure leather shoes over patent leather as they tend to overpower your outfit. Airlines tend to focus on the uniform, so avoid shoes with lacquer surfaces. A heel height of 3-5 cm is the most comfortable for ground crews to wear all day. Flight attendants have in-flight and out-flight shoes. In-flight shoes are worn during boarding for safety and service reasons, and higher heels are not recommended due to safety concerns. Out-flight shoes should complement your body shape and give a professional appearance. During interviews, simple and

Neat makeup and grooming

covered shoes are best, without straps or thick-soled heels. Avoid boots, as they may be seen as inappropriate or informal.

- Socks: Some aviation personnel prefer medical compression stockings due to long periods of standing. A pressure of 150 Dan is moderate and provides good support without looking tight or prosthetic. Be careful with color selection as compression stockings can give off a swelling effect. When wearing compression stockings, put them on slowly to ensure an even fit. Skin-colored stockings are recommended, or choose colors that match the company uniform you are applying for.

Aviation Interview Response

While some budget airlines may accept candidates with high school vocational degrees, most airlines require a college degree or higher. Some students have asked me whether they should drop out of school once they secure a position in a budget airline. My response is always the same: students should carefully consider their options. After all, obtaining a degree opens up many opportunities. Airline exams typically take place during mid-March every year, one after another. While there are many things that should be prepared before the exam, there are also certain things that should be avoided.

I. Things you should not do before the exam

- To prevent any injuries prior to the interview, one should refrain from engaging in extreme or adventurous outdoor activities. It's crucial to keep your physical and mental condition at their best state. Activities like riding a bike around the island or surfing at the beach are not recommended, as it could leave scars that might affect your self-esteem and appearance. Some airlines avoid recruiting candidates with obvious traumatic scars on their bodies, and if you get sunburnt just before the interview, your skin will eventually peel, making it hard to conceal with makeup.

- Avoid dyeing your hair to absurd colors or cutting it too short or too strangely before the interview date. It will be too late to fix your hair for the interview, and companies usually reject candidates that look odd. ∘

- Refrain from getting braces or laser eye surgery before the exams, even if the purpose is to have a better appearance. Plan ahead so that it doesn't interfere with your exams.

- Keep your weight in check by avoiding overeating or consuming heavy meals. Airlines are very particular with their staff's appearance, and the ideal weight is when you take your weight and subtract it by about 110 to 120. For example, a woman who is 165 cm tall and weighs between 45 to 55 kg is the ideal weight, and she will look more professional in uniform.

- It's important to avoid excessive weight loss when preparing for an airline job. After admission, many airlines conduct health checks, and abnormal weight loss can lead to health issues like irregular blood pressure and low hemoglobin value. In some cases, airlines may even rescind a job offer if they're concerned about a candidate's health. It's also important to stay hydrated and drink enough water to prevent inflammation of the urethra which results in a failed health check.

- Avoid getting eyelash extensions or acrylic nails. Airlines typically discourage overly flashy appearance. Remember, the focus should be on your skills and qualifications rather than your appearance. Airlines interview is not a beauty contest.

- It's important to prepare your attire well in advance of the exams, rather than waiting until the last minute. This is particularly true for shoes, as your feet may need some time to adjust to new footwear. You don't want to risk losing a job opportunity due to leg cramps or discomfort caused by ill-fitting shoes. Keep in mind that interviewers are unlikely to accept excuses related to ill-fitting attire, so it's important to plan ahead and make sure everything fits properly.

II. The preparations that should be done before the exam

- Consider checking the airline's website for recruitment information or forming a study group to keep each other updated on the latest news from airline companies.

- Moderate exercise can help keep your body limber and flexible, which is beneficial for working in the aviation sector - a service-oriented industry. During interviews, some airlines may assess candidates' ability to carry heavy objects to overhead bin, and there may also be height requirements for potential crew members. While there are regulations against discrimination based on height and weight, it is important to note that cabin crew members typically need to be tall enough to assist passengers with storing their luggage in the overhead compartments, which are typically around 208cm in height. Shorter crew members may be able to tiptoe, which is why flexibility is important.

- To make a good impression during interviews, girls may want to practice their makeup application and hairstyling, while boys may benefit from getting comfortable with wearing leather shoes and suits to avoid looking uncomfortable. It's also a good idea to practice walking in the shoes you plan to wear during the interview, particularly if the airline requires you to do a catwalk. Regular practice can help you feel more confident and comfortable during the interview process.

- To maintain good posture, try standing with your back against a wall and make sure your neck and head are straight, and your chest is lifted. Practicing in front of a mirror or recording yourself can help you make adjustments and improve your posture.

- When preparing for your airline application, make sure to have your ID photos taken in advance. Look for a reputable photography company to ensure quality photos. Keep in mind that ID photos may not be as flattering as real-life appearance, as not everyone is photogenic.

- It is advisable to prepare personal photos in advance as some airlines may require them. While casual photos are acceptable, it's important to choose appropriate ones. Avoid pictures taken in professional workshops or those that are unclear or with filters. You may want to consider using a photo of yourself with the airline company, or choose life photos taken during travel. Note that you as the main object should not be too small to be clearly seen. Also, pay attention to avoiding complicated backgrounds that make the characters out of focus.

- To prepare for aviation exams, one can practice answering questions using resources such as "One Hundred Questions for the Aviation Exam" and self-assess. Pay attention to your articulation, facial expressions, and eye contact. Avoid losing focus, as it can make you appear unprofessional. For applicants to foreign airlines, it is also important to practice answering questions in English to feel more prepared for the exam.

- To prepare for the interview, you can create two versions of self-introduction - a 30-second and a 1-minute version. This will allow you to introduce yourself in a clear and concise manner when given the opportunity during the interview. Remember to maintain a pleasant smile throughout the interview. It's also important to pay attention to how other candidates introduce themselves while you wait for your turn. This will give you an idea of what works and what doesn't, and help you refine your own introduction.

- Prepare a complete resume and autobiography: Ensure that your resume and autobiography are complete and free of any errors or corrections. Avoid repeating information already mentioned in your resume when writing your autobiography. Instead, focus on highlighting your unique qualities and characteristics that make you stand out. Remember that your autobiography is like a letter of self-introduction, and it should have four parts: personal background, education and achievement, character and strength, show gratitude and emphasize your enthusiasm for airlines job.

①In the first paragraph, introduce your family background, emphasizing any unique aspects that demonstrate your independence and excellence. For instance, growing up in a single-parent family and how it has shaped your character.

②In the second paragraph, highlight your achievements during your studies, focusing on those that are relevant to the job you're applying for. Mention any positions you held, clubs you participated in, awards and internships you received, and how these experiences have prepared you for the job.

③In the third paragraph, share a true story that shows your passion for serving others or why you love interacting with people. This story should touch the hearts of your interviewers and give them a deeper understanding of who you are.

④Finally, in the last paragraph, express your gratitude to the interviewer for the opportunity and explain why you are a strong candidate for the job. Instead of focusing on the benefits of working for the airline company, explain how your strengths will be an asset to the company.

III. Interview day

To ensure that you arrive at the interview venue on time, it's important to be familiar with the location of the interview room, the mode of transportation available, and the estimated journey duration. It's also essential to get enough rest the night before the interview so that you're rejuvenated and ready to perform at your best. If the interview venue is far from your home, consider staying in a nearby hotel or with a friend to avoid rushing on the day of the interview.

- Make sure to wake up early on the day of your interview to give yourself enough time to prepare. Check your grooming and attire to ensure that you look presentable. If your suit tends to wrinkle easily, consider changing into it at the venue. The same goes for your shoes. It is recommended that you take a cab to the interview venue to avoid any unfortunate events, such as getting your attire dirty on public transportation. Arrive at the venue at least an hour ahead of time to allow yourself to get changed and relax. Stay calm during the interview so that you don't panic or become anxious.

- Ensure that you arrive at the venue on time with all the necessary items. Airline companies value punctuality highly, and it is important to be respectful and courteous while at the venue, as your conduct is being observed. Remember that cabin crew members cannot keep passengers waiting, so it is essential to be punctual and prepared.

- When you arrive at the interview room, knock on the door, and wait for a response before entering. Once inside, close the door gently and maintain a friendly smile. Walk confidently to your designated spot. If you are participating in a group interview, be polite to your fellow applicants. If there is an unoccupied chair, ask for permission before taking a seat. Remember to maintain a professional and respectful demeanor throughout the interview.

- Be assertive and seize any opportunities given to you to answer questions during the interview but avoid being overly aggressive. Remember that time is limited, so make the most of every chance you have to speak. If it's an open question and answer session, you don't have to be the first to respond. However, try to participate in the discussion by answering second or third, and continue to engage with the interviewer.

- Show your appreciation by giving your biggest smile to the interviewers before leaving. Nod your head to express your gratitude for their time and consideration. Remember that everyone has put in their best effort, and now it's time to wait for further notice.

- Upon receiving an admission notice from the airline company, it is crucial to reply within the given deadline. Take the opportunity to reflect on your previous interview, identify your mistakes, and work on improving for the next round. Remember to showcase the best version of yourself during the interview. Congratulations if you receive further admission notices! Be sure to prepare all the necessary documents requested by the airline. If many candidates make it through the recruitment process, you may be reporting separately. Always ask for your reporting batch as it is based on seniority. Crew members in the earlier batches get to choose their shifts and vacations before others.

- Before becoming an official part of the airline company, it's important to pay attention to important dates and schedules that are notified by the airline. This includes things like health checks, tea parties, and newcomer orientation. Being aware of these important events will help ensure that you are prepared and able to fully participate in all aspects of your new role with the airline.

IV. Actively attend training after shortlisted

After being shortlisted, you will be required to attend various training sessions. As a flight attendant, you will undergo basic training on the aircraft, including on-board safety training and exams. If you fail the exams, you will usually be given a second chance. However, if you fail again, it may suggest that you are not capable of working well under stress, and in the event of an emergency, you may not be reliable enough to escort passengers. In this case, you may be deemed unfit for the company. The initial few training sessions are always the most challenging yet crucial. If you remain persistent and able to pass every test, you will successfully pass the exam and earn your aviation badge. Congratulations on this achievement!

The above-mentioned tasks are necessary preparations for applying to an airline company. Air crews usually have more responsibilities compared to ground staff, but this does not imply that one position is superior to the other. Pilots have more stringent requirements such as language proficiency, physical fitness, and a series of tests that focus on multi-tasking, teamwork, and stress management. In the aviation sector, the goal is to find the most qualified candidates.

Class activities 12

1. Get students to practice good standing posture by leaning against the wall
2. Get students to practice walking, standing and sitting posture by using mirrors.
3. Design a mock airline interview

延伸閱讀

Evans, V., Dooley, J., & Coocen, L., (2016). *Career Paths: Flight Attendant Student's Book with Cross-Platform Application.* 東華。

Wards, K., (2000). *The Essential Guide: To Becoming a Flight Attendant.* Kiwi Productions.

空中老爺（資深座艙長）（2017）。《空中老爺的日常》。寶瓶文化。

Part 5

Hospitality Etiquette

Accommodation is a vital part of travel, and besides airfare, it's often the biggest expense. It's almost fair to say that the choice of accommodation shapes the type, quality, or level of the entire trip. Travel motivations range from seeking escape, relaxation, and rejuvenation to prestige, well-being, adventure, learning, sightseeing, and shopping. These motivations determine the type of lodging, and each option offers a distinct travel experience. The quality of accommodation during travel is all-encompassing. On the practical side, it involves factors like cleanliness, hygiene, and the convenience of public facilities. On the personal side, it concerns the politeness and professionalism of the hotel staff. Hence, proper accommodation etiquette matters significantly for both travelers and those working in the hotel industry.

Chapter

13

Accommodation Etiquette

- International Hotels
- Japanese hotels
- Bed and Breakfasts and huts
- New Type of Accommodation - Airbnb

What are the classifications for accommodation in the tourism industry? According to the regulations outlined in the "Architectural and Equipment Standards for Tourist Hotels" by the Construction and Planning Agency of Taiwan's Ministry of the Interior, international tourist hotels are required to have a minimum of thirty rooms, including single rooms, double rooms, and suites. There are detailed specifications regarding the size standards of these rooms as well as the proportions of facilities like restaurants within the hotel.

The accommodation service industry includes both the hotel industry and other lodging service sectors. Within the hotel industry, there are various types of tourist hotels with facilities such as cafés, conference rooms, bars, shops, and recreational amenities. Another category is the general lodging service industry outside of tourist hotels, encompassing guesthouses, inns, motels, and budget hotels. The other lodging service sector refers to accommodation services beyond hotels, including bed and breakfasts, camping centers, and hostels.

The Choice of Accommodation Determines the Type, Quality, or Level of Travel

Classification of Accommodation Service Industry and Content

Classification of Accommodation Service Industry	Content
Tourism Hotel Industry	Hotels (including hotel services with cafés, conference rooms, bars, shops, and recreational facilities)
General Lodging Service Industry	Guesthouses, Inns, Motels, Budget Hotels
Other Lodging Service Industry	Bed and Breakfasts, Camping sites, Hostels

These accommodation establishments can also be classified based on their nature. For instance, they can be categorized by geographic location, such as airport hotels and hot spring resorts. Depending on the size of the hotel, they range from star-rated hotels to bed and breakfast inns. The purposes of hotels vary as well, including hostels, business hotels, vacation resorts, and backpacker accommodations. From a market positioning perspective, there are boutique hotels, casino resorts, and private lodgings. According to the type of guests, there are family-oriented hotels and pet-friendly accommodations.

Classification of other lodging service industry

Classification	Types	Needs
Geographic Distinctions	Airport Hotels, Hot Spring Resorts	Convenient Location, Distinctive Features
Size	Star-Rated Hotels, Bed and Breakfast Inns	Standards, Unique Attributes
Purpose Differentiation	Hostels, Business Hotels, Vacation Resorts, Backpacker Accommodations	Catering to Pursue Goals
Market Positioning	Boutique Hotels, Casino Resorts, Private Lodgings	Specific Needs of Different Traveler Groups
Guest Segmentation	Family-Oriented Hotels, Pet-Friendly Accommodations	Providing Comprehensive Accommodation Services

Different types of hotel service personnel provide the necessary services according to the needs and preferences of guests. For example, star-rated hotels require well-defined standards and specifications to ensure consistency in the services guests receive. On the contrary, various surprises are welcomed by guests in bed and breakfast inns and such unexpected delights are embraced.

International Hotels

Staying at an international star-rated hotel should be the most relaxing and enjoyable time during a journey. According to a 2020 survey and statistics by the magazine "Hotel" on the global hotel groups and alliances, the top five leading global hotel groups are: Marriot International, Jin Jiang International, Oyo rooms, Hilton Worldwide and IHG InterContinental Hotels Group respectively. Basic services in regular hotels are expected to adhere to SOP (Standard Operating Procedure), while star-rated hotels strive for customization beyond SOP. Achieving customization involves "listening" to guests' needs and providing meticulous and thoughtful services that go beyond their expectations. These star-rated international hotels often host various celebrities and dignitaries, hence safeguarding customer privacy is of utmost importance.

Checking in star-rated hotel

I. General Process of Staying at a Star-Rated Hotel

- The hotel offers airport shuttle services. Guests should proceed to the designated meeting point where the hotel's dedicated vehicle will be waiting. After handing over their luggage to the driver, guests board the vehicle. Inside the vehicle, there will be welcome juice or bottled water, along with wet towels. During the ride back to the hotel, guests can engage in casual conversation with the driver, keeping in mind that the driver's primary duty is safe driving and excessive interference should be avoided.

- Upon arrival at the hotel, guests can proceed to the front desk for check-in procedures. The doorman or bell captain will directly deliver the luggage to the room.

- Upon entering the room, you should

  ①Inspect the Room: Check if the room amenities are sufficient or if any additional requirements are needed. For instance, assess whether the pillow's firmness suits your preference, if the blankets and sheets are adequate, and if the room's bottled water supply is enough. Hotels typically provide towels in three sizes: the smallest square towel for hand wiping, the next size for drying hair, and the largest for drying the body. Gym facilities often have dedicated towels, so there's no need to take them from the hotel room.

  ②Reserve Facilities and Services: You can inquire about the operating hours of hotel facilities, such as making reservations for restaurants, sauna rooms, gyms, and other amenities. Some hotels offer shoe polishing services. You can place your shoes in a designated shoe tray or bag for housekeeping to attend to.

  ③Plan Your Itinerary: Familiarize yourself with the hotel's location and arrange local sightseeing activities.

  ④Room Entry and Exit Guidelines: If you need housekeeping services during your absence, secure valuable items in the safe and tidy up personal belongings to facilitate the housekeeping process. When leaving the room, remember to set the "Please Clean Up" mode on the door instead of the "Do Not Disturb" mode.

"Do not disturb" and "Please clean up" signs

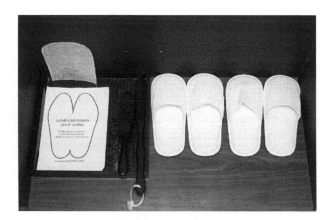

Shoe polishing services in hotel

Source: hutchgo.com

II. Behaviors to Avoid When Staying in a Hotel:

Whether it's a splendid grand lobby or elegantly comfortable furnishings, staying at a hotel instantly creates a relaxed atmosphere. However, basic etiquette should not be disregarded even during vacations. Here are some things to avoid when staying at a hotel:

1. Casual Attire

Upscale hotels often have dress codes for different occasions, particularly in dining areas. It's important to adhere to dress code requirements. Avoid moving from the pool in swimwear covered by a towel to the bar or hotel lobby. Wandering around the hotel in unkemp attire gives off a negative impression and lowers the overall hotel's image.

2. Service Staff are Not Servants

Service at high-end hotels is often meticulous and customer-centered, but it's essential to treat the staff with the respect they deserve. They aren't personal servants. Hotel staff have many routine tasks. Hotel service personnel often interact with dignitaries and celebrities from around the world. Instead of flaunting your influence, demonstrate your character and manners.

3. Respect Privacy

Maintaining customer privacy is a fundamental duty of upscale hotels. Inquiries about the whereabouts of celebrities for curiosity's sake are inappropriate. Hotel staff are trained and required to maintain strict confidentiality. Respect the privacy of fellow guests, especially if you happen to encounter a celebrity during your stay. Do not take photos or videos without permission, and do not disturb them for autographs.

4. Avoid Taking Hotel Items

Some items in hotel rooms are provided complimentary, such as coffee, tea bags, bottled water, welcome fruit, and toiletries. These can be used during your stay or taken as souvenirs. However, refrain from packing items for personal use back home. Items like bathrobes, towels, hairdryers, coffee makers, ice buckets, and glasses from the minibar are intended for guest convenience during the stay.

According to a survey by Wellness Heaven, the list of stolen items from hotels ranges from the smallest, such as pens, to large furniture like televisions, mattresses, and tables. The most commonly taken items include towels, bathrobes, glassware, hangers, and cutlery.

III. General Guidelines for Hotel Stays

1. Dress code

Apart from your room, all other areas within the hotel are considered public spaces. This includes the lobby, restaurants, business center, gym, pool, sauna, and even hallways outside the rooms. Some guests, for their convenience, might move around in their pajamas between different rooms, which is considered inappropriate. Dress code etiquette to consider while staying at a hotel includes:

- Proper swim attire, including a swim cap, should be worn in the pool area. When leaving the pool area, change into appropriate clothing. Wearing swimwear or walking barefoot in indoor slippers into elevators, restaurants, bars, or sitting in the lobby is not allowed.
- Entering a formal restaurant requires neat attire. Overly casual clothing like shorts, tank tops, and flip-flops are not suitable. Be aware of the dress code requirements to avoid being denied entry.
- Avoid wearing overly revealing attire in public areas, and refrain from engaging in intimate interactions that may make others uncomfortable or uneasy.
- When using the gym, wear proper workout attire and sports shoes. Avoid running on the treadmill or using gym equipment in slippers, flip-flops, or even the paper

slippers provided in the room. Doing so can result in injuries and is hazardous.

2. Volume Etiquette

Maintaining an appropriate volume within the hotel premises is a basic courtesy. Here are specific points to be mindful of:

- While checking in at the reception, keep your voice low, especially when discussing room numbers with friends. Avoid loudly sharing your room number, as it can attract unwanted attention and risk.

- When watching TV or having conversations, close your room door to ensure both your peace and others'. Also, refrain from using your room as a party venue, engaging in loud activities, singing, or causing disturbances that disrupt the tranquility of other guests.

- If traveling with children, avoid allowing them to loudly play or scream, causing inconvenience to other guests. Some guests might be from different time zones, requiring sleep at different hours. Respect their need for rest.

- Avoid practicing instruments or singing loudly in your room. If you need to rehearse for a performance or competition, inquire with the hotel if alternative spaces are available.

3. Safety Etiquette

- Smoking is prohibited within the room. This rule is in place for safety and hygiene reasons. Smoking in a non-smoking room might result in an additional cleaning fee.

- Avoid hanging clothes randomly in the room, especially on lamps, as this could pose a fire hazard.

- Do not display valuable items openly in your room to prevent attracting unnecessary attention or danger. Luggage tags often have names written on them; keep them hidden to avoid potential disruptions.

- Refrain from loudly mentioning your name and room number in public areas to avoid potential unwanted interactions or disturbances.

- If someone unfamiliar knocks on your door, observe through the peephole to confirm their identity. If unsure, avoid opening the door or use a door chain until you can ascertain the visitor's intent.

- Use electrical appliances in the bathroom with caution. Particularly, avoid using them while in the bathtub to prevent potential electrocution.

- In the event of a power outage or alarm, follow the hotel staff's instructions and swiftly exit through emergency exits if needed.

4. Basic courtesy

- When receiving services, timely nodding and smiling to express gratitude is appropriate. Payment doesn't warrant an entitled attitude.

- Men should allow women to enter elevators and hotel entrances first, showing chivalry.

- In restaurants, signaling for service with eye contact or a slight hand raise is sufficient. Loudly calling for attention disturbs others' dining experiences.

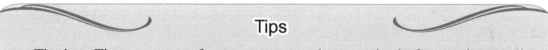

Tips

Tipping: Tips are a way for customers to show gratitude for service quality. There's no set amount for tips, but in countries where tipping is practiced, there's usually a certain percentage.

- Dining: In Europe and the United States, tips generally range from 10% to 20% of the total bill. Lunch tips are around 10% to 15%, while dinner tips can range from 15% to 20%. In upscale fine dining establishments, tips can extend to 25% to 30%, or even higher, based on satisfaction.

- Luggage Handling and Other Services: Bell Captains/Doormen who assist with luggage in the hotel lobby receive tips based on the luggage's size. This generally ranges from around $2 to $5 USD, or up to $10 USD for multiple pieces. If the assistance is provided by external transportation services like limousines or shuttle buses, the tipping can follow a similar percentage of the fare model, aligning with the dining etiquette.

- When checking out, roughly tidy up your room to avoid leaving personal items behind. Hotel property should not be damaged or tampered with, burdening the housekeeping staff, and potentially leading to being blacklisted by the hotel.
- Tipping Etiquette: Except for hotel reception, tipping is customary in various situations:

  ①Tip to Bell Captain/ Doorman for assisting with luggage.

  ②Tips are customary for dinning in Bar or Restaurant.

  ③Tip to housekeeping for additional service or daily cleaning.

  ④Tip to the server delivering your in-room dining order.

Japanese hotels

Based on the 2020 statistics from the Directorate-General of Budget, Accounting, and Statistics, Japan has held the top spot as Taiwanese people's favorite travel destination for four consecutive years, accounting for 30% of preferences. Mainland

A wonderful relaxing Get-Away stay

China ranks second, while South Korea has surpassed Hong Kong, making its debut in the top three. Whether traveling to Japan or exploring domestic destinations, staying in a Japanese-style hotel is a favored choice among Taiwanese travelers. Japanese-style hotels are renowned for their traditional architectural style, the experience of soaking in hot springs, and the unique service they provide. As Japanese people place a high emphasis on etiquette, staying in these hotels involves adapting to local customs, especially focusing on etiquette. By doing so, travelers can better enjoy and immerse themselves in Japanese culture. So, what are the etiquettes to be observed during a stay in a Japanese-style hotel?

- Japanese people are highly attentive to details and always strive not to inconvenience others. Therefore, they exhibit a strong self-awareness, such as lowering their voices. In some older Japanese-style inns with creaky wooden floors, even a slight footstep noise might disturb neighbors' sleep. Hence, whether it's closing doors or walking up stairs, it's essential to step lightly, minimize noise, and when taking off shoes, place them in the designated area or with the toe facing out.

- Japanese inns usually have the assistance of "okami" (female innkeepers) and "nakai" (maids). After checking in, the okami personally greets each guest in their rooms to ensure service quality and enhance the guest experience. Typically, Japanese inns offer a one-night stay with two meals included, which can be enjoyed either in-room or in the restaurant. Nakai are responsible for meal services and reception. Additionally, the task of arranging the cotton futons in rooms is performed by the "bantou" (male staff), who comes to set up the futons after dinner. For those with no time for a soak before dining, taking a short rest after the meal and then enjoying the onsen is recommended, while paying attention to the designated times for soaking. When staying in a Japanese onsen resort, guests can move around public spaces wearing the provided "yukata" and wooden clogs. The yukata can even be worn to the restaurant. In onsen towns with nearby tourist spots, guests can stroll around in the yukata, always mindful of maintaining a neat appearance.

- Onsen areas in Japanese inns are segregated by gender, and bathing is conducted naked. Before entering the bath, it's customary to warm the body with warm water and cleanse thoroughly. Towels and hair must not touch the bathwater, and wearing swimsuits is prohibited. Before entering the bath, a preliminary shower is important to maintain bathwater cleanliness and acclimate the body to the temperature. Body and hair cleaning products should not enter the bath and should be used in the designated "sit-bath" area. Laundry should not be done in this area, and large towels should not be placed in the water. Vigilance against splashing is also crucial. For foreigners, public nudity can be uncomfortable, so maintaining a composed attitude is essential. Avoiding staring or making others feel uncomfortable is a matter of politeness.

- To prevent damaging the tatami flooring, it's recommended not to step on the middle line between two tatami mats. Excessive play or moving around of tatami should be avoided, as well as spilling food or drinks.

- Being punctual is highly regarded in Japan. Being late for a reservation for in-house dining can cause great inconvenience to the staff and disrupt the dining schedule for the next guests.

- Guests are free to arrange and move items within the Japanese-style inn. However, the "tokonoma," a recessed alcove often displaying valuable artworks or flower arrangements, should be treated with care. It signifies the host's welcome to the guests.

Attire Provided by Japanese Onsen Inns.

Source: jlan.net

- The correct way to wear a Japanese yukata is to have the left side over the right, secured with a belt. Wearing it right over left is reserved for the clothing of the deceased. If the weather is cold, a "haori" can be layered over the yukata. Some inns provide a thicker version called "dantai."

Bed and Breakfasts and huts

According to the regulations for managing bed and breakfast establishments, accommodations with eight rooms are classified as bed and breakfasts. With the changing trends in travel, more people are opting for bed and breakfasts. Unlike the luxurious experience of five-star hotels, bed and breakfasts offer a welcoming, relaxed, and down-to-earth atmosphere. What should you keep in mind when choosing a bed and breakfast?

- Avoid Canceling Reservations Unnecessarily: Bed and breakfasts have limited room availability. Consider the difficulties faced by the owners. Last-minute cancellations make it challenging to fill the room. Be a responsible traveler and refrain from last-minute cancellations.
- Adhere to Designated Occupancy: Bed and breakfasts have specific occupancy limits. Do not exceed these limits to avoid additional charges or even being denied accommodation. Violating these rules might impact the establishment's operational license.
- Maintain Appropriate Noise Levels: Activities such as late-night karaoke, setting off fireworks, or loud play and laughter can disturb neighboring residents. Keep noise levels reasonable.
- Respect Provided Facilities: Be considerate in using resources like water, electricity, and gas. When using amenities like grills or stoves, treat them with care and follow guidelines.
- Exercise Caution with Candles in huts: Avoid smoking or cooking flammable items in cabins. Huts are typically located in rural areas, providing proximity

to nature. Expect insects and pests that come with the outdoors. Use mosquito repellents and similar products to prevent their intrusion. Keep doors and windows closed to prevent them from entering.

- Accommodation options are becoming more diverse, including capsule hotels and youth hostels as budget-friendly choices. In such places, guests often share communal spaces. Ensure the safety of your belongings and yourself during sleep. When booking, consider online reviews and choose safe accommodation rather than solely focusing on price.

New Type of Accomodation-Airbnb

Founded in 2008, Airbnb emerged when two designers rented out their home space to three travelers in search of accommodation. Today, Airbnb is a global phenomenon, showcasing a unique chapter in the lodging industry through the concept of the "sharing economy."

I. Airbnb: Airbnb check-in

For those accustomed to traditional hotels, staying overnight in a stranger's house during travel might evoke some concerns and uncertainties. While Airbnb provides detailed check-in regulations on its website, confirming a reservation implies accepting these terms. What else should you consider?

- Communicate with the Airbnb host before your trip. Maintain polite communication and respect response times. Avoid treating the host as a tour guide, as this can consume a significant amount of their time.
- Arrive on time to prevent keeping the host waiting to open the door for you. If a delay is unavoidable, notify them promptly.
- Do not bring extra guests or pets without informing the host. Doing so without notification may result in fines or denial of accommodation.

- When sharing common spaces with others, respect the host's or other guests' daily routines. If using shared facilities like the kitchen, it's courteous to inquire beforehand. Additionally, when using shared bathrooms, be considerate of time, maintain cleanliness, and remove personal items.
- Mind your noise levels to avoid disturbing neighbors.
- Safeguard your belongings and avoid displaying valuables.

II. HomeAway and Campinmygarden

The sharing economy has transformed our lives, saving us money, and facilitating new friendships. Besides Airbnb, there are other platforms that offer a more diverse range of accommodation options:

- HomeAway: This is a well-known vacation rental online booking platform based in the United States. It provides a variety of choices, from single rooms to entire villas, with the unique feature of offering an immersive experience of local culture.
- Campinmygarden: this platform enables hosts to offer their gardens for camping. Travelers only need a simple tent for an overnight stay.

These new modes of accommodation are sprouting up like mushrooms after rain, offering people more versatile choices. It's important to pay attention to online reviews before booking and not to expect hotel-level standards. Furthermore, one should seek an approach that suits them best or find options that align with their personal style. This way, a pleasant stay experience can be ensured.

Class activities 13

1. Please have the students share their experiences of staying in various types of accommodations. (Including international tourist hotels, Japanese-style lodgings, Airbnb, etc.)
2. Encourage the students to discuss the impact of new types of accommodations on traditional hotels, along with their advantages and disadvantages.

延伸閱讀

Leigh, G., (2017). *The Airbnb Story: How Three Ordinary Guys Disrupted an Industry, Made Billions... and Created Plenty of Controversy*. Houghton Mifflin.

中華民國統計資訊網，行業統計分類，https://www.stat.gov.tw/public/Attachment/6427152602. pdf

日高民子（2003）。《日本文化巡禮》（春夏秋冬四集）。統一出版社。

周明智（2011）。《旅館管理》。五南圖書。

蔡惠仔譯（2021）。Robert Chesnut著。《Airbnb改變商業模式的關鍵誠信課》。商業週刊。

蘇芳基（2013）。《旅館服務技術》。揚智文化。

Chapter

14

Basic Competency and Etiquette for Hotel Personnel

- Basic Competency of Hotel Personnel
- Hospitality Etiquette for Guests from Different Countries

Many young individuals aspire to join the hotel industry, with international hotel chains being a particularly appealing goal. After all, luxury hotels boast magnificent settings, and the opportunity to work and dress smartly in suits without having to face the elements outside is alluring. This often places such positions as the top choice for students in hospitality and tourism programs. However, it's important to note that work in this field isn't a vacation; it involves crafting the best possible guest experience. Every aspect constitutes details and challenges, testing the professionalism and etiquette of hotel service staff.

Courtesy and quality are the key elements of star hotel personnel.

Basic Competency of Hotel Personnel

When checking into a hotel, what guests most hope to receive is a sense of being at home. To provide such attentive and appropriate service, apart from enthusiasm and comprehensive on-the-job training, cultivating the fundamental qualities and etiquette of service personnel is crucial. One of the most significant aspects is possessing interpersonal communication skills. Working in the hotel industry comes with long hours and various challenges, but the most complex aspect remains the "people." People can be considered the industry's biggest variable, asset, challenge, and source of happiness. Therefore, to excel in hotel industry roles, it's best to select service personnel with a natural "service industry DNA", individuals inherently well-suited for the service sector. This should be combined with both innate qualities and training to ensure a comprehensive skill set. Additionally, attention to detail and thoughtfulness, meaning an unparalleled level of thoroughness, is required. These qualities collectively form the essential attributes of an ideal hotel service professional.

I. Appearance

The appearance of service personnel is not only their facade but also a crucial criterion in the service industry. A neat and pleasant appearance can bridge the gap with people, while a smile serves as the key to unlocking exceptional service. When recruiting hotel service personnel, attention is usually given to their appearance, as their image is an integral part of "service" and should not be taken lightly. Generally, the following aspects of appearance should be considered:

Presenting professional image as the hotel staffs is also part of the service

1. Facial Features

- Kind and upright demeanor with a proper appearance, avoiding expressions that may evoke fear and distance.

- Avoid having tattoos on the face, piercings on the eyebrows, or tongue rings that deviate from good social norms.

- Pay attention to facial skin issues. Address acne and pimples early to maintain a fresh complexion.

- Men should regularly shave their facial hair, trim nose hair, and groom eyebrows to maintain a pleasant appearance. Men prone to chapped lips can carry a lip balm for use.

- Women should wear makeup, but avoid heavy makeup that doesn't match the uniform. Contact lenses that enlarge pupils and false eyelashes are not required for hotel staff and should be avoided.

2. Hairstyle

- Women's hair should be neatly combed. Those with short hair should blow dry it well, avoiding excessively long bangs to reveal a fresh face. Women with long hair should tie it up, often in a bun or French twist, with simple and elegant hair accessories. Hair color should not be overly unusual or attention-grabbing.

- Men's hair should be regularly trimmed to an appropriate length. Simple hair products can be used, and the hair should be styled daily to maintain a clean and stylish look.

3. Attires

- Clothing should be regularly changed and cleaned, ensuring cleanliness, and eliminating odors. Clothes should be properly ironed for a professional appearance.

- Attires should fit properly, not too loose or too tight. Avoid exposing clothes. Women's skirts should not be too short for convenience during work.

- Name tags are part of the uniform and should be neat and visible for guests to identify staff easily, symbolizing professionalism and facilitating guest assistance.
- Men generally wear dark-colored socks, such as blue or black. If the elastic band becomes loose, it should be replaced. Women should choose appropriate-colored stockings, usually skin-toned or black to match the uniform. Some lower-denier medical elastic stockings (150 deniers) look natural and are beneficial for jobs involving prolonged standing, promoting blood flow to prevent varicose veins.
- Shoes should be frequently polished to maintain a shiny appearance. Women wearing high heels should avoid making loud clicking noises. Adding anti-slip pads to shoes can make them more comfortable and quieter.

4. Others

- Men should regularly trim their nails and wash their hands to maintain clean fingernails.
- If women wear nail polish, they should choose natural colors to avoid overly striking or attention-grabbing shades that may seem unprofessional.
- If wearing perfume, it should be used appropriately, without being overpowering or discomforting to others.

II. Characteristics

1. Individual characteristics

The hospitality industry falls under the service sector, and what are the individual characteristics that are essential for service personnel? According to a survey by the labor market, the key characteristics that service personnel should possess are as follows:

- Affability: Maintain a constant smile and warmth to bridge the gap with strangers.
- Warm Communication: Avoid using scripted lines that can make interactions feel detached and lacking in personal touch.
- Reflective: Each customer interaction is unique, and the ability to learn from

these experiences and seek improvement is crucial. Lessons learned from customer complaints can also contribute to refining service quality.

- Resilience: Given the diverse and sometimes urgent nature of situations that arise daily in the service industry, personnel must be able to cope with pressure while maintaining a high standard of service across various aspects.

- Attentive and Adaptability: Being attentive signifies observation skills, while adaptability represents the ability to respond on the spot. Both are indispensable qualities in the service sector.

It can be said that the service industry should embody the three degrees of service: speed, precision, and warmth. First is speed, as the service industry often deals with high demand situations. Staffing may not always be adequate, and even during the off-peak times, unexpected situations can arise. Service personnel must not only address situations promptly but also digest the circumstances with optimal speed. Secondly, precision is vital. Rushing through tasks without attention to detail can lead to customer complaints and worsen the situation. Lastly, warmth generates customer satisfaction and ensures that the service provided is successful and valuable.

Keeping reception neat and tidy at all time

2. *Personality traits*

In terms of the "Big Five" personality traits, employees in the service industry should have four of them:

◆Extraversion

This refers to being communicative, socially adept, enthusiastic, proactive, and people-oriented.

- Communicative: Given the frequent interactions with customer in the service industry, individuals who are too reserved or less inclined to engage in conversation might not be suitable. Being communicative means being able to discuss a wide range of topics and tailor conversations to suit preferences while maintaining appropriate boundaries. However, it's also essential to have good observational skills, recognizing when quieter customers prefer more privacy and space, thereby striking a balance.

- Sociable: Enjoying interactions with people and being open to various social situations is fundamental.

- Enthusiastic: Demonstrating enthusiasm towards people, tasks, and things, even exhibiting a slightly proactive and involved nature.

- Proactive: Averse to apathy, the service industry thrives on proactive anticipation of customer needs—delivering before the request is made. This reflects a sense of "care" and "perceptive ability." Passive service only meets the basic level, while proactive service involves predicting customer needs in advance. This also extends to offering proactive support and care to team members.

- People-oriented: Focusing on people and considering the customer's feelings rather than just completing tasks, achieving comprehensive and harmonious handling in all aspects.

◆Openness

This trait includes being curious, creative, and non-traditional in thinking.

- Curious: In the service industry, indifference is a pitfall. Being curious about people, events, and things is essential. Such a disposition truly enjoys the fast-paced, interactive nature of the service industry.

- Creative: The service industry demands flexible thinking, not following a rigid script. To provide "Heartfelt service," a thoughtful and creative approach is crucial.

- Originality and Non-traditional Thinking: Contemporary service strives to break free from rigid SOP standards. Having original and non-traditional thinking in service responses can exceed customer expectations, allowing for flexible and unbounded personalities to shine.

◆Agreeableness

This trait includes being trustworthy, gentle, helpful, kind-hearted, forgiving, and benevolent. Agreeableness is fundamental in the service industry. Being entrusted with tasks by customers requires reliability. Within a team, an agreeable individual is a dependable teammate. Furthermore, a helpful nature, coupled with kind interactions with colleagues, reflects a benevolent and forgiving personality, which is essential in addressing customer complaints rationally.

Service personnel requires careful and
responsive characteristics

◆Conscientiousness

This trait encompasses qualities like diligence, self-discipline, organizational skills, responsibility, and perseverance. Service professionals often humorously refer to themselves as "Oshin", signifying the need for unyielding persistence. After all, matters involving "people" are not resolved simply with a logical approach. Thus, having the capability to persist and a clear conscience is essential. Additionally, a good service team operates with organization and discipline. Each team member taking responsibility in their respective roles ensures that every aspect of the process is well-executed.

III. Language Ability

Language proficiency is a fundamental requirement for hotel service personnel. It encompasses not only proficiency in various foreign languages but also proficiency in Mandarin, dialects, and even sign language. After all, the tool for interacting with people is language. With a diverse array of guests staying at hotels, each individual should receive proper "care," and the most direct way to communicate is through language. The fundamental ability of language is "communication," meaning saying the right words at the right time, in a pleasant and agreeable manner. Furthermore, it should convey a sense of "quality" to the listener, as guest expectations in a five-star hotel are holistic. Apart from the physical amenities, hotel staff should also adhere to a five-star standard of service.

1. Right time, right words

◆Conveying Accurate Message Content

Conveying accurate message content requires thinking about the who, what, when, where, and why, which demands strong logical thinking. The ability to convey the "key" message accurately and concisely, without beating around the bush, while also delivering the 5W1H (What, When, Who, Why, Where, How) effectively. Furthermore, an advanced approach involves anticipating the potential areas of misunderstanding and reiterating them at the end of the conversation, somewhat like "highlighting" the key points. For instance, reminding someone that the meeting is at "2 PM" in the lobby and emphasizing the meeting point at the "front desk."

◆Conveying Appropriate Emotional Concern

Conveying appropriate emotional concern involves "feeling what others feel." For example, if you observe a family of multiple generations enjoying themselves, you can naturally compliment the joyous atmosphere and express how admirable their happy family outing is. On the other hand, if you notice a guest feeling frustrated and helpless due to a missed flight, empathize with their frustration and helplessness. Try to assist in resolving the issue and acknowledge their distress.

◆Purpose of Speaking on this Occasion

Since speaking involves a positive purpose rather than creating a negative impact, it's better not to speak if it doesn't serve a positive objective. For instance, in handling customer complaints, every communication should aim at resolving the issue. Remember the purpose of speaking – is it to solve a problem, manage emotions, or address a company crisis? Avoid getting lost in the conversation's direction due to emotional influence.

2. Speak with texure

Speaking with texure means using proper language and tone when using Mandarin, and displaying an affinity by using local dialects like Taiwanese, Hakka, or indigenous languages. The quality in speech helps people perceive your profound expertise and knowledge, which is built over time. This entails staying informed about global events, reading popular books from bestseller lists, being aware of trending topics, knowing tourist attractions globally for convenient recommendations, and mastering your own professional field within your work context. This forms the essence and self-cultivation of hotel service personnel.

3. Five-Star Conversations

Five-star conversations encompass both proper etiquette and well-chosen language. In the service industry, responses should not be purely colloquial or unpolished. The choice of words should align with the so-called "service language," adjusted appropriately. This aspect requires training. However, conversations shouldn't be monotonously polite to the point of sounding robotic. Lack of variation might result in a scnsc of discomfort, often referred to as "language cancer" in the service industry. For instance, continuously apologizing without offering follow-up actions could feel insincere, which is counterproductive.

IV. People skills

Interpersonal communication skills are a manifestation of socialization abilities, and they hold particular significance in the service industry. Strong interpersonal communication skills require keen observation and the ability to perceive and respond to others' needs. This skill set cannot be applied universally; it necessitates the right personality traits and the cultivation of a robust inner self before practicing responsive techniques.

1. Clarifying One's Role

Establishing the fundamental qualities of the service industry starts with an internal understanding – clarifying one's role within the job position. Many individuals, at the outset, assume that the service industry is glamorous, merely involving talking and chatting with people. However, after working in this field for a while, they begin to perceive the service industry as entirely centered around "customer-first" principles, leading to dissatisfaction following unfavorable interactions and customer complaints. This often results in self-repression and self-devaluation. Feeling that the service industry is subservient or even degrading work stems from a lack of clarity about one's role within it.

◆Cultivating the Right Mindset

Working in the service industry doesn't mean being subservient; clarifying your role and establishing the right mindset are crucial. When approached with dedication and sincerity, all jobs deserve respect. It all depends on how you perceive the work and how you interpret it. There are two essential mindsets that hotel service personnel should adopt:

- Utilize your expertise to assist customers during their stay, aiming to create a more enjoyable experience.
- Fulfill your duties and utilize your skills to collaborate with team members in accomplishing each aspect of the service process.

Hence, the value of hotel service personnel isn't determined by customers' praise or criticism but rather by their adherence to these two correct mindsets when performing their tasks. The source of a sense of accomplishment should also originate from these two mindsets.

Establish the correct mentality and professionalism to
provide customer a wonderful stay experience.

◆Creating Your Own Value

The service industry is quite remarkable. When you understand that your role is about "giving," you will be inclined to give willingly. You'll be surprised to discover that, with a healthy mindset, giving in the service industry can be boundless. Your service isn't exhausted after providing for one person, leaving nothing for another. Of course, everyone has limited time and energy, so there's no need to drain your emotional well-being needlessly. Instead, focus on how to create your own value. Put your heart into customer service, creating a meaningful interaction at every encounter. Offer your sincerest welcome, your best service, and your brightest smile. Truly empathize with the customers' needs and provide them with 「heartfelt service」.

2. Interpersonal Communication Skills in the Service Industry

The role of hotel service in creating a win-win-win scenario, involving customers, employees themselves, and the hotel brand, constitutes a successful and pleasant experience. This hinges on the establishment of a mindset. Firstly, employees must identify with the brand they serve, loving and taking pride in it. This means working for a company they admire, and once this alignment is achieved, they can promote and embody the hotel's values and principles, each employee becoming an ambassador of the brand. As for customers, they come in two categories: external customers, encompassing all hotel guests, including potential ones, and internal customers, consisting of supervisors, subordinates, colleagues within the department, and across different departments. In terms of interpersonal communication skills, the primary focus should be on avoiding service errors, followed by addressing customer complaints.

◆Avoiding Service Errors

- Every Day is a Good Day: Maintain good physical health and a positive mindset. Arrive a few minutes early to your workstation, familiarize yourself with the day's workflow and important customer lists. Coordinate with colleagues who are involved in the process and rehearse various scenarios in advance. This minimizes

Maintain good physical strength and healthy mind to
minimise mistakes

unexpected situations.

- Resources are Everywhere: Cultivate positive relationships with colleagues from various hotel departments, treating them with the same courtesy as external customers. Understand the challenges and efforts of different departments and focus on how to collaborate and assist each other in the workplace. Newcomers should approach experienced employees with humility, seeking advice while offering respect. This approach ensures that resources are accessible in critical moments.

◆Handling Customer Complaints Techniques

- Avoid Getting Hooked and Maintain Inner Stability: Practice emotional control to prevent conflicts with customers. When customers express dissatisfaction with the service, it's often due to their perception of the hotel, brand, or team, not a personal attack against you. Possible scenarios include customers becoming impatient due to prolonged waiting times, which could result from high occupancy or understaffing. Other situations involve disappointment with food choices or dissatisfaction with the hotel room's physical condition. These issues are not personal, so it's essential to avoid getting emotionally involved and responding on a personal level. Getting emotionally caught up in such situations would transform the issue into a personal matter.

- Avoid Arguing Back to Prevent Further Damage: When customers express dissatisfaction with the service, it's typically due to a service failure. Maintain your professionalism by not engaging in arguments or responding emotionally. Adding emotional responses to the situation could lead to irreparable consequences, which is the least intelligent approach for a service professional. Such reactions not only risk impacting your work but could even result in legal action or penalties.

- Attempting to Understand and Find Feasible Solutions: The approach involves:

①Try to Understand: It's not just about right or wrong, understanding the emotional gaps on the other side is essential. The issue might be related to saving face or even inner beliefs. Frequent conflicts and disputes aren't just about surface-level correctness.

②Changing the mood: This includes:

► Change of Environment: For instance, guiding an angry customer to a VIP lounge to prevent disruptions for other guests. The serene ambiance of the VIP lounge can help both parties calm down.

► Change of Focus: Sometimes, the problem is merely not getting along with a particular service staff member. Switching to a different staff member can resolve the issue. Or if the customer wants their feedback to reach higher management, involving the duty manager can make them feel heard. Additionally, during this handover, the customer may need to repeat their situation, which can help alleviate their emotional state.

③Seeking feasible solutions

► Customized Compensation Approaches: Tailor compensation based on the specific aspects where the guest experienced inconvenience. Some guests might solely seek understanding, while others desire sincere apologies. Some may expect tangible compensations. Address these needs according to how the guests perceive the situation.

▶ Rationalized Compensation Plans: Reference industry practices or company policies to create compensation strategies that cover both psychological and material aspects. Address the situation with a sincere and immediate attitude. If a customer insists on specific demands, inquire or escalate to higher authorities rather than outright rejecting the request. If the escalated solution is still not feasible, provide a genuine response and actively discuss alternative options with the customer.

▶ Post-Incident Handling and Follow-Up: Providing compensation should not mark the end of the interaction. Approach emotionally affected guests with utmost respect, ensuring that their remaining time at the hotel is filled with impeccable service. It's crucial to avoid further mistakes. After the guest checks out, send a letter expressing gratitude for providing the hotel with a learning opportunity.

All customer complaints should be addressed outwardly by focusing on resolving service gaps. Internally, there should be a thorough review and enhancement of education and training. Education and training should encompass not only professional skills but also courses aimed at improving psychological well-being. Simultaneously, reflecting on the past, learning from it, and avoiding repeating the same mistakes in the future is crucial.

V. Developing a Global Perspective

Regardless of the type of hotel, whether it's a guesthouse or a luxury international hotel, hotel service personnel have the opportunity to interact with travelers from different countries. Therefore, cultivating a broad international perspective is an essential quality for hotel staff. Hotel service personnel often have busy work schedules and spend long hours at their posts. So, how can they develop a global perspective?

1. Enhance Language Skills

Hotel service personnel have a great advantage – they have numerous opportunities to communicate. Utilize this advantage to improve language skills

◆Native Language / Local Dialect

Language skills aren't solely limited to foreign languages. Practicing local dialects can also be valuable. Incorporate idioms, proverbs, and phrases from the local dialect into conversations, showcasing your unique skills.

◆Foreign Languages

Focus on a foreign language you want to learn. Seek opportunities to interact with guests from that country. Practice daily conversations beforehand and engage in conversations with foreign guests using your learned language. This demonstrates your effort and growth to both guests and supervisors. If you lack immediate opportunities, listen closely, imitate, practice at home, and be prepared for the moment when an opportunity arises.

Cultivating an international perspective is an essential
quality for hotel staff.

2. Travel for Learning

Use holidays to travel and explore. While reading thousands of books during your spare time is beneficial, traveling thousands of miles during holidays can broaden your horizons. Experiencing foreign cultures firsthand can help you better understand the difficulties faced by foreign hotel guests, fostering empathy when you return to your workplace. Even if time is limited, exploring your own country can provide insights on how to introduce local beauty to foreign guests.

3. Stay Informed on International Affairs

Keep up with international news through newspapers, magazines, and media. Pay attention to the habits of the guests you serve. For instance, departments frequently hosting Western guests should stay informed about international situations or popular sports events and updates. Similarly, those interacting with Southeast Asian guests should be knowledgeable about the trending topics and widely discussed issues in those countries. This will provide conversation topics for meaningful interactions and firsthand international insights.

4. Learning from Your Environment

The hotel industry closely follows international trends. Large international conferences and high-profile social events are common in hotels. Your environment is a constant source of learning materials. The multilingual facility explanations in the hotel are also readily available sources of international knowledge.

5. Seek Learning Opportunities

Pursue learning opportunities, whether through on-the-job training, self-education, courses, or even formal education. Applying what you learn at work will allow you to engage in more diverse conversations with foreign guests, enhancing your interactions and broadening your perspectives.

Hospitality Etiquette for Guests from Different Countries

Hotel staff etiquette includes various aspects beyond personal demeanor. In your role at the workplace, it's crucial to be aware of your position and the expected decorum. Often, we say that service work is like being on a stage, and don't forget, you are the main character on this stage. As long as you are within the work environment, every word and action you take is highly scrutinized. When interacting with guests from different countries, hotel service personnel need to be mindful of:

I. Be mindful of your roles

Many hotel employees have long working hours and tend to view the workplace as their home. While it's good to be committed to your job, this might lead you to overlook the distinction between personal and professional life and neglect the presence of other guests. This is unprofessional behavior.

- Be aware of your actions and speech at all times during work. When wearing your uniform, you represent the hotel, not yourself.
  ①Avoid lounging in public areas while wearing your uniform. Others might not know your work status and might perceive you as being too casual and inappropriate.
  ②Refrain from engaging in lengthy conversations with others while wearing your uniform. Observing guests or colleagues from different departments might assume you're working but spending too much time chatting, giving the impression of not taking your job seriously or neglecting your responsibilities.
- After your shift, ensure you change out of your uniform and leave the work area immediately. Avoid wearing casual clothes while engaging in conversations with colleagues in public areas. Also, avoid being present in work-related areas, such as the hotel front desk or kitchen. Such behavior disrupts colleagues who are

working and may confuse guests. It's an unprofessional display without clear rules or standards.

- If you have personal matters or visitors during work hours, report to your supervisor and take visitors to the employee break area to handle matters quickly. Some male employees might have uniforms similar to regular suits. If in public spaces, consider removing the name tag to signify that it's not official business time. Regardless, maintain a clear boundary between personal and professional life to uphold a positive image.

II. Be mindful of appropriate discourse

As discussed earlier, it's important for hotel service personnel to choose their words carefully. Here, the focus shifts to being mindful of one's own speech, whether directed towards team members or hotel guests.

- In the workplace, superiors shouldn't chastise team members in front of guests. Doing so amidst the hustle and bustle only portrays the superior's inadequacy and exacerbates the chaotic situation. Team members also shouldn't engage in mutual blame during work, as this will only dampen team morale and worsen the situation.

- Whether on duty or off, avoid criticizing guests in the workplace. Be aware that walls have ears. If the person in question or other guests hear such remarks, it can have a profoundly negative impact, making it seem like you engage in constant criticism of customers.

- Avoid discussing sensitive topics in public areas, such as nationality, race, and religion. Not only should you refrain from discussing these topics with hotel guests, but you should also avoid such conversations with colleagues in public spaces. Consider optics; your remarks can sometimes be misconstrued as reflecting the company's stance.

III. Catering to different types of travelers

Travelers from various countries have unique preferences and expectations when it comes to hospitality. By paying attention to these nuances, one can create a "home away from home" experience for them. Adapting reception according to the habits and preferences of different nationalities can lead to the guests' appreciation and make a particular country's accommodations their preferred choice. Below are some examples of different types of travelers and the appropriate etiquette for service personnel:

1. United State

Americans are known for their warm and friendly nature, valuing freedom. Many enjoy outdoor activities and prefer comfortable attire while traveling. They often use facilities like gyms and swimming pools during their stay. Socially, greeting and initiating conversation are considered polite. Hotel service personnel can greet them with enthusiasm, inquire about their experience, engage in small talk about their trip's purpose, and wish them a wonderful time in the country. Open-body gestures and a sunny smile can be used to welcome them, rather than strictly formal gestures.

2. United Kingdom

British social traditions used to be hierarchical, and while this is changing, they still value politeness. Addressing guests as "Sir" or "Madam" and using refined language is crucial. Courteous greetings and well-wishes should suffice in conversation. It's important not to be overly intrusive in discussions unless the guest initiates further conversation.

3. Japan

Japanese guests are generally polite and reserved, their everyday life characterized by bowing and polite language. Despite their quiet nature, service personnel should not overlook their feelings. A respectful, formal approach is necessary. Bowing with full sincerity while greeting them shows proper respect. The service quality of high-end

Japanese hotels is a good model to understand the service preferences of Japanese guests.

4. Southeast Asia

Guests from Southeast Asia, including Thailand, Vietnam, Indonesia, and Malaysia, tend to be easygoing. It's important to consider their dietary habits and religious beliefs, such as providing prayer rooms for Muslims. Also, be cautious not to point using the index finger to Malaysians and avoid touching a Thai person's head, as they highly value it.

5. Singapore

Singaporeans are friendly but assertive about their rights. Treating them with the same respect as Western guests is essential. English is widely spoken, though many Singaporeans understand Mandarin. However, not all Singaporean Chinese read Chinese, so using English for official communication is advisable.

6. China

Chinese guests are generally relaxed and comfortable in Taiwan. Effective communication can usually be achieved, even if simplified characters differ from traditional ones. Courteous and respectful treatment is key. Avoiding political topics is wise. Focus on discussing local culture, cuisine, and attractions, which usually interest them.

The aforementioned types don't encompass all guests from each country, as individual preferences vary. Overall, Western guests assert their rights but usually won't pose difficulties if hotel service meets the expected standards. Asian guests may be more reserved, but that doesn't mean their feelings should be overlooked. Attentiveness and cultural understanding should be emphasized for successful service. By providing quality service and accommodating diverse cultural differences, service personnel can effectively care for guests from different countries and become exceptional hotel staff. This approach will likely lead to positive feedback from customers, making work more enjoyable and helping to truly appreciate the service industry.

Class activities 14

1. Ask students to share experience of staying in hotel. What are some of the best service experiences you have encountered? And on the contrary, what led to the worst service experience you've had?

2. Ask students, Do you believe the customer is always right? How would you handle a difficult customer situation? Have you ever found yourself being a difficult customer?

3. Discuss whether you enjoy the service industry, and if your personality is suitable for it. Why or why not?